Latchkey Children in the Library & Community

Latchkey Children in the Library & Community

Issues, Strategies, and Programs

by Frances Smardo Dowd

Oryx Press 1991

The rare Arabian Oryx is believed to have inspired the myth of the unicorn. This desert antelope became virtually extinct in the early 1960s. At that time several groups of international conservationists arranged to have 9 animals sent to the Phoenix Zoo to be the nucleus of a captive breeding herd. Today the Oryx population is nearly 800, and over 400 have been returned to reserves in the Middle East.

Copyright © 1991 by The Oryx Press
4041 North Central at Indian School Road
Phoenix, Arizona 85012-3397

Published simultaneously in Canada

All rights reserved
No part of this publication may be reproduced or transmitted in any form or by any means, electronic or mechanical, including photocopying, recording, or by any information storage and retrieval system, without permission in writing from The Oryx Press.

Printed and Bound in the United States of America

∞ The paper used in this publication meets the minimum requirements of American National Standard for Information Science—Permanence of Paper for Printed Library Materials, ANSI Z39.48, 1984.

Library of Congress Cataloging-in-Publication Data
Dowd, Frances Smardo.
   Latchkey children in the library and community : issues, strategies, and programs. / Frances Smardo Dowd.
      p.   cm.
   Includes bibliographical references and index.
   ISBN 0-89774-651-1
   1. Libraries, Children's—United States—Activity programs.
2. Libraries, Children's—United States—Security measures.
3. Latchkey children—Services for—United States. 4. Public relations—Libraries—United States. 5. Libraries and community—
—United States. I. Title.
Z718.2.U6D69   1991   91-3580
027.62´5—dc20   CIP

To all latchkey children and to adults who work with, help, and care for them in schools, libraries, homes, and community agencies

Contents

Preface ix

PART I: CHILDREN IN SELF-CARE AFTER SCHOOL 1

Chapter 1: Statistics and Contributing Factors 3
Definitions 3
Historical Background 4
Problems in Estimating Numbers of Latchkey Children 4
Estimates of Numbers of Latchkey Children 6
Factors Contributing to the Latchkey Phenomenon 7
References 8

Chapter 2: Implications and Impact of Leaving Children in Self-Care 12
Background Information/Overview 12
Latchkey Experience: Research Indicating a Detrimental Impact 13
Latchkey Experience: Research Indicating a Beneficial Impact 18
Latchkey Experience: Research Indicating No Impact 19
Effects of the Latchkey Experience Upon the Community 22

Additional Research Needs 23
References 25

PART II: LATCHKEY CHILDREN IN THE COMMUNITY 29

Chapter 3: Local and National Responses to Latchkey Children 31
Adult Care Programs 31
Self-Care Supportive Programs 42
Combination Programs: Adult Care and Self-Care 51
Publications 54
Project Home Safe 55
References 58

Chapter 4: Recommendations for the Future 62
Recommended Latchkey Strategies 62
References 72

PART III: LATCHKEY CHILDREN IN PUBLIC LIBRARIES 75

Chapter 5: Why Latchkey Children Present a Dilemma for Public Libraries 77

Definitions 77
The Nature of the Public Library
  Dilemma 78
Philosophy of Public Library
  Service to Children: A Historical
  View 80
References 82

Chapter 6: What National Research Tells Us About Library Latchkey Children 84
1988 National Survey of Latchkey
  Children in Public Libraries 84
1990 National Survey of Latchkey
  Children in Public Libraries 95
References 103

Chapter 7: Library Responses 105
Overview 105
The Response of Organizations
  Working with Libraries 106
The Response of Libraries:
  Individual Case Studies 115
References 159

Chapter 8: Recommendations for Future Library Service 163
Recommendations of Librarians
  (1988) 164
Recommendations of Librarians
  (1990) 169
Author's Recommendations
  (1988) 172
Author's Recommendations
  (1990) 173
References 174

APPENDICES 175

Appendix A: 1988 Questionnaire 177

Appendix B: 1990 Questionnaire 186

Appendix C: Annotated Bibliography 191

Appendix D: Latchkey Organizations and Agencies 198

Appendix E: Names, Addresses, and Telephone Numbers of Public Libraries in Case Studies 201

Index 205

Preface

"A generation ago, when the final school bell of the day sounded, most children went home for milk and cookies with their mothers" (Campbell and Flake, 1985). Today, over half of all mothers with preschool children are in the labor force, and by 1995 more than four-fifths of all school-age children and two-thirds of all preschool children will have working mothers (Children's Defense Fund, 1988). Consequently, as many as 15 million children, or 20 percent of elementary-age youth, are regularly left without adult supervision for several hours each day until an adult arrives home from work (Nienhuis, 1987).

They are called latchkey children, and their rapidly increasing numbers have made them a vital concern to all those interested in children's welfare, primarily because the effects of the self-care experience are largely unknown (Peterson and Magrab, 1989). The existence of latchkey children has been cited as the most pressing national problem involving the social policy and health care of children (Zigler, 1982). This phenomenon is not exclusive to the United States; government agencies in Canada, for example, are also addressing the issues and concerns raised by latchkey children (Baynham, 1990).

This book is about what is happening and what could happen to latchkey children, in terms of the community as a whole, and, more specifically, in regard to public libraries. Because of its broad perspective, *Latchkey Children in the Library and Community: Issues, Strategies, and Programs* provides librarians with an overall understanding of latchkey children as a community issue. It addresses the need for a definitive work to guide librarians in serving latchkey children more effectively. Children's librarians, branch managers, library administrators, other library practitioners, library educators, library researchers, and library students can gain valuable insights and ideas for service to this clientele from reading the results reported herein of the author's research, and especially from considering the successful strategies of public libraries throughout the nation described in the individual case studies. Since many of the innovative, effective techniques for serving library latchkey children are inexpensive and even informal, it is hoped that librarians will tailor and implement them to suit the need in their own communities.

Conversely, *Latchkey Children in the Library and Community* assists educators and professionals in related fields in understanding the impact of the sociological phenomenon of latchkey children, particularly in regard to public libraries. This book meets the needs of practitioners and professionals interested in the welfare of children for a comprehensive but readable text/handbook about latchkey children. The information contained in the chapters, and especially in the appendices, makes this book an authoritative reference source.

Part I, "Children in Self-Care After School," deals broadly with the phenomenon of latchkey children, providing definitions and background and discussing consequences. Chapter 1, "Statistics and Contributing Factors," presents historical background about latchkey children, estimates of their numbers, and sociological and economic factors contributing to this phenomenon. Chapter 2, "Implications and Impact of Leaving Children in Self-Care," discusses the effects of the latchkey experience upon children's social, emotional, physical, and cognitive development, as evidenced from research findings in the fields of sociology, psychology, education, and social welfare. The effects of the latchkey experience upon the community, as well as research needs related to this topic, are also described.

Part II, "Latchkey Children in the Community," describes current community efforts and recommends future community strategies for serving latchkey children. Strategies in place in communities throughout the United States and Canada to address the needs of children in self-care are examined in Chapter 3, "Local and National Responses to Latchkey Children." These strategies include, but are not limited to, various types of school-age child care, supportive services (such as telephone reassurance lines, the buddy system, and survival skills training), combination adult care and self-care programs, publications, and "Project Home Safe," a national education and advocacy effort operated by the American Home Economics Association (AHEA) with a grant from the Whirlpool Foundation.

Potential programs, policies, and services that communities could implement on behalf of latchkey children and their families are presented in "Recommendations for the Future," Chapter 4. In particular, suggestions are made for teachers (including physical education and recreation leaders), school counselors, school administrators, employers, institutions of higher learning, home economists, parents, state officials/legislators, organizations, researchers, and librarians.

The sole focus of each of the four chapters of Part III is upon latchkey children in public libraries. Chapter 5, "Why Latchkey Children Present a Dilemma for Public Libraries," explains why service to this group both coincides and conflicts with the very mission of the public library as an institution, causing uncertainty among the profession as to the appropriate role of librarians in serving these children. A historical perspective of the development of children's rooms and departments in public libraries and of the philosophy of public library service to children is offered as a background to understanding the challenge that latchkey children pose for these institutions. However, while library literature and especially the media have reported adverse effects resulting from large numbers of unsupervised children in public libraries in the after-school hours, a positive approach is taken throughout Part III. The opportunity that latchkey children create for public libraries to develop library and reading habits in this built-in clientele is emphasized.

Chapter 6, "What National Research Tells Us About Library Latchkey Children," describes in detail the goals, methodology, and findings from the author's 1988 national survey of latchkey children in public libraries, concerning the description and magnitude of the situation, the content and extent of policies and procedures, and programs and services. Findings not previously published are reported, including results of the narrative open-ended section of the questionnaire, which addressed library interaction with community agencies, the role of libraries in regard to latchkey children, and success of libraries in meeting the needs of this group.

Chapter 6 also contains the complete findings, never before published, of the author's 1990 national survey of latchkey children in public libraries, which investigated a new aspect—personnel. Consequently, this same chapter includes information regarding librarians' level of knowledge in serving latchkey children, sources of their training and experience, and the most desirable methods to increase their knowledge of this clientele. Chapter 6 contains the only national study on the topic of latchkey children in public libraries published to date.

Chapter 7, "Library Responses," highlights innovative, successful strategies undertaken by public libraries throughout the United States (and Canada) to address the problems of latchkey children. Thirty-one individual public libraries, identified via the author's survey research or literature search, are presented as mini case studies, and are arranged alphabetically by state. Among the diverse effective strategies public libraries employ are the following: changing the architectural design/layout of the facility; providing homework/tutoring assistance, drop-in activities after school, or 4-H club programs; transporting students from school to the library; implementing an "engagement policy" and "child-friendly management plan"; offering bookmobile service after 3:00 P.M. at public schools; and utilizing retired senior volunteers to work with children, read to them, and listen to them read.

In addition, Chapter 7 gives an overview of and contains excerpts about policy development from the American Library Association's "position paper," *"Latchkey Children" in the Public Library*, which was written concurrently with but independently of the author's initial survey research. Lastly, Chapter 7 describes efforts by library-related institutions on behalf of latchkey children, such as R.S.V.P. Intergenerational Library Assistance Project grants, the Metropolitan Cooperative Library System's National Clearinghouse on Library Latchkey Children, and Whirlpool and AHEA's "Project Home Safe" at one branch of the Prince George's County Memorial Library system.

Chapter 8, "Recommendations for Future Library Service," presents, primarily from the author's survey and interviews of librarians, recommendations regarding public library service to latchkey children, in terms of programs and services, policies and procedures, personnel, the physical facility, and materials.

The appendices provide readers with the questionnaires used in the author's 1988 and 1990 national surveys, an annotated bibliography of print and nonprint fiction and factual materials for youth about latchkey children, a list of organizations and agencies concerned with latchkey children, and a list of names, addresses, and telephone numbers of public libraries in each of the case studies.

REFERENCES

Baynham, P. 1990. Latchkey children in the public library. Paper presented at the Canadian Library Association Annual Conference, June 15, Ottawa, Ontario, Canada.

Campbell, L. and A. Flake. 1985. Latchkey children—What is the answer? *The Clearing House* 58(May): 381–83.

Children' Defense Fund. 1988. *A call for action to make our nation safe for children: A briefing book on the status of American children in 1988.* Washington, D.C.

Nienhuis, M. 1987. 7.2% of children characterized as "latchkey" in 1984 census survey. *Education Week* (February 18): 6.

Peterson, L. and P. Magrab. 1989. Introduction to the special section: Children on their own. *Journal of Clinical Child Psychology* 18(March): 2–7.

Zigler, E. 1982. Current social policy issues related to children and families. Paper presented at the American Psychological Association, August, Washington, D.C.

PART I
Children in Self-Care After School

Chapter 1
Statistics and Contributing Factors

DEFINITIONS

On any given weekday in the United States, between 3:00 P.M. and 6:00 P.M., millions of children are left without adult supervision. Called "latchkey children," they come from all racial, cultural, and socioeconomic backgrounds and reside in urban, suburban, and rural communities (U.S. Bureau of the Census, 1985). Findings from a study of over 4,000 eighth grade students in the Los Angeles and San Diego metropolitan areas revealed that self-care was associated significantly with higher rather than lower socioeconomic status, possibly because a greater proportion of families living in higher socioeconomic status communities have both parents working outside the home (Dwyer, Danley, Sussman, and Johnson, 1990).

The term "latchkey" is used because these youth often carry a house key on a chain or string around their neck to let themselves in their homes independently after school. But the definition of the term "latchkey children" is ambiguous, and is frequently implied rather than stated. The following is one of the most comprehensive definitions of latchkey children:

> Children who are regularly left during some part of the day to supervise themselves, whether during the time they use group recreation programs, play in the street, stay home alone, join a gang, or for whom child care arrangements are so loosely made that they are virtually ineffective... Latchkey here refers to children who are regularly left unattended; this includes both children left alone and those left in the care of an underage sibling (Long and Long, 1983).

Because "latchkey" has a negative connotation, the designation "self-care" may be considered more acceptable (Pitney, 1989; Coolsen, Seligson, and Garbarino, 1985). A child in a "self-care" arrangement is defined as one between the ages of 6 and 13 who spends time alone or with a younger sibling on a periodic basis (Cole and Rodman, 1987). Another definition describes children in self-care as "those who take care of themselves or younger siblings on a regular basis during the out of school hours" (Coolsen, Seligson, and Garbarino, 1985). Other less value-laden alternatives for "latchkey" include "unsupervised," "children with working parents," and "children on their own" (Peterson and Magrab, 1989). But, as Peterson and Magrab emphasize, "whatever label is used, the phenomenon is of vital concern to all those interested in the welfare of children."

HISTORICAL BACKGROUND

Although the topic of latchkey children has been highlighted in the media during the last few years, this sociological phenomenon is not new. Unsupervised children have probably existed as long as the family has been recognized as a social unit (Padilla and Landreth, 1989), or, perhaps, at least since the Industrial Revolution (Toenniessen, Little, and Rosen, 1985). At the turn of the twentieth century, latchkey children were even called "dorks" because latches became uncommon and doorkeys were used to gain entry (Seligson, et al., 1983).

One of the first published reports of latchkey children in the United States was during World War II. Child welfare professionals expressed concern at the numbers of "latchkey" or "doorkey" children, also referred to as "eight-hour orphans," who were left to shift for themselves while their mothers worked (Zucker, 1944). The war sent fathers away from home in the military and caused mothers to join the labor force in large numbers. Latchkey children became so highly visible that in 1943 the central theme of the annual meeting of the American Association of School Administrators was the plight of "doorkey" children (Strohman and Duff, 1982). The superintendent of schools in Cleveland called attention to these children in his annual report for the year 1941–42; he cited a recent survey of selected elementary schools that indicated as many as 25 percent of the children had both parents working (Zucker, 1944).

PROBLEMS IN ESTIMATING NUMBERS OF LATCHKEY CHILDREN

An accurate count of latchkey children currently in the United States is lacking. Although surveys at the national, state, and local levels have attempted to determine their numbers, estimates vary greatly. One problem is attitudinal or value-laden. Parents may be reluctant to reveal that they leave their children without adult supervision, since this is a violation of the law in many states (Fosarelli, 1984; Coolsen, Seligson, and Garbarino, 1985). Consequently, figures may reflect "some level of deliberate misrepresentation of child supervision because of a perceived illegality (child neglect) of leaving children unattended, fear for children's safety, and a perception of social undesirability associated with forms of child care labeled 'latchkey'" (U.S. Bureau of the Census, 1987). Difficulty in obtaining accurate statistics, then, is directly related to the emotionally sensitive nature of the latchkey phenomenon.

Another problem in obtaining an accurate count of latchkey children is definitional, since no clear statement exists as to what constitutes a child in self-care or a latchkey arrangement (Coolsen, Seligson, and Garbarino, 1985). Cole and Rodman (1987) list five variables that make it difficult to define the latchkey arrangement, and consequently create problems in estimating latchkey numbers:

1. employment status of parents
2. what time children are at home
3. presence of siblings
4. age of children
5. amount of time children spend alone

For example, some researchers confine latchkey children to those unsupervised solely after school rather than before school. Others disagree as to whether lack of supervision at other times (i.e., during school vacations, on weekends, evenings, etc.) constitutes a genuine latchkey arrangement. Disparity also exists as to age level. Are preschoolers deemed latchkey? Are adolescents in their mid-teens considered latchkey? Another debatable aspect regards the presence of siblings. If an older sibling cares for a younger one, is this a latchkey situation? And if so, are both counted, or just one? The amount of time a child spends alone (both in terms of duration and frequency) also raises issues that cloud definitions. Where is the time spent? Are children left unsupervised for reasons other than the parents' need to work (i.e., parents socializing, shopping, etc.)? Children in such situations can be categorized as latchkey children (Cole and Rodman, 1987; San Antonio Cares, 1987). The fact that these children are not in a formalized setting, making them difficult to reach, is yet another reason for the lack of accurate latchkey numbers.

ESTIMATES OF NUMBERS OF LATCHKEY CHILDREN

At the national level estimates of the number of latchkey children vary from 2 to 15 million, or from 7 percent to 45 percent of all elementary school children (Nienhuis, 1987). However, there are an appreciable number of preschool children under 6 years of age as well. In 1982 the Census Bureau reported that 9.3 percent of all children under 6 were either alone or cared for by siblings (Wright, 1990). In 1985 the Census Bureau released what is probably the most conservative estimate to date of the number of latchkey children nationwide. Based on interviews with a scientifically developed sample, the Bureau identified 7 percent of 5- to 13-year-olds as latchkey (U.S. Bureau of the Census, 1985). But this figure is an underestimate because siblings over 14 years old were classified as adults (Chelton, 1988; Rosenzweig, 1988).

Twelve percent of parents of elementary school students acknowledged leaving their children alone at home, according to findings from a Metropolitan Life Study of American teachers (Harris, 1987). Researcher Thomas Long, President of the National Institute of Latchkey Children and Youth and author of two books on the topic, believes that a more accurate accounting is 20 percent of all American youth (Long, 1985); the National PTA estimates that an even greater percentage of children are regularly left in self-care (Chepesiuk, 1987). According to a Department of Labor report, 30 percent of mothers of children under 13 allow their children to stay home unattended after school (Whirlpool Corporation and American Home Economics Association [AHEA], 1987). In the Metropolitan Life Study, which polled a random sample of teachers and parents from various socioeconomic levels, 40 percent of the children were identified as unsupervised from 3:30 P.M. to 6:00 P.M. (Harris, 1987).

Local studies in a wide variety of communities have yielded estimates of self-care and sibling care in the 15 percent to 25 percent range for children in the lower elementary grades, with percentages rising sharply after grades four or five (Seligson and Fink, 1989). For example, a sampling in the greater Minneapolis area conducted by Pillsbury Company found 15 percent of children in kindergarten through third grade and 35 percent of children in the fourth through sixth grades were home alone or with siblings at least three days a week after school (Hedin, et al., 1986).

In the city of Dallas, 35 percent of the children were without adult supervision for more than three hours. The Dallas report concluded that "data presented indicate that the latchkey phenomenon is not limited to certain locations or groups," but that "supervision of children before and after school is an issue which affects families of all racial/ethnic groups and all income levels" (Redlinger and Letteer, 1989).

In Houston, some officials believe that 40 to 60 percent of their school children are on their own until parents come home from work (Wellborn, 1981). A survey of working mothers in New York City revealed that 9 percent left their children alone regularly and 10 percent occasionally (McMurray and Kazanjian, 1982).

Less than 10 percent of 1,806 children 5 to 14 years old in Charlotte, North Carolina, have their needs met through planned programming. This was the finding from a survey of a random sample of parents by a task force to determine needs of children for care both before and after school during the holidays and vacation time (Council on Children, 1984).

Long (1985) believes that "self care has become the second most prevalent form of child care in America today," with care by parents the most prevalent type. Some researchers believe that there are more children in self-care than in day care (Rodman, Pratto, and Nelson, 1985). Regardless of the exact figures, authorities maintain that the number of children in self-care is substantial and that their numbers will continue to increase (Bundy and Boser, 1987; Cole and Rodman, 1987).

FACTORS CONTRIBUTING TO THE LATCHKEY PHENOMENON

A variety of sociological, demographic, and economic factors contribute to changes in the American family, which consequently affect latchkey children. First, the proportion of women in the workforce, particularly mothers of young children, has increased dramatically, as women may be employed due to economic necessity and/or to achieve a sense of personal satisfaction (O'Connell and Bloom, 1987). Fifty percent of all mothers with preschool children are in the labor force. By 1995 more than four-fifths of all school-age children and two-thirds of all preschool children will have mothers in the labor force (Children's Defense Fund, 1988).

Second, single-parent families have become the norm. High divorce and teenage childbearing rates have led to an increase in single-parent, female-headed households (U.S. Bureau of the Census, 1987). The "traditional family"—with a nonworking mother and a father present—accounts for only 7 percent of American families (San Antonio Cares, 1987). Twenty-three percent of all families in the United States are single-parent families, and if current trends continue, 60 percent of all children will live in a single-parent home for some period of their lives (Jellinek and Klavan, 1988).

Third, there is a decline in the number of adults available to children after school in their local neighborhoods. This is partially due to high geographic mobility, as well as to age-segregated housing, which results in neighborhoods composed of families of similar ages (Pitney, 1989). This situation in turn results in the separation of the extended or nuclear family and fewer adult relatives or friends who might otherwise serve as surrogate caregivers to children. Fourth, homelessness has increased nationwide, including families with children. Thus, the latchkey phenomenon has been said to "represent one profound aspect of the modern family's adaptation to changing times and circumstances" (Messer, Wuensch, and Diamond, 1989).

Lastly, but perhaps most importantly, there is an acute lack of affordable high quality child care available to parents (O'Connell and Bloom, 1987; U.S. Bureau of the Census, 1987). According to Senators Dodd and Kildee, co-sponsors of the Act for Better Child Care Services, fewer than 3 million licensed day care positions exist, yet there are 21.6 million children under 6, and two-thirds of their mothers work (Fairhall, 1987). For example, in 1986 more than three-quarters of Maryland mothers with children under 6 worked, but only 10 percent of their children under 14 were enrolled in registered day care centers. Consequently, more than half a million children in Maryland spend part of every day unsupervised (Gambill, 1988).

In the state of Illinois, according to a 1985 University of Chicago study, 642,555 children under 10 would need day care in 1989, yet in January 1989 the Illinois Department of Children and Family Services had licensed spaces for only 152,000 children. The University of Chicago study suggested that the need for latchkey care will peak at 341,000 around 1996 (*When School Is Not in Session*, 1989). In Boston, almost one-third of the 1,447 parents of students in public and parochial elementary schools who responded to a 1989 survey stated that they looked for care for their school-age children in the past two years and could not find it, and for an equal fraction child care options were too expensive (Parents United for Child Care and the Wellesley College Center for Research on Women, 1989).

REFERENCES

Bundy, M. and J. Boser. 1987. Helping latchkey children: A group guidance approach. *The School Counselor* 35(September): 58–65.

Chelton, M.K. 1988. Kids with keys. Paper presented at the Public Library Association National Conference in Pittsburgh, Pennsylvania, April 29.

Chepesiuk, R. 1987. Reaching out: The Greenville County library's latchkey kids program. *Library Journal* 112(March): 46–48.

Children's Defense Fund. 1988. *A call for action to make our nation safe for children: A briefing book on the status of American children in 1988.* Washington, D.C.

Cole, C. and H. Rodman. 1987. When school-age children care for themselves: Issues for family life educators and parents. *Family Relations* 36(January): 92–96.

Coolsen, P., M. Seligson, and J. Garbarino. 1985. *When school's out and nobody's home.* Chicago: National Committee for Prevention of Child Abuse.

Council on Children. 1984. *Taking action for latchkey children.* Charlotte, North Carolina.

Dwyer K., K. Danley, S. Sussman, and C. Johnson. 1990. Characteristics of eighth-grade students who initiate self-care in elementary and junior high school. *Pediatrics* 86(September): 448–54.

Fairhall, J. 1987. Lawmakers champion child care plan. *Baltimore Evening Sun*, November 20, 10A.

Fosarelli, P. 1984. Latchkey children. *Developmental and Behavioral Pediatrics* 5(August):173–77.

Gambill, A. 1988. Kids of working parents find refuge in libraries, schools. *Harford County Sun*, January 31, 2+.

Harris, L. 1987. *The Metropolitan Life survey of the American teacher 1987: Strengthening links between home and school.* New York: Metropolitan Life.

Hedin, D., et al. 1986. *Summary of the family's view of after-school time.* Minneapolis: Pillsbury Company.

Jellinek, M. and E. Klavan. 1988. The single parent. *Good Housekeeping* (September): 58.

Long, L. and T. Long. 1983. *Handbook for latchkey children and their parents.* New York: Arbor House.

Long, T. 1985. Advice for parents of latchkey children. Paper presented at Nova University Ed.D. Program on Early and Middle Childhood Summer Institute. Washington, D.C.

McMurray, G. and D. Kazanjian. 1982. Day care and the working poor: The struggle for self-sufficiency. ERIC Document ED 221 266.

Messer, S., K. Wuensch, and J. Diamond. 1989. Former latchkey children: Personality and academic correlates. *Journal of Genetic Psychology* 150(September): 301–09.

Nienhuis, M. 1987. 7.2% of children characterized as "latchkey" in 1984 Census Survey. *Education Week* (February 18): 6.

O'Connell, M. and D. Bloom. 1987. *Juggling jobs and babies: America's child care challenge.* Washington, D.C.: Population Reference Bureau.

Padilla, M.L. and G. Landreth. 1989. Latchkey children: A review of the literature. *Child Welfare* 68(July/August): 445–54.

Parents United for Child Care and the Wellesley College Center for Research on Women. 1989. *Challenges facing Boston families: The need for school-age child care.* Parents United for Child Care, Boston. September.

Peterson, L. and P. Magrab. 1989. Introduction to the special section: Children on their own. *Journal of Clinical Child Psychology* 18(March):2–7.

Pitney, M. 1989. Children in self-care. In *Counseling young students at risk: Resources for elementary guidance counselors*, edited by J. Bleuer and P. Schreibner. Ann Arbor, Michigan: ERIC Clearinghouse on Counseling and Personnel Services, ED 307 524.

Redlinger, L. and M. Letteer. 1989. *Child care arrangements for elementary and intermediate school children in Dallas County: Executive summary.* Dallas: University of Texas at Dallas.

Rodman, H., D.J. Pratto, and R.S. Nelson. 1985. Child care arrangements and children's functioning: A comparison of self-care and adult-care children. *Developmental Psychology* 21(May): 413–18.

Rosenzweig, S. 1988. Kids with keys. Paper presented at the Public Library Association National Conference in Pittsburgh, Pennsylvania, April 29.

San Antonio Cares. Child Care Working Group of the United Way of Texas. 1987. *Latchkey children in Texas.* Austin.

Seligson, M., et al. 1983. *School-age child care: A policy report.* Wellesley, Massachusetts: School-Age Child Care Project, Wellesley College, Center for Research on Women.

Seligson, M. and D. Fink. 1989. *No time to waste: An action agenda for school-age child care.* Wellesley, Massachusetts: School-Age Child Care Project, Wellesley College, Center for Research on Women.

Strohman, S.H. and R.E. Duff. 1982. The latchkey child: Whose responsibility? *Childhood Education* 59(November/December): 76–79.

Toenniessen, C., L. Little, and K. Rosen. 1985. Anybody home? Evaluation and intervention techniques with latchkey children. *Elementary School Guidance and Counseling* 20(December):105–13.

U.S. Bureau of the Census. 1985. *After-school care of school-age children: December, 1984.* Series P-23, No. 149. Washington, D.C.: U.S. Government Printing Office.

U.S. Bureau of the Census. 1987. *Household and family characteristics: March, 1986.* Series P-20, No. 419. Washington, D.C.: U.S. Government Printing Office.

Wellborn, S. 1981. When school kids come home to an empty house. *U.S. News and World Report* (September 14): 42–47.

When school is not in session: Report of the ad hoc committee on latchkey children of the Illinois Association of School Boards. 1989. Illinois Association of School Boards, Springfield. November.

Whirlpool Corporation and American Home Economics Association (AHEA). 1987. Press packet on Project Home Safe. Alexandria, Virginia.

Wright, R. 1990. Who's watching the children? *McCall's* 117(January): 22–24.

Zucker, H. 1944. Working parents and latchkey children. *Annals of the American Academy of Political and Social Science* 236: 43–50.

Chapter 2
Implications and Impact of Leaving Children in Self-Care

BACKGROUND INFORMATION/OVERVIEW

Because of the increasing numbers of latchkey children, educators, politicians, child welfare specialists, sociologists, and professionals from various related fields interested in the welfare of children have become concerned as to whether the consequences of being in self-care are beneficial or detrimental to children (Robinson, Rowland, and Coleman, 1986). The phenomenon of children being on their own before and after school has grown so rapidly that even its short-term effects, let alone its long-term effects, are largely unknown (Peterson and Magrab, 1989). While some claim that self-care has deleterious consequences upon children, others argue that it may be beneficial with respect to the learning of responsibility and the development of independence.

However, very little systematic research has verified either view, as studies of the impact of the latchkey experience upon children have neither been very extensive nor very conclusive. Mixed findings shroud each claim with controversy. Some results indicate that self-care children are at a distinct disadvantage. Other studies reveal no significant differences between latchkey children and children supervised by adults, and a few suggest that the experience may actually be advantageous. The empirical studies that have been undertaken are recent—the majority since 1982. Research on this topic is in its infancy; only a limited number of variables has been systematically investigated. Therefore, the effect of self-care upon children's development, in terms of their academic performance; interaction with peers, parents, and teachers; or emotional well-being is still undetermined (Vandell and Corasaniti, 1988).

In addition, much of the research has many shortcomings, making conclusions impossible or at best risky. For example, most studies have been based on latchkey versus nonlatchkey children without taking into account that not all latchkey children are alike. Research must take into consideration the ways in which children in self-care differ. Among the factors requiring consideration are: the child's age when first left in self-care, the child's sense of self, and the child's attitude toward self-care (Fosarelli, 1984).

Other drawbacks of existing research about children in self-care concern leading interviews, potentially nonrepresentative samples, unproven measures, and inadequate controls (Peterson and Magrab, 1989). In most studies the sample has been too small; the focus is upon only one school district per study. Such a focus can cause selection bias and difficulty in generalizing findings (Fosarelli, 1984). Reliance upon a sole approach to data collection, rather than use of observational techniques in combination with self reports and interviews, is another problem (Robinson, Rowland, and Coleman, 1986).

In spite of the limitations described above, the major existing research regarding the impact of self-care on children is discussed in this chapter. Studies indicating an adverse effect, a positive effect, and no significant impact are all described. In addition, the following pages discuss the impact of the self-care experience upon parents, schools, and the community, since Bronfenbrenner (1979) suggests that, when examining environmental forces on an individual's development, multiple levels of influence should be considered, comparing such influence to a "set of nestled structures, each inside the next, like a set of Russian Dolls."

LATCHKEY EXPERIENCE: RESEARCH INDICATING A DETRIMENTAL IMPACT

Emotions—Worry and Fear

The Longs, a husband and wife team, interviewed inner city minority children in Washington, D.C., and reported that latchkey children had a high incidence of loneliness, fear, stress, and conflict, as well as problems in their peer relationships and schoolwork. From interviews the Longs found that children who routinely cared for themselves experienced more fear than children supervised by adults. The fear most often mentioned was that someone would break into their homes and hurt them. The Longs also reported that latchkey children worried about noises in the dark, fire, severe weather, and losing house keys (Long and Long, 1983). However, this highly publicized study is considered by many researchers to be seriously flawed by methodological problems (Cole and Rodman, 1987). One researcher advocates cautious interpretation of the findings because characteristics of the sample were not specified, interview procedures were not explained, and no comparable interviews were reported for children in other forms of after-school care. Consequently, the generalizability of the Longs' observations is questionable (Vandell and Corasaniti, 1988).

Nevertheless, other studies have supported the Longs' findings. In a national survey 32 percent of the males and 41 percent of the females between 7 and 11 years of age reported worrying about staying home without an adult. The primary concern was that "someone bad would get in the house" (Zill, 1980). One of the most revealing negative portraits of latchkey children, albeit unscientific, came about as an accidental outcome of a survey by *Sprint*, a language arts magazine for fourth- through sixth-grade children published by Scholastic, Inc. Readers were invited to respond in writing to the theme: "Think of a situation that is scary to you. How do you handle your fear?" Editors received more than 7,000 letters, and 5,000 of these dealt with the fear of being home alone, usually in the after-school hours while parents were working (*School-Age Child Care [SACC] Newsletter*, 1984).

Analysis of calls children in self-care made to the telephone intervention program, "PhoneFriend," provides additional clues as to how the latchkey experience affects children. Of the 1,370 calls received during the first year of operation, 60 percent were classified as "lonely" and 15 percent as "scared," "worried," "sad," or "crying." Relatively few dealt with practical emergencies, such as cuts and scrapes (4 percent) or home maintenance problems (3 percent). (The system allowed multiple classification of each call, which is why the numbers add up to more than 100 percent) (Guerney and Moore, 1983).

In another study with over 4,000 eighth-grade students in San Diego and Los Angeles, those in the highest category of self-care (i.e., 11 or more hours per week) were 1.5 to 2 times more likely than those not in self-care at all to score high on risk-taking, anger, family conflict, stress, and fear of being left alone (Dwyer, Danley, Sussman, and Johnson, 1990).

Use of Drugs and Alcohol

According to a recent study financed by the National Institute on Drug Abuse and conducted in metropolitan schools in San Diego and Los Angeles, eighth-grade latchkey children who spend 11 or more hours a week alone are twice as likely to use cigarettes and alcohol, and 1.7 times as likely to use marijuana as are children cared for by adults after school ("Latchkey Kids More Apt to Use Drugs," 1989; Richardson, et al., 1989). This finding was independent of children's sex, race, family income, academic performance, family structure (two parents versus single parent), or involvement or noninvolvement in sports or other extracurricular activities. Moreover, these risks increased as latchkey children spent more time alone. This study suggests that the role transitions faced by 12- to 13-year olds, combined with decreased parental monitoring, may place adolescents at risk for problem behavior, particularly alcohol and other drug use ("Latchkey Children at Risk for Alcohol and Other Drug Use," 1990).

Controversial Television Viewing

A Fort Worth mother, Lynda Beams, is concerned about the potential detrimental effects of unsupervised children's television habits—particularly their watching "Geraldo" and the "Oprah Winfrey Show," which often air sexually explicit topics (Visser, 1989). The Texas PTA supported Beam's efforts and plans to publish an article about this case in the *PTA Communicator,* which is distributed to 8,000 members across the state.

Sexual Activity

Because latchkey children are alone much of the time, they have increased opportunity to participate in sexual activity. Their sexual development is as likely to be influenced as much by their peers, older siblings, television, movies, and books, as by their parents (Long and Long, 1987). The Longs collected interview data from 362 randomly selected adolescents who attended parochial schools in the Middle Atlantic states. While the information obtained did not indicate that the latchkey children surveyed were significantly more involved in sexual behavior than those young people who were continually supervised by adults, the data revealed that a significant minority (20 percent) of the young people sampled were sexually active in their own homes during the hours when they were on their own.

Sexual activity increased proportionately with the amount of time adolescents spent in self-care. Sexual activity increased particularly in the summer months, when teenagers regularly were left to care for themselves for eight to ten hours per day.

Safety

The most drastic outcome of the latchkey arrangement is that unsupervised children's safety is at risk. Accidents are the leading cause of death in young children, accounting for more deaths than the next six leading causes of death combined, and affecting one in every three children (Dershewitz and Williamson, 1977). Not surprisingly, research indicates that children are more likely to be seriously injured at home when they do not have an adult caregiver available (Haller, 1970; Tokohata, Colflesh, Digon, and Mann, 1972).

According to data gathered from a telephone survey of more than 1,000 Texas households, in over 15 percent of the homes there was a firearm as well as an elementary-age latchkey child. Researchers applied this 15 percent estimate to the nation and calculated that almost 1.2 million homes combine the potentially "deadly" risk factors of a firearm in the home and an unsupervised child. The researchers suggested that parents and other caretakers be educated about how to protect children from weapons at home. In particular, parents were advised to store weapons in locked boxes and use trigger locks; child proof safety catches and loading indicators were also advocated ("Latchkey Kids in Gun-Owning Families May Be at Risk," 1991).

Unsupervised children are also more likely to be the victims of home fires (Wheatley, 1973). Six thousand children die each year as a result of in-home accidents and fires that take place almost entirely in the absence of adults (Whirlpool Corporation and American Home Economics Association [AHEA], 1987).

In Texas, for example, reports of children playing with fire significantly increased after 3:00 P.M. when children leave school and are unsupervised (Patton, 1990; State Board of Insurance and State Fire Marshall's Office, 1987). Over 50,000 children under age 14 are permanently disabled annually (National Coalition to Prevent Childhood Injury, 1988). Results of a national study of household tasks performed by school children revealed that 71 percent of latchkey children regularly operated home appliances, frequently without adult supervision, and that parents were concerned about their children's use of these appliances, citing fires, burns, and electric shock as their major fears (Research and Forecasts, Inc., 1987).

Of course the extent of children's safety in taking care of themselves depends in part upon their level of knowledge of how to cope with emergencies. If children are without supervision for some portion of the day, they should be well prepared by parents to stay home alone. Ironically, research suggests that parents greatly overestimate their children's self-care competency (Peterson, Mori, and Scissors, 1986). The researchers independently gathered written answers from parents and spoken answers from 8-year-old children concerning rules for dealing with everyday situations (such as safe snacks) and for handling emergencies (such as housefires). Parents were asked to rate how well prepared each child was to be in self-care. Children rated themselves in this regard, along with acting out what they would do in various emergency situations. Results suggest a strong disparity between the preparation parents believed children had and the amount of preparation children actually had. Children were almost totally unaware of rules for emergencies and for daily safety decisions. They did not know a fraction of what they needed to know or what their parents believed they knew. The conclusion was that latchkey children need better preparation in avoiding injuries, dealing with emotional problems, and selecting appropriate activities (Peterson, 1989). Children who are not developmentally ready to handle self-care arrangements, in terms of their reasoning, coping skills, emotional maturity, and independence, may risk the consequences of the "hurried child" syndrome (i.e., may be pushed too quickly into adulthood) and may suffer both physical and emotional harm (Elkind, 1981).

Unsupervised children have also been found to be at-risk sexually. They are easy targets for child molesters (Forgione, 1976), and they typically show naive and trusting reactions to adult strangers (Poche, Brouwer, and Swearingen, 1981).

School and Education

Both parents and teachers consider the common practice of leaving children alone after school to be the primary cause of student difficulties in public school. Both parents and teachers rank unsupervised children as a factor more detrimental to educational progress than "poverty," "automatic promotion," "boring curriculum," or "teacher's failure to adapt to individual student needs" (Harris, 1987). Moreover, 62 percent of the teachers surveyed thought that "most" parents leave their children alone too much after school. Of the parents surveyed, 59 percent agreed with this criticism, and 41 percent stated that their child was often on his or her own between the end of school and 5:30 P.M. This situation was found to exist at all socioeconomic levels and in all parts of the country.

Children's education is adversely affected by the latchkey experience in a number of ways. Many students in self-care do not eat breakfast and the resulting nutritional deficiency reduces their ability to learn (Long and Long, 1983). Often children in self-care are tardy or absent from school because no one is home to wake them and to be responsible for their arrival on time. Or they may fall asleep in class, adding to their inability to learn effectively (San Antonio Cares, 1987).

Advertising and Marketing

Marketeers consider latchkey children an ideal target audience for consumable products. This is because marketing research indicates that, in addition to watching television, latchkey children are much more likely to wash dishes, prepare meals, do laundry, shop for groceries, and operate major appliances than are nonlatchkey children (Rothenberg, 1988; Whirlpool Corporation and American Home Economics Association [AHEA], 1987). Peanut butter, ketchup, and soft drink companies are among those directing after-school advertisements specifically toward unattended children. Because food companies are now targeting latchkey children, spending for national advertisements on commercial television between 3:00 P.M. and 5:00 P.M. on weekdays skyrocketed from nothing in 1982 to $107 million in 1987 (Rothenberg, 1988).

LATCHKEY EXPERIENCE: RESEARCH INDICATING A BENEFICIAL IMPACT

Hedin (1986) found 80 percent of the fourth through eighth graders in self-care or sibling care that she studied enjoyed being home without adult supervision. Strohman and Duff (1982) suggest in their literature review that latchkey children, because of early responsibilities, become more independent, self-reliant, and resourceful than their constantly supervised peers. Still other research has found that latchkey children learn earlier than they otherwise might to master self-help skills, take on responsibility, and solve problems (Kieffer, 1981).

In one study in North Carolina underwritten by a grant from Project Home Safe, teachers rated students in kindergarten through grade six for their level of school adjustment. As a group, children in self-care after school were rated as significantly better adjusted to school than either children in mother care or children attending a child care center after school (Rodman and Payne, 1990).

In an attempt to focus on the possible medical risk to latchkey children, researchers from the University of Arizona Health Sciences Center tried to answer the following questions: Are children in self-care more obese? Do children in self-care miss more school days? Do they make more visits to the school health office? The answers obtained from analyzing school records, school health exams, and physical exams performed by nurse practitioners for over 500 fifth-grade students in 10 public elementary schools in Tucson, Arizona, were somewhat surprising. There were no differences in height or weight between children in self-care and those in adult care. Abnormal physical findings were relatively infrequent and no different in self-care children from those in adult care. There were no differences in the number of school days missed between the two groups nor in the number of visits to the school health office. These researchers concluded that the 11-year-old self-care children in this study did not suffer more ill health than their counterparts in adult care ("Are Latchkey Kids More Unhealthy?," 1989).

LATCHKEY EXPERIENCE: RESEARCH INDICATING NO IMPACT

Several researchers have reported no significant differences—in terms of emotional, social, or academic development—between children in self-care and those supervised by adults. In a study of 150 white, predominantly middle class third graders from a suburban Dallas school system, no differences were found between latchkey children and mother care children in terms of sociometric nominations (children they liked or disliked playing with), academic grades, standardized test scores, conduct, children's own reports of their competence, or parent and teacher ratings of children (Vandell and Corasaniti, 1988).

D'Agostino (1987) examined the effect of the presence or absence of adult supervision on the academic, behavioral, and social development of fifth- and eighth-grade students. Results indicated virtually no difference in supervised and unsupervised children's perceptions of themselves. The self-concept of unsupervised children was also no different from that of supervised children. Similarly, another study found no difference between latchkey and adult care children in North Carolina in regard to either self-reported sense of control and self-esteem or to teachers' ratings of children's social adjustment (Rodman, Pratto, and Nelson, 1985).

Studying fifth and seventh graders in rural New York State, Galambos and Garbarino (1983) found that latchkey children did not perform any differently in school than nonlatchkey children in regard to academic achievement, fear of going outdoors alone, classroom orientation, and teacher-rated school adjustment. Galambos and Garbarino concluded, based upon the research on latchkey children to date (then 1983), that the environmental context may be the single most important factor in how well latchkey children adjust to self-care. Therefore, they advocated that future studies take into account differences in community characteristics, including the number of playgrounds, friendliness of neighbors, and neighborhood and family support systems.

No differences were found between 97 latchkey children and 19 nonlatchkey control children in a Midwest study, in regard to anxiety, self-perceived social ability, or behavioral problems (Lovko and Ullman, 1989). Interestingly, the amount of variance in the adjustment of the 116 children which was accounted for by whether or not the child was latchkey was normal when compared to amounts accounted for by the demographic/background variables (i.e., age, race, and sex of child; community size; family income; parents' marital status; and recent life stress) and latchkey situation variables. In particular, sex, income, and the presence of, or interaction with, other children during the self-care period were among the best "predictors" of the three adjustment indices.

A team of researchers studied the behavioral and academic correlates of latchkey status among 10- and 11-year-old children in a rural town, with subjects divided into three groups. "Latchkey children" were defined as those alone or with younger siblings for two hours or more each weekday after school; "semi-latchkey children" were classified as being without supervision three to five hours per week; and "non latchkey children" had a parent figure 17 or older at home daily after school. Questionnaire results indicated few differences between latchkey and nonlatchkey children, supporting the theory that community differences may account for children's response to self-care arrangements (Diamond, Kataria, and Messer, 1989). In addition, no significant differences were found between latchkey and nonlatchkey groups on personality and academic achievement measures in a study which examined the prevalence and correlates of former latchkey status, using a sample of 188 university students who had been unsupervised by an adult during their elementary or middle school years for at least two hours per day over a year or more (Messer, Wuensch, and Diamond, 1989).

Researchers at the University of North Carolina at Greensboro reported in their study of 354 children in grades kindergarten through six from randomly selected schools across their state that teachers felt latchkey children did as well in math and reading as children in mother care and center care after school (Rodman and Payne, 1990).

Steinberg (1986) found no overall difference in the responses of latchkey children and mother care children in Wisconsin to a set of story dilemmas assessing susceptibility to negative peer pressure. In other words, unsupervised adolescents who reported home after school were no more susceptible to peer pressure than adolescents supervised by parents at home during after-school hours. However, a subset of latchkey children *was* vulnerable. Those latchkey children who were allowed to "hang out" were more likely to report that they could be negatively influenced by their peers. Steinberg's study demonstrates that there are important differences within the self-care population. Adolescents who are more removed from adult supervision are more susceptible to peer pressure from their friends. Perhaps the most important conclusion from this study is that variations within the latchkey population—i.e., within the setting in which self-care takes place—are more important than variations between adult care and self-care, broadly defined.

In a follow-up study to Steinberg's, researchers contrasted sixth graders in adult care with sixth graders in self-care, and using a series of hierarchical multiple regression analyses they examined the effects of sex of adolescent, self-care status, and parental work hours on peer experience and self-image. Results indicated that variation in the self-care experience was more important for predicting behavior than the number of hours both parents worked. The kinds of arrangements made for children when parents were away had more import for understanding adolescent behavior than how long the parent worked (Galambos and Maggs, 1989).

EFFECTS OF THE LATCHKEY EXPERIENCE UPON THE COMMUNITY

Parents and Their Work

Parents of children in self-care are especially concerned about their children's safety and exposure to dangers inside and outside the home. Employers feel that this increased level of parental stress interferes with work performance, and they see evidence of decreased productivity, loss of concentration, and absenteeism resulting from such stress (Bureau of National Affairs, 1988). Declining production and work quality are especially likely around 3:00 P.M. when school is dismissed and working parents are anxiously calling to check on children and give them instructions or are awaiting a phone call from their children confirming that they have arrived home safely. This phenomenon is referred to as the "Three O'Clock Syndrome" or "Angst Hour" (Long and Long, 1983). Studies indicate that this stress is detrimental to employees and increases mistakes (Fernandez, 1986).

Libraries

Another significant aspect of the latchkey phenomenon is that throughout the country, in lieu of day care, children are increasingly spending their after-school hours at public libraries until picked up by a working parent. The existence of latchkey children in libraries is not unique to the United States; Canadian libraries have found that the situation is a regular occurrence in their system (Budziszewski, 1990). A recent survey found that 38 percent of Toronto Public Library's 32 branches experience some kind of problem related to unattended children, as only the minority read, browsed, or did their homework at the library (Ling, 1990).

Usually latchkey children are not at libraries by choice but because their parents consider these institutions to be safe, appropriate, or convenient places for children to wait. Unattended children, referred to as "library latchkey children," come from various income brackets and all types and sizes of localities (Leigh, 1987; Mitgang, 1988; Stefansson, 1988). Latchkey children often present space and control problems for libraries having too few staff to work with them. Until recently few libraries implemented solutions which addressed this phenomenon as an opportunity rather than as a problem.

Library media centers are also somewhat affected by latchkey children; school librarians may feel increasing pressure to provide school-based after-school programs (Connor, 1990). Although unattended children can be considered an opportunity for libraries, the media have portrayed latchkey children in the library negatively. This issue is the focal point of Part III of this book.

ADDITIONAL RESEARCH NEEDS

Steinberg's study (1986), as well as the research of Galambos and Garbarino (1983), indicate that simply studying latchkey versus nonlatchkey children is inadequate, since it is not the child care arrangement per se but the context of the situation that seems to affect children most. Moreover, it is probably overly simplistic to expect that being in self-care would have a single, unidirectional effect on all children. Although research has not adequately addressed these possibilities, it seems more likely that children who receive self-care are heterogeneous on several dimensions and that there are factors both about the latchkey situation itself and about the child that may well influence or mediate the presence, extent, and direction of any effects on the child's adjustment (Lovko and Ullman, 1989).

Consequently, Robinson, Rowland, and Coleman (1986) advocate that: "Studies should distinguish between the various types of latchkey situations (e.g., strictly alone, cared for by an older sibling, etc.) as potential negative environments, rather than simply comparing variations between adult care and self care." Furthermore, parameters such as the age at which a child enters the latchkey arrangement, number of hours in self-care, elected versus forced latchkey status, extent of parental supervision "in absentia," and recent life stressors affecting the child, must be considered in evaluating the impact of self-care upon children (Messer, Wuensch, and Diamond, 1989).

Longitudinal research is especially needed to investigate the long-term effects of self-care during the early elementary school years (Powell, 1987; Fosarelli, 1984). Negative effects may be cumulative and differences may be hidden until children are older (Vandell and Corasaniti, 1988).

Developmental theories, such as those of Piaget and Erickson, could be used as a basis for future research about children in self-care (Robinson, Rowland and Coleman, 1986; Magnusson and Allen, 1983). Seligson and Fink (1989) find the lack of strong data on the effects of being a latchkey child to be a critical gap in the research on child development, and believe that "it is hard to imagine how the total lack of such opportunities" as sports, arts, and informal play, which have been traditionally available in the out-of-school hours, "could not have at least a covert impact on the overall development of personality, intellectual inquiry and social relations." They urge that researchers study the effect on children of participation in school-age child care programs as compared to the effects of self-care. They also advocate a cost-benefit analysis documenting savings made possible by expenditures in quality school-age child care.

Research based on larger and less homogenous samples of supervised and unsupervised children is needed. For example, a national collaborative study of latchkey children would ensure sufficient numbers of children of various ages, ethnicities, races, and geographic locations. Some of these characteristics may be crucial in determining a profile of children who would or would not do well unsupervised (Fosarelli, 1984).

Certain characteristics of the parents and family which may influence the child's latchkey experience should also be investigated, such as family size, socioeconomic status, educational levels, methods of preparing children for self-care, attitudes of working mothers and children in self-care, and, especially, the father's attitudes and expectations. In addition, the health status of children in self-care needs to be studied in comparison to the health of children in adult care. Do these groups differ in regard to their nutritional status or junk food intake? (Fosarelli, 1984).

Finally, research is needed to evaluate the effect of different approaches to supporting children during the after-school hours, such as telephone hotlines, parent training, and school-age child care (Powell, 1987). Studies concerning intervention programs for latchkey children are just now beginning to appear (Padilla and Landreth, 1989). However, here too the quality and the numbers of children in groups must be considered, as "reports of questionable practices of staff-child ratios of 1:100 where children are herded into a gymnasium to do homework for several hours can be as startling as stories of unattended children at home" (Powell, 1987). Powell concludes that the overriding question for evaluating alternatives to self-care should not be whether harm or risk has been prevented, but whether a child's development has been enhanced. These intervention programs are the focus of Chapter 3.

REFERENCES

Are latchkey kids more unhealthy? 1989. *Pediatric Reports* 6(May): 30.

Bronfenbrenner, U. 1979. *The ecology of human development.* Cambridge, Massachusetts: Harvard University.

Budziszewski, M. 1990. Latchkey children in the public library now common. *Feliciter* (July/August): 2.

Bureau of National Affairs. 1988. *Latchkey children: A guide for employers.* National report on work and family. Special Report #11. Washington, D.C.: Bureau of National Affairs. November.

Cole, C. and H. Rodman. 1987. When school-age children care for themselves: Issues for family life educators and parents. *Family Relations* 36(January): 92–96.

Connor, J. G. 1990. *Children's library services handbook.* Phoenix: Oryx Press.

D'Agostino, R. 1987. Supervision: A study of the effects that the presence or absence of adult supervision has on the academic, behavioral, and social development of school-age children. *Dissertation Abstracts International* 48A, no. 4: 785-A.

Dershewitz, R.A. and J.W. Williamson. 1977. Prevention of childhood household injuries: A controlled clinical trial. *American Journal of Public Health* 67(December): 1148–53.

Diamond, J., S. Kataria, and S. Messer. 1989. Latchkey children: A pilot study investigating behavior and academic achievement. *Child and Youth Care Quarterly* 18(Summer): 131–40.

Dwyer, K., K. Danley, S. Sussman, and C. Johnson. 1990. Characteristics of eighth-grade students who initiate self-care in elementary and junior high school. *Pediatrics* 86(September): 448–54.

Elkind, D. 1981. *The hurried child.* Reading, Massachusetts: Addison-Wesley.

Fernandez, J. 1986. *Child care and corporate productivity: Resolving work-family conflicts.* Lexington, Massachusetts: Lexington Books.

Forgione, A.G. 1976. Use of mannequins in behavioral assessment of child molesters. *Behavior Therapy* 7(October): 678–85.

Fosarelli, P. 1984. Latchkey children. *Developmental and Behavioral Pediatrics* 5(August): 173–77.

Galambos, N.L. and J. Garbarino. 1983. Identifying the missing links in the study of latchkey children. *Children Today* 12 (July/August): 2–4+.

Galambos, N. and J. Maggs. 1989. The after-school ecology of young adolescents and self-reported behavior. ERIC Document ED 311 315. Victoria, B.C., Canada: University of Victoria.

Guerney, L. and L. Moore. 1983. PhoneFriend: A prevention oriented service for latchkey children. *Children Today* 12 (July/August): 5–10.

Haller, J.A. 1970. Problems in children's trauma. *Journal of Trauma* 10: 269–71.

Harris, L. 1987. *The Metropolitan Life survey of the American teacher 1987: Strengthening links between home and school.* New York: Metropolitan Life.

Hedin, D., et al. 1986. *Summary of the family's view of after-school time.* Minneapolis: Pillsbury Company.

Kieffer, E. 1981. The latchkey kids—how are they doing? *Family Circle* (February 24): 28–35.

Latchkey children at risk for alcohol and other drug use. 1990. *Observer: News from the Johnson Institute* (Summer): 12(3).

Latchkey kids in gun-owning families may be at risk. 1991. *The Washington Post*, January 8: 10.

Latchkey kids more apt to use drugs. 1989. *The Baltimore Sun*, September 6, 1A+.

Leigh, S. 1987. Chicago's latchkey kids. *Today's Chicago Woman* (September): 50–51.

Ling, F. 1990. Latchkey children in the public library. Paper presented at the Canadian Library Association Annual Conference, June 15, Ottawa, Ontario, Canada.

Long, L. and T. Long. 1983. *Handbook for latchkey children and their parents.* New York: Arbor House.

Long, T. and L. Long. 1987. Sexuality and latchkey children. *Peabody Journal of Education* 64 (Summer): 173–83.

Lovko, A.M. and D. Ullman. 1989. Research on the adjustment of latchkey children: Role of background/demographic and latchkey situation variables. *Journal of Clinical Psychology* 18(March): 16–24.

Magnusson, D. and V.L. Allen. 1983. *Human development: An interactional perspective.* New York: Academic Press.

Messer, S., K. Wuensch, and J. Diamond. 1989. Former latchkey children: Personality and academic correlates. *Journal of Genetic Psychology* 150(September): 301–09.

Mitgang, L. 1988. Libraries new haven for latchkey children. *Denton Record Chronicle*, February 21, 4F.

National Coalition to Prevent Childhood Injury. Leader's Guide. 1988. *Safe kids are no accident!* Washington, D.C.

Padilla, M.L. and G. Landreth. 1989. Latchkey children: A review of the literature. *Child Welfare* 68(July/August): 445–54.

Patton, C. 1990. *What do I do until you get home?! School-age child care in Texas.* Houston: Houston Committee for Private Sector Initiatives.

Peterson, L. 1989. Latchkey children's preparation for self-care: Overestimated, underrehearsed, and unsafe. *Journal of Clinical Child Psychology* 18(March): 36–43.

Peterson, L. and P. Magrab. 1989. Introduction to the special section: Children on their own. *Journal of Clinical Child Psychology* 18(March): 2–7.

Peterson, L., L. Mori, and C. Scissors. 1986. Mom or Dad says I shouldn't: Supervised and unsupervised children's knowledge of their parents' rules for home safety. *Journal of Pediatric Psychology* 11 (June): 177–88.

Poche, C., R. Brouwer, and M. Swearingen. 1981. Teaching self-protection to young children. *Journal of Applied Behavior Analysis* 14(Summer): 169–76.

Powell, D. 1987. After-school child care. *Young Children* 42(March): 62–66.

Research and Forecasts, Inc. 1987. *The Whirlpool report on children's use of appliances.* New York: Research and Forecasts, Inc.

Richardson, J.L., et al. 1989. Substance use among eighth grade students who take care of themselves after school. *Pediatrics* 84(September): 556–66.

Robinson, B., B. Rowland, and M. Coleman. 1986. Taking action for latchkey children and their families. *Family Relations* 35(October): 473–78.

Rodman, H. and C. Payne. 1990. Predictors and consequences of amount of time children spend in self care. Unpublished manuscript, University of North Carolina at Greensboro.

Rodman, H., D.J. Pratto, and R.S. Nelson. 1985. Child care arrangements and children's functioning: A comparison of self-care and adult-care children. *Developmental Psychology* 21(May): 413–18.

Rothenberg, R. 1988. Advertisers take aim at latchkey children. *Dallas Morning News*, May 10, 1C+.

San Antonio Cares. Child Care Working Group of the United Way of Texas. 1987. *Latchkey children in Texas.* Austin.

School-Age Child Care (SACC) Newsletter. 1984. Home alone after school is worse than snakes and book reports! Wellesley, Massachusetts: Wellesley College, Center for Research on Women. 2(Fall): 12.

Seligson, M. and D. Fink. 1989. *No time to waste: An action agenda for school-age child care.* Wellesley, Massachusetts: School-Age Child Care Project, Wellesley College, Center for Research on Women.

State Board of Insurance and State Fire Marshall's Office. 1987. *Fire in Texas.* Austin: State Fire Marshall.

Stefansson, J. 1988. Kids with keys: San Marino Public Library—A case study. Paper presented at the Public Library Association National Conference in Pittsburgh, Pennsylvania, April 29.

Steinberg, L. 1986. Latchkey children and susceptibility to peer pressure: An ecological analysis. *Developmental Psychology* 22(July): 433–39.

Strohman, S.H. and R.E. Duff. 1982. The latchkey child: Whose responsibility? *Childhood Education* 59(November/December): 76–79.

Tokohata, G.K., V. Colflesh, E. Digon, and L. Mann. 1972. Childhood injuries caused by consumer products. Pennsylvania Department of Health, Division of Research and Biostatistics, Harrisburg.

Vandell, D. and M.A. Corasaniti. 1988. The relation between third graders' after-school care and social, academic, and emotional counseling. *Child Development* 59(August): 868–72.

Visser, N. 1989. Mother wants to switch times of "Oprah," "Geraldo." *Fort Worth Star Telegram*, February 20, 1+.

Wheatley, G.M. 1973. Childhood accidents 1952–1972, an overview. *Pediatric Annals* 2(January):10–30.

Whirlpool Corporation and American Home Economics Association (AHEA). 1987. *Press packet on project home safe*. Arlington, Virginia.

Zill, N. 1980. *American children: Happy, healthy, and insecure*. New York: Doubleday-Anchor.

PART II
Latchkey Children in the Community

Chapter 3
Local and National Responses to Latchkey Children

ADULT CARE PROGRAMS

School-Age Child Care

Coolsen, Seligson, and Garbarino (1985) believe that the best supervised programs for latchkey children are staffed by adults; offer a carefully designed curriculum based on knowledge about the cognitive, social, and emotional development of children; and use the resources of the community. One approach widely implemented throughout the country is that of before- and after-school child care for school-age children (or "extended day programs") at school sites. Schools can administer their own programs or can contract with community agencies that take responsibility for designing the program, recruiting children, hiring staff, and managing the day-to-day operation (Coolsen, Seligson, and Garbarino, 1985). School-age child care programs are housed, funded, and administered by diverse agencies. A program may be initiated by one organization, offered at the site of another organization, administered by a third organization, and funded by a fourth.

The number of latchkey children participating in school-age child care programs is enormous, and their numbers are increasing. Agencies providing school-age child care include: the YMCA, the YWCA, Boys Clubs of America, Girls Clubs of America, Camp Fire, Inc., parks and recreation departments, private and public schools, independent organizations, and even the nation's largest employer—the U.S. Army. The latter has decreed that no child under 12 should be left without adult supervision after school, and, consequently, plans to bring school-age child care to every Army post (Seligson and Fink, 1989).

The following statistics give some indication of the extent and variety of sponsors of school-age child care programs throughout the United States. In 1987 the YMCA reported that 962 of its 2,200 local units offered school-age child care programs. About 54 of the YWCA's 400 units now serve between 30,000 and 35,000 children via school-age child care programs. At least 18 percent of the 200 Boy's Clubs of America provide school-age child care. In a 1987 survey, 50 percent of the 112 units of Girl's Clubs of America responded affirmatively when asked about extended day services. At least 17 of the 300 local councils of Camp Fire, Inc. operate full-time before-school and after-school care, primarily in public schools. Another 10 operate drop-in programs and 10 more provide vacation time care. According to a survey, the National Association of Independent Schools reports that at least half or approximately 300 of their 604 private elementary schools have active extended day programs. Although no figures are available, an increasing number of local park and recreation departments switched from their traditional drop-in recreational programs to school-age child care (Seligson and Fink, 1989).

NAESP Survey on School-Age Child Care

The National Association of Elementary School Principals (NAESP) queried 1,175 principals about before- and after-school care (National Association of Elementary School Principals [NAESP], 1988). Although 84 percent of the principals responding believed that children in "most communities" need supervision before and after school, and although 60 percent reported a "definite need" for before- and after-school child care, less than one-fourth actually offered this service. Given adequate resources (i.e., staff, money, and authority), two-thirds of the principals stated that they would provide school-age child care, with more than one-third giving as the primary reason for this willingness the belief that the "in school performance of children who are left alone too long could improve with adequate care." Nearly two-thirds believed schools should provide school-age child care, and about one-third stated that they felt this way because school buildings are the logical sites for such programs.

Of those respondents who provided school-age child care, the majority offered programs paid for by parents and combining recreational activities with academic enrichment. The "problem" with school-age child care most frequently cited by principals (22 percent) was that of building use—flexibility. However, 54 percent felt that their school-age child care programs were "very successful." The major benefits cited were that children received adequate before- and after-school care and that the school had better relationships with the community and parents. According to Dr. Samuel Sava, NAESP Executive Director, findings from this survey indicate the vast gap between supply and demand for before- and after-school supervision of children in grades kindergarten through eight.

In regard to the advantages of school-age child care programs, Strother (1984) states the above reasons as well as the fact that they build parental support, attract students to public schools, put empty classrooms to work, and reduce vandalism. On the negative side, Strother feels that administrators and teachers are often confused about the schools' responsibility, that heavier professional workloads lead to stress, that tax increases may be needed to cover expenses, and that legal or policy issues may pose problems.

In 1989 the Texas legislature recognized the needs of latchkey children and passed Senate Bill 914, which requires school districts with student populations of 5,000 or more to hold public hearings annually for the purpose of considering the needs and availability of out-of-school care for children in prekindergarten through grade seven. The bill addresses funding issues for school districts choosing to assume direct responsibility for providing programs rather than contracting for these services (Baker, 1990).

Examples of School-Age Child Care

Murfreesboro's Extended School Program

An example of a school-based program offered by a school system and completely funded by users (parents) is that of ESP—the Extended School Program—in Murfreesboro, Tennessee. Begun in 1986 at one school in that city's school system, ESP now is available in seven schools. Of the 4,000 children enrolled in the school system, 1,635 participate in the Extended School Program, with an average daily attendance of 900 (Lee, 1990). ESP provides year-round child care and enrichment activities before school begins (6:00 A.M. to 7:45 A.M.), after school is finished (2:25 P.M. to 6:00 P.M.), and all day from 6:00 A.M. to 6:00 P.M. on snow days, teacher in-service days, and during summer vacation. Planned activities include physical education, snacks, violin, guitar, art instruction, computer clubs, foreign language experience, and special homework time. Children may also participate with no additional charge in Boy Scouts, Brownies, 4-H Club activities, typing, handwork, and movies.

A unique feature of ESP is that tutors from the local university—Middle Tennessee State University (MTSU)—assist children with homework, tutoring, and special activities. MTSU students benefit from the opportunity to obtain quality training for their professional careers and to apply the latest teaching techniques they have learned. Since children participate in ESP at their normal school site, the program does not require interim transportation, and is very convenient for both children and parents. The local business people support ESP because they believe that it alleviates the "three o'clock syndrome" at work and increases their employees' productivity by lowering parental preoccupations with children's whereabouts and safety after school. The chairman of the School Board of the Murfreesboro City School System has stated that ESP has been significant in eliminating "latchkey" children in that area. The Extended School Program has become a state model for innovative, cost-efficient programs that serve business, the community, and student needs. It is an example of how parents, businesspeople, elected officials, and school administrators can work together to turn "a problem into an opportunity" (Murfreesboro City School System, 1989; Lee, 1990).

Osborn's Cactus Club

Another example of a school-based program completely supported by parent fees is the Cactus Club of Osborn School District in Phoenix, Arizona. Children participate in R.A.F.T. (Reading Aloud and Following Through). Each day a child care teacher reads a book which the children extend by a creative project to enhance the book's theme. For example, if the book is about pink lemonade the children make lemonade from fresh lemons. As part of R.A.F.T., children also write and illustrate their own books (Chambers, 1990).

Sacramento and Yolo County's Kids-On-Kampus

One example of a school-based program operated by a private business is Kids-On-Kampus, which runs 12 latchkey centers in seven school districts in Sacramento and Yolo counties in California. The centers are open from 7:00 A.M. to 6:00 P.M. during the school year and full-time during summer and school holidays. The program is staffed by highly qualified directors and teachers and includes supervised homework, educational specialty, outdoor recreation, and choice time. Parents are involved through the elected Parent Advisory Council. Cost is $160 per month for full-time care (Press-Dawson, 1987). In districts experiencing a space crunch, children are bused from other schools to a facility leased to Kids-On-Kampus. Some Kids-On-Kampus centers are housed in churches adjacent to schools.

Jackson's Park and Recreation Program

In Jackson, Tennessee, the Recreation and Parks Department works with the Education Department in providing after-school care. The program includes crafts, games, storytelling, music, movement, and creative dramatics. Parental response has been very positive (Campbell, 1988).

Hawaii's A+ After-School Program

Currently, 22,500 elementary students are enrolled in Hawaii's very successful A+, the after-school program funded almost entirely by the state. Parents pay $25 per month for A+, regardless of their income. A+ is not only open to children whose parent(s) work, but is also available to children whose parents are registered in educational courses or job training programs. A+ is set up to put almost total control in the hands of each individual principal. But the principal designates a site coordinator to run the program, assisted by a group leader and program aides. Each program must include five basic components: snack/free time; study time; content enrichment, such as language arts, math, or science; creative enrichment, such as art or drama; and character development through interaction and instruction.

The A+ program was the result of a crisis situation in funding affordable, quality child care in Hawaii, which has the highest percentage of the nation (66 percent) of mothers in the work force. Hawaii is in a unique position to institute such a massive social program because, unlike other states that have local school jurisdictions, Hawaii—the second oldest public school system in the nation—has a statewide school system that is financed with state funds instead of with local taxes. Dr. Herman Aizawa, assistant superintendent in charge of instructional programs, stated that "the state identified A+ as an essential service" (Sullam, 1990).

EARTHNAUTS After-School Care

Some students in Austin, Texas, would like to see and participate in a unique concept of school and corporate child care programs for school-age children, which has as its focus environmental science. Those students have formed EARTHNAUTS, a nonprofit service organization concerned with the endangerment of the earth's biosphere and which is composed of and operated by students at the secondary level under adult supervision. They propose that EARTHNAUTS work toward becoming a multi-national organization of students involved in preserving and restoring the earth's environment. Because students in EARTHNAUTS believe that existing after-school care programs lack a central focus, except to keep children safe, do not usually consult children regarding what they would like to do after school, and do not offer enjoyable science/technology education for lack of qualified personnel to administer them, they have proposed "A Kid's Concept" of meaningful after-school care.

EARTHNAUTS envision their program as a component in existing after-school care programs, offering an option for children who desire a challenge, even in the after-school hours. Their program would consist of hands-on environmental science at selected elementary schools. Environmental awareness, application of information, and active participation in experimentation and creative problem-solving strategies would be stressed. Average to high quality students who are potential leaders, and curious, independent workers would be eligible for the program. Program activities would include learning about pressing environmental issues; hands-on analysis of soil, water, vegetation, etc.; organization and leadership training; creative environmental dramatic presentations; and wildlife rehabilitation training (EARTHNAUTS, 1990).

YMCA School-Age Child Care

In Dallas, the YMCA operates school-age child care programs at 66 sites after school from 3:30 to 6:00 or 6:30 P.M., serving 21,000 kindergarten through sixth-grade students of all socioeconomic groups at an average cost of $30 per week. The activities include homework assistance, indoor and outdoor play, snack, art, one special activity per day, and field trips. In some cases the YMCA contracts with the school system to use the building and the school system charges rental fees each month but provides utilities, janitorial service, air/heat, and overhead. In most cases in Dallas, however, the YMCA hires its own staff (Petrick, 1990).

Boys and Girls Clubs of Ontario: C.A.R.E. Programs

In September 1990, four Creative After School Recreation and Enrichment Pilot Projects (C.A.R.E.) for children ages 10 to 12 were initiated in Ontario, Canada, via the Boys and Girls Clubs, with funding from the Ministry of Community and Social Services. The programs, which will be evaluated in Fall 1991, are exploring various methods of combining recreational activities with a supervised care component aimed at helping children achieve an independent approach to self-care during their leisure time.

One of the four C.A.R.E. programs is offered by the YMCA of Hamilton/Burlington. It includes a walk-in center where children can relax, play games, participate in gym, or do homework; a telephone support service; and a community-link component in which parents can register their children in after-school recreational activities while using the center as a check-in and check-out point. Program base hours are Monday through Friday from 3:30 P.M. to 6:30 P.M. during the academic school year, and fees are $3 per day. Nutritional snacks, a "kid's" council to assist in program development and evaluation, family involvement in planning, and specialized activities for pre-teens (i.e., skateboarding instruction, rap dance, self-defense) are also unique features (Groves, 1990).

Another C.A.R.E. program, provided by the Dilico Ojibway Child and Family Services of Thunder Bay, Ontario, focuses upon the vast cultural resources available in the local community and the needs of native youth. Program features include youth work with community elders; native arts, crafts, dance, and traditions; nutritional supplements; and referrals from community agencies (Baynham, 1990).

A third C.A.R.E. program is available through the St. Christopher House in Toronto, Ontario, and involves the Parks and Recreation Department. Program features include an after-school and a full summer program, a "warmline" telephone access, and specialized creative visual and performing arts events by local residents (Baynham, 1990).

A fourth C.A.R.E. program involves a public library and is described in Chapter 7.

Sugar Mill's Theatre Arts Program for Children at Risk

At Sugar Mill Elementary School in Volusia County, Florida, a special after-school drama program is being funded by the U.S. Department of Health and Human Service's Office of Substance Abuse and Prevention

(Van Driel, 1990). The $400,000 grant (the only one of its kind awarded to an elementary school in the United States) allows Sugar Mill to operate a model drug and alcohol education/prevention program as an after-school Theatre Arts Program over the next two years. Each of the 50 participants in grades four through six—many are latchkey and all are high risk—auditioned for a spot in the group by writing and presenting a one-minute speech about drug and alcohol abuse. They meet from 2:00 P.M. to 5:30 P.M. each weekday, and after snacks and a roll call they divide into groups that rotate between homework/study hall, drama, music, and dance classes, each lasting 45 minutes.

The focus is on educating youth about the dangers of drug and alcohol abuse and building self-confidence and self-esteem to resist peer pressure to try drugs and alcohol. Many of the group's skits deal with drug and alcohol problems, and adults from the community speak to the group about substance abuse. Harry Burney III, professional actor and singer who performed on Broadway in "Driving Miss Daisy," is the artistic director for the project. The three-year grant provides for extensive research, including pre- and post-testing students concerning their attitudes toward themselves, school, peer pressure, and other people, in order to determine the effects of the program upon pupils.

School of the 21st Century

Edward Zigler, Sterling Professor of Psychology at Yale University, developed a model for the School of the 21st Century, which was implemented in September 1988 in Independence, Missouri, and in nearby Platte County. These two locales now boast 13 schools serving 1,000 children in school-age child care. Currently, three other states are implementing the School of the 21st Century—Connecticut, Ohio, and Wisconsin (Watson and Fitzgerald, 1989). Zigler's idea was that the public school buildings already in existence could be used for more than formal schooling—they could also provide much needed services. Those services are on-site day care for 3- to 5-year-olds; before- and after-school (latchkey) care for 5- to 12-year-olds; support and training for neighborhood family day care providers; assistance and home visitation to new parents; and information and referral services for parents, starting from the time of pregnancy. In this model of school-age child care, physical education activities, computer and arts and crafts classes, practice time for music, and unstructured time is offered both before and after school is in session (Zigler and Ennis, 1988;

Watson and Fitzgerald, 1989). A specially trained day care worker visits homes of newborns in the district, offering parents support and information. A special bus delivers school-age children to their homes at 4:30 P.M., or children may stay at school until parents pick them up (Wright, 1990).

The Lighted School House

The Houston Independent School District (Texas), with the assistance of the American Red Cross, Boy and Girl Scouts of America, Coalition for the Homeless, United Way, and other social and religious agencies, provides a well-organized comprehensive latchkey program that is more than ordinary school-age child care. The Lighted School House program is available from 3:30 P.M. to 10:00 P.M. weekdays at the Gregory-Lincoln School. Its mission statement reads:

> ... to provide for the homeless, unattended and displaced child some relief from the often unhealthy and dangerous atmosphere of the streets by extending security of the school day beyond 3:00 P.M. and giving him/her some measure of stability, reinforcement of identity and worth, and a continued opportunity to learn basic study and social skills (Houston Independent School District [HISD], 1990).

Via the Lighted School House a target group of almost 60 children in grades kindergarten through fifth and 80 students in grades nine through twelve are provided not only a range of educational and recreational after-school activities, but also guidance, counseling, and emergency overnight shelter. The program was begun in 1989 when Superintendent Joan Raymond, learning of reports that students were living on the streets, presented a proposal to the board for a network of support from community agencies (Smith, 1989). Staffing for this program consists of two full-time coordinators and contracted services of the YMCA, as well as "loaned" personnel who are crisis, drug, and family counselors; social workers; and child psychologists.

Employer-Sponsored Child Care

Increasingly businesses are establishing child care assistance programs and "family friendly" work policies to address issues raised by growing numbers of women in the workforce. In 1970 only a handful of employers offered any form of child care assistance, but by 1989 more than 4,000 corporations did so (Wilks, 1990).

The most frequently offered programs are information and referral services and dependent care assistance plans, which enable employees to pay for child care with pre-tax dollars. Some corporations provide financial assistance through vendor or voucher agreements or corporate-sponsored child care centers on-site. As companies strive to be responsive to the needs of the changing American family, many have expanded or modified existing personnel policies to incorporate such features as maternity/paternity leave, paid sick leave to care for an ill child, flexible work hours, permanent part-time employment, and stress counseling for employees and their family members (Wilks, 1990).

One study found that 1,800 U.S. companies offer either on-site or off-site child care centers for their employees' children ("Kids with Keys," 1986). Moreover, a recent survey by the Union Bank in Los Angeles found that for every three dollars spent aiding employees, four dollars were saved in reduced absenteeism, increased productivity, and good public relations ("Child-Care Patchwork," 1989).

Child Care at Apartment Sites

In the city of Richardson (a suburb of Dallas) an apartment manager who is a former teacher started an after-school activity center for children of working parents who live in the complex. She reconverted a two-bedroom apartment into a center where school-age children can congregate between 3:45 P.M. and 5:45 P.M. for games and structured activities ranging from making a pinata to painting a cardboard stage (Barker, 1988).

Child Care at Housing Projects

A number of cities, including Dover, Delaware; Baltimore, Maryland; and Minneapolis, Minnesota, have school-age child care programs within housing projects. The Dover program is available from 6:00 A.M. to 6:00 P.M., serving half-day kindergarten children from five elementary schools. Housing authorities donate space and utilities. Funds for the program come from parent fees, Title XX, and subsidies parents receive for work incentive programs (Seligson and Fink, 1989).

Intergenerational Programs

A number of intergenerational programs have been developed to meet the needs of school-age children and working parents. One example is a senior center latchkey model in which children in nearby schools attend a planned after-school program at a local senior center. After-school programs staffed by older workers and situated in schools or other community sites, and telephone reassurance programs, often called intergenerational hotlines, in which older volunteers are regularly in touch with latchkey children when they return from school to an empty house, are other examples of intergenerational programs (Ventura-Merkel, Liederman, and Ossofsky, 1989). Successful and exemplary intergenerational programs appear to have several distinguishing characteristics. They address major social issues and problems, rebuild natural helping relationships, and are mutually supportive and beneficial to all generations involved. In addition, noteworthy intergenerational programs provide optimum use of financial resources, build upon existing services of the institutions, and provide opportunities for communities to design programs appropriate to local needs (Ventura-Merkel, Liederman, and Ossofsky, 1989).

Shared Heritage Grandparent Child Program: One unusual adult-care intergenerational program, which is based on a grandparent-grandchild type of relationship, is the Shared Heritage Intergenerational Child Care Program in Iowa (Hawkeye Area Community Action Program, 1985). For this program people over 55 are recruited as family day care home providers.

AgeLink: Another example of a program with an intergenerational approach is AgeLink, which was begun in 1985 and operated from Western Carolina University's Center for Improving Mountain Living (CIML). AgeLink brings together 11,000 latchkey children with some of the area's 80,000 people over 65. Elders are encouraged to share with children their special talents in crafts, music, and storytelling. Program planners see AgeLink as having at least two benefits: elders pass along skills that might otherwise be lost to future generations, and children who would otherwise spend many hours home alone can be in the company of caring adults (Coolsen, Seligson, and Garbarino, 1985). AgeLink offers four different models: after-school group care in schools or senior centers; family day care; transportation for unsupervised older children to attend after-school activities; and telephone contact between older volunteers and children home alone. As of March 1989, 50 AgeLink volunteers were working with 600 children at 11 after-school sites (Rickman, 1990).

SELF-CARE SUPPORTIVE PROGRAMS

Self-care may be appropriate for older children or in circumstances in which the alternative is poor supervision (Coolsen, Seligson, and Garbarino, 1985; Fosarelli, 1984). Cole and Rodman (1987) provide parents with minimum guidelines for determining children's developmental readiness for self-care. Physically, children should have enough control of their body so as not to be susceptible to injury. They should be able to manipulate doors and locks and to safely operate equipment, such as the stove and vacuum. Emotionally, children should be capable of handling unexpected situations and of tolerating separation from adults without much loneliness or fear. They should also be able to follow important rules. In regard to cognitive development, children should be able to understand, remember, and receive verbal and written instructions and to solve problems rationally. If children can solicit help as appropriate from designated persons, understand the role of community resource persons, and maintain friendships, socially speaking, they may be ready for self-care.

Some solutions are available to backup adult supervised child care programs and to enhance the potential for healthy, safe, self-care situations. These supportive efforts include the use of pets as companions, the "buddy system," educational materials or curricula about "survival skills" to train latchkey children, and telephone hotlines and warmlines.

Use of Pets as Companions

Since social support for self-care children is important to their wellbeing, one often overlooked yet appropriate support strategy is the use of pets (Heath and McKenry, 1989). A pet can play a role in alleviating fears and loneliness (Blue, 1986). Because self-care children are the first family members to arrive home, they benefit from the pet's initial and often enthusiastic greeting. Consequently, as animals sense the child returning home they become active and eager for the predictable interaction with the child. Self-care children who live with companion animals may not perceive themselves as returning home to an empty house, but rather as returning to an animal who needs them to let it in or out, or to feed it. Companion animals may also have therapeutic benefits for self-care children, which researchers are just beginning to examine.

Bachman (1975) found that 9 percent of first and second graders queried in his sampling of 108 public elementary school students in a middle class neighborhood in New Hampshire named pets as their first choice of "helper." Another 14 percent chose pets as their second choice of "helper." Of the 173 third, fourth, and fifth graders Bachman queried, 14 percent chose pets as their second choice (compared to 11 percent choosing fathers). Data gathered as to why they selected pets as a "helper" indicated that it was because the "helper" does not criticize. But "mothers" were the first choice as helper because they gave good advice and understood. This suggests that children this age understand the benefits and limitations of animal companions as compared to humans. The study also suggests that pets can make a significant contribution in an area that adults have assumed to be solely their role.

Wynn (1987) surveyed 93 third and fifth graders and their parents to compare children's satisfaction with self-care and adult care as a function of dog ownership and neighborhood safety. Contrary to other studies, the self-care children (who had dogs as companions) were generally less fearful than adult care children.

In a recent study psychologist Michael Levine found that "people who were raised with a pet showed greater social responsibility, personal adjustment, and better social skills." "A pet can make a special difference for latchkey children who are home on their own after school," as a furry friend can provide security against real and imagined threats, can fill the gap left by missing family and friends during those hours, and can offer unfailing friendship and love in an uncritical, noncompetitive way. In addition, pets can help in stressful situations by "triangling," or serving as a neutral party to reduce tension and diffuse conflict (Jabs, 1989).

The Buddy System

In the "buddy system" a child walks home from school with another child every day. This arrangement provides children with the comfort of knowing that they are not the only ones in a self-care situation and that there is someone with whom to share feelings or problems. Older children can be paired with younger ones (Toenniessen, Little, and Rosen, 1985).

Survival Skills Training

Numerous comprehensive programs have been developed to help prepare children and their families to deal with the challenges of the self-care arrangement. "Despite the recent proliferation of survival skills programs, few empirical studies have examined the impact of self-care training on children's knowledge, behaviors, or emotional well-being" (Koblinsky and Todd, 1989).

I'm In Charge

In five sessions (one for parents, three for children, and one for parents and children) the course "I'm In Charge," covers personal safety skills, emergency responses, and care of younger siblings (Swan, Briggs, and Kelso, 1985). This guidance unit developed by the Kansas Committee for Prevention of Child Abuse has been conducted in 47 states and abroad (McHenry, 1990). It was designed to assist families in determining whether self-care is appropriate for their 8- to 12-year-old children as well as to provide children with the skills to cope more effectively with self-care. Each 45-minute session begins by asking students to complete sentence stems, such as: "When I'm home alone I feel. . . ." Responses are then shared with the group. Because parent involvement and parent-child communication are two of the goals of "I'm In Charge," students are given "homework" which involves discussing with parents material distributed in class.

The National Committee for the Prevention of Child Abuse evaluated the impact of the "I'm In Charge" program on more than 1,800 parents and children in eight states in urban, suburban, and rural communities with white and minority populations. Program participation significantly increased parent-child agreement about how children should handle a housefire, a possible poisoning, a peeping Tom, and an approach from a potential child molester. However, program attendance did not influence parent-child agreement about how the child should deal with an invitation to play with a friend after school (Gray and Coolsen, 1987).

Being In Charge

A second but similar self-care skills training course is "Being In Charge." Researchers examined the influence of this guidance unit on lower and middle class fifth and sixth graders' knowledge of self-care procedures, after they attended a six-session course regarding family rules, personal safety, handling emergencies, home management, and methods of establishing a self-care arrangement. Students who completed the unit demonstrated greater gains in their knowledge of safety and self-care practices than did children in a control group. Moreover, after five months their knowledge about self-care only slightly lessened (Bundy and Boser, 1987).

Safe at Home Game and Prepared for Today

Peterson (1984) compared the effectiveness of a behavioral program ("Safe at Home") and a discussion-oriented program ("Prepared for Today") to teach self-care skills to 8- to 10-year-old children without parental supervision from lower socioeconomic status families. Each of the 16-session programs addressed personal safety, handling emergencies, dealing with strangers, and sibling care. Following the intervention program, children in "Safe at Home" demonstrated better self-care skills than those trained with "Prepared for Today," and those skills were maintained in a five-month follow-up evaluation.

Keys for Kids

A curriculum kit developed by Ohio State University and the Ohio Cooperative Extension Service to train children for being alone is entitled "Keys for Kids: A Learning Packet for Self Care/Latchkey Children and Their Parents." The packet contains an educational game to help families confront problems, dilemmas, and decisions children face when home alone. The game consists of a game board, one die, four game markers, 48 key cards, and five sets of cards (12 to a set) on food and fitness, telephone and home responsibilities, and self-esteem and safety. The object of the game is to travel through the house and finish with the most keys. In the guidebook for parents is a certificate of recognition for a "clean kitchen cook" and a "super cook award." Role playing situations, objectives, and discussion of how to deal with strangers, fire safety, telephone calls, self-esteem, helping at home, and health and fitness are included in the guidebook. The children's workbook teaches by listing rules and offering crossword puzzles, yes and no questions, recipes, etc. (Ohio Cooperative Extension Service, 1985).

On Your Own

Still another self-reliance training program to assist latchkey children in caring for themselves responsibly is entitled "On Your Own" (Mock, n.d.). The six-session course designed for third and fourth graders includes information similar to the other units described above—i.e., crime prevention, first aid, coping with such crises as lockout or bad weather, nutritional snacks, homework, care of younger siblings, and leisure time activities. One suggestion for preventing boredom is to "visit your library" to get a free library card and to borrow books and records. A four-part letter series for parents and children can be used with "On Your Own" lessons. Letters for parents cover goals for self-care, hassle-free good nutrition, school, home work, and TV alternatives. Letters for children cover safety, snacks, study, and fun. The Texas Agricultural Extension Service prepared "On Your Own" and the average enrollment is 3,000 children per year (Corporate Child Development Fund for Texas [CCDFT], 1988).

K.I.D.S.

K.I.D.S. is a self-care survival skills program developed by the Camp Fire Council (Fosarelli, 1984). In Dallas the Camp Fire Council offers self-reliance and crime prevention classes for children that cover safety at home, including kitchen practices (Floria and Effren, 1988; South, 1988). Some local Camp Fire councils offer the program "I Can Do It," which is an eight-week course designed for second and third graders who spend time alone at home. Taking care of belongings, escaping a fire, telephone usage in emergencies, and responsibility for family members are all covered in this program (Camp Fire, Inc., n.d.).

Police Partners

"Police Partners" is a successful survival training program for latchkey children with a slightly different approach and goal. Offered by the Police Department and Neighborhood Watch in Altamonte Springs, Florida, the goals of this program, which over 300 children, ages 9 to 14, have completed, are competency in handling basic emergency situations when home alone, building relationships between youth and law enforcement officers, and establishing a children's "Neighborhood Watch." "Police Partners," which is scheduled into five two-hour sessions, covers the police department and the community, Neighborhood Watch, crime and consequences, juvenile arbitration, a mock trial, drugs and alcohol, the fire department in the community, home safety, and CPR and basic first aid. While the primary instruction is done by the police department, guest instructors, such as fire department personnel, assist. Participants receive "The Official Kid's Survival Kit" and special "Police Partners" t-shirts, with costs underwritten by the business community. This program benefits the police by creating better rapport with community youth and by creating extra eyes and ears for the police station. Children learn confidence in reacting to emergencies and handling the responsibilities of being alone, and parents appreciate the assistance given children (Liquori, 1990; Murphey and Viner, 1986).

Basic First Aid

The American Red Cross' nursing intervention course on Basic First Aid Training (BAT) has been utilized to teach latchkey children first aid techniques. Research conducted to determine whether the BAT course would increase fourth graders' first aid knowledge and reduce their stress levels revealed that children who received BAT showed a significant increase in knowledge of first aid as well as a significant decrease in stress (May, 1989).

Adventure Addison

The Town of Addison (a suburb of Dallas) piloted "Adventure Addison" in March 1990, a program aimed at an estimated 400 latchkey children within the city limits—mainly 6- to 14-year-olds whose parents work and live in apartment complexes. In this interdepartmental experiment, latchkey children were offered supervised recreational activities, including fishing, swimming, games, and movies, as well as safety instruction on what to do in emergency situations. Children also had a quiet time and lunch. "Adventure Addison" was offered from 7:30 A.M. to 5:30 P.M. once in March and once in April on a teacher in-service day when the public schools were not in session, as well as once in June after summer vacation had begun. The entire program, including transportation to the sites at an apartment clubhouse and to the Addison Athletic Club, was free, provided parents signed the registration and release form attached to the publicity flyer (Addison Parks and Recreation Department, 1990). A total of 260 children participated in the events during the three days.

As a result of piloting "Adventure Addison," the following three goals were achieved: an informal base was established upon which a recreation curriculum could be developed for youth in Addison; a rapport was established between the town of Addison and social service agencies which serve youth in particular; and the staff of "Adventure Addison" ascertained that there is a need and a desire on the part of children and parents in the town to have recreational activities designed for them (Dixon, 1990a). Although the staff of "Adventure Addison" recommended the continuance of the program as activity-based recreation for children after school and on weekends, the decision of the City Manager and City Council, after a particularly difficult year of falling property assessments and budget constraints, was not to consider "Adventure Addison" as a funded program for fiscal year 1990–1991 (Dixon, 1990a). The Parks and Recreation Department of Addison attributes the success of "Adventure Addison" to the cooperation of persons in various community agencies. The Department advises towns desirous of replicating this type of endeavor to be certain that governmental authorities and appropriating agencies are very committed to such a program from its inception, so that long-term funding is assured (Dixon, 1990b).

Telephone Hotlines

Telephone "warmlines" or "hotlines" are another viable option for children in self-care. Designed as a support system, these telephone services provide opportunities for contact with an adult, but do not offer direct supervision. The child must initiate the contact (which is beyond the means of low-income children and difficult for shy children), and there is no on-going responsibility by the organization for the child's welfare. However, "warmlines" are cost-effective and a few of them utilize contacts which are geographically close enough to children to actually provide help if an emergency arises (Todd, Albrecht, and Coleman, 1990). During the last decade more than 200 hotlines for children home alone have come into operation in the United States, and they respond to over one million calls per year (Long and Long, 1988).

Several common denominators underlie successful reassurance phone lines for children:

1. Pro-family philosophy in which the guidance provided is confidential, is not intended to supplant parents' role, and is geared toward encouraging communication between parents and children
2. Highly trained volunteers
3. Consultation and support
4. Sensitivity to cultural and language differences
5. Close supervision of volunteers
6. Professional backup
7. Close contact with other agencies

8. Record keeping and evaluation
9. Confidentiality (Long and Long, 1988).

PhoneFriend: The PhoneFriend project, a prevention-oriented community service begun in 1982, was the first telephone support line in the country and is the most widely followed (Guerney and Moore, 1983). Phone lines are staffed by volunteers from 2:30 P.M. to 5:30 P.M. and all day when school is not in session during the academic year. The goals of PhoneFriend, which is operated out of State College, Pennsylvania, are to create a helping network, to provide information and support to children home alone after school, and to increase community awareness of these children's needs. PhoneFriend is not intended as a crisis line or counseling/referral service, but is rather a "friend-in-need" outreach service. Its name intentionally highlights the aspect of social contact for children. During the five hours adult volunteers spend in training they learn how to use a cardex file describing anticipated situations and appropriate actions (such as handling first aid, coping with power failures, etc.). While in training volunteers role play in pairs, alternately taking the roles of children and of telephone workers. PhoneFriend provides technical assistance to other children's hotlines around the country and has distributed over 2,000 start up kits to agencies expressing interest in establishing such lines (Long and Long, 1988).

In Washington, D.C., the public school system has run PhoneFriend for five years after school and during holidays and vacations ("Latchkey Children," 1988). After preliminary and more extensive year-long evaluations in two communities having varied demographic characteristics, PhoneFriend administrators concluded that a telephone program is an effective way of providing emotional and informational support to children alone after school (Guerney and Moore, 1983). Records kept during the first year of service indicated that callers ranged from 4 to 16 years of age, but were an average of 8. The number of calls from males and from females was about equal. The most frequent types of calls were categorized as "lonely/bored" (24 percent); immediate hang ups or saying a few words and then hanging up without interaction between volunteer and child (23 percent); and "wants to talk" (23 percent) (Guerney and Moore, 1983). For those few calls requiring a referral, children were most frequently referred to the "Tell-A-Tale" number, a phone company service that narrates children's stories.

Recently, PhoneFriend received a President's Citation for a Private Sector Initiative (PhoneFriend, 1989).

KIDLINE: A second similar telephone reassurance or warmline is called KIDLINE. It provides a point of contact for children who need assistance, information, or support. Begun in November 1984, KIDLINE, which receives an average of 1,500 calls per month, operates out of the Tucson Association for Child Care (TACC) from 2:00 P.M. to 9:00 P.M. weekdays and from 1:00 P.M. to 6:00 P.M. Saturdays. During summer it operates six days a week. Telephones are answered by trained volunteers under supervision of a paid staff person. KIDLINE'S objectives are to teach children home safety and instruction in 911 usage, to make referrals to community resources, and to provide guidance for homework problems and accidents (Nichols and Schilit, 1988).

During a three-month period in 1986 calls coming into KIDLINE were analyzed according to types/categories (i.e., conversational, support, guidance, counsel, conflicts, safety, fear/worry, and referral). Of the 2,495 analyzable calls which were received, the majority were conversational. Twice as many calls were from girls, who were more likely to seek emotional support or safety information, while boys were more likely to call about conflicts. Eighty-one percent were from children ages 7 to 11, with 19 percent from children 12 to 16. Adolescent calls were more heavily concentrated on specific problem situations (i.e., interpersonal relations and safety), while younger children made significantly more conversation calls just to talk to someone and guidance calls to obtain advice (Nichols and Schilit, 1988).

KIDTALK: Since 1986 a confidential telephone counseling service in Dallas called KIDTALK has been available for latchkey children weekdays from 3:00 P.M. to 6:00 P.M. Housed with and administered by the Lone Star Council of Camp Fire, KIDTALK received more than 25,000 calls in its first year of operation, making it the busiest telephone line of its kind in the United States. The majority of calls are those categorized as "bored" or "just want to talk." Many questions are food related, such as how to operate a can opener (Floria and Effren, 1988). Although KIDTALK is a collaboration of more than 40 Dallas organizations, it is funded by corporations, foundations, individuals, and United Way. Each volunteer receives four hours of structured training and four hours of general orientation covering child development, communication, problem solving strategies, encouragement, support services, etc. (Corporate Child Development Fund for Texas [CCDFT], 1988). Administrators of KIDTALK would like to expand the program to include more teenage or high school students as volunteers who would be supervised by a teacher or school counselor (Austin, 1990).

"Grandma, Please": Begun in 1984 in Chicago, "Grandma, Please" links older adults with latchkey children; even seniors with limited mobility receive calls to their homes between 3:00 P.M. and 6:00 P.M. daily. This serivce, which attempts to combat the isolation experienced both by younger and older people, has recently begun a national franchise system (Long and Long, 1988). More than 800 calls are received by seniors per month in Chicago, and 28,000 school children have used "Grandma, Please" since its inception (Larkin, 1989).

COMBINATION PROGRAMS: ADULT CARE AND SELF-CARE

Family Day Care Check-In Project

The Family Day Care Check-In Project in Fairfax, Virginia, is an example of a combined adult care and self-care program for latchkey children. Funded by the Department of Health and Human Services in 1982, the Fairfax County Office of Children developed a model for a Family Day Care Check-In Program providing flexible care for children 10 to 14. Two groups in Fairfax County—the Reston Children's Center and the Potomac Area Council of Camp Fire—piloted the program for one year and each continues to operate it today (Fairfax County Office for Children, 1989).

Children are required to check-in daily after school with their designated neighborhood adult caregiver. Each child has an individual contract about how he/she will spend the after-school hours—from checking-in with an adult to spending the entire time at home. The contract also defines the role that the providers play in the supervision of children and the responsibilities parents assume. The Family Day Care Check-In Project allows for children's increasing developmental readiness for more and more time alone (McKnight and Shelsby, 1984).

The Reston Children's Center Family Satellite Program for older children is designed to respond to adolescents' increasing needs for independence and responsibility. Children check-in with a neighborhood provider after school, are offered a snack, and spend time with friends. Individual schedules are worked out by the provider, the child, and the parent. Children may spend time visiting friends, playing in the neighborhood, doing homework, having a snack at the day care provider's house, or attending community activities (e.g., sports). Carefully planned check-in programs such as this can be a cost-efficient way of providing some degree of supervision for children ready to handle the responsibility (Todd, Albrecht, and Coleman, 1990).

Telephone Plus Counselor Programs

Houston's "Children Home Alone Telephone Reassurance Service" (CHATTERS) is a telephone warmline with an adult component—an adult counselor. CHATTERS was begun in 1980 as a program that provides children 8 to 13 years of age with a place to call weekdays between 2:00 P.M. and 6:00 P.M. during the school year in emergencies, when they have questions about personal or school problems, or if they just want to talk to someone. Run by the Neighborhood Centers-Day Care Association, a nonprofit organization, CHATTERS assigns each child a counselor who lives 15 minutes away; child and counselor meet prior to any telephone contacts. Children make routine calls to their counselor and in emergencies a counselor goes to the child's home (Coolsen, Seligson, and Garbarino, 1985). CHATTERS reassures parents by having a competent, caring adult nearby to help children in a crisis, and it offers latchkey children emotional support (Rosenthal, 1982). Parents register their children and pay a $5 fee to cover the cost of printing and mailing a monthly newsletter containing stories written by children, advice to families and children, informational exchanges, and birthday acknowledgements. Originally funded by the Hogg Foundation, CHATTERS is currently available through United Way (Corporate Child Development Fund for Texas [CCDFT], 1988).

Early Adolescent Helper Program

A second example of a combination adult care and self-care program is the Early Adolescent Helper Program, a school-based endeavor sponsored by the Center for Advanced Study in Education of the City University of New York Graduate College. Initiated in 1982, it addresses the multiple needs of 11- to 15-year-olds, recognizes their developmental needs and capacity for productive community participation, and offers them age-appropriate opportunities. Over 200 inner-city youth from 15 schools in New York City, Bridgeport (Connecticut), and Phoenix are involved in the Early Adolescent Helper Program, serving in day care, recreational and senior centers, in Head Start, and in latchkey programs. Their activities include storytelling, reading aloud, recording oral histories, escorting children on trips to neighborhood sites, supervising children at play, and helping with homework. Schools prepare youngsters for their roles in a weekly seminar with an adult leader (usually a teacher or guidance counselor). The Helpers Program provides structured settings after school when many students would otherwise be unsupervised latchkey children at loose ends. It motivates young people to stay in school, teaches them in a firsthand way about the world of work, bolsters their self-esteem, and provides extra hands for community service agencies (Schine, 1989; City University of New York [CUNY], Graduate School and University Center, 1990).

As the special nature of the helper-child relationship was recognized, a two-year research study was undertaken to determine whether the presence of the helper made a difference in the centers. Another purpose of the study was to discover whether the helper's presence encouraged the development of skills the young child needs for success in school, such as language development and the ability to seek and receive help from another. The analysis of observer's reports, videotapes and reviews with teachers, child care staff, and helpers themselves revealed that children had more opportunities to talk with an older person and that they sought and received help more consistently when helpers were present (Schine, 1989).

One specific recent project of the Early Adolescent Helper Program is "Helpers Promoting Reading." After a demonstration year, the project has been expanded to six child care and after-school Helpers programs in the Bronx, Manhattan, and Brooklyn, with over 50 helper participants. Adolescents in "Helpers Promoting Reading" receive two training workshops, which begin with examining a display of children's books. Through discussion, practice, and role playing, helpers learn about reading aloud, how to keep children's interest, and how to help children discuss and understand books and stories. During the training, adolescents work in pairs reading aloud to each other and critiquing each other's reading. The technique of "sandwiching" one negative comment between two positive ones is employed. Helpers select books to read with the children, using criteria they generate, such as interest, story line, quality of illustrations, and appropriateness of reading level. Helpers assist children to write reviews for the books they have read together. These reviews become the "Helper Review of Books," a special section of the Helper Program *Newsletter* distributed to Head Start and early childhood centers as an aid to book selection (City University of New York [CUNY], Graduate School and University Center, 1990).

A new type of helper, the math/science helper, is planned to be implemented in 1991. Math/science helpers will perform hands-on science and math activities with children in child care centers and in after-school programs. As part of their training, math/science helpers will set up "activity kits" using everything from corn starch and water to balances and balls (Schine, 1990).

The staff of the Early Adolescent Helper Program has created program guides and videotapes which describe the program, and are available for use by teachers and program leaders. For more information, see Appendix D.

Block Parents

Block parents is another example of a program for latchkey children in which adults provide a limited amount of supervision without the resource demands of formal school-based or other community or institution-based programs. Block parents programs use trained neighborhood volunteers who make themselves and their home available to children needing a place to go in an emergency (Coolsen, Seligson, Garbarino, 1985). Communities in Detroit, Phoenix, and Shawnee Mission, Kansas, are just a few places where block parents have been implemented ("Latchkey Children," 1988). In Chicago, neighborhood support groups and block persons act as safety mechanisms for children going to and from school or playing unsupervised outside. The appointed block parent is available to receive a daily call from unattended children upon their arrival home. Block parents serve as check-in persons encouraging children to begin homework or to perform household tasks. The block parent arrangement has the advantage of providing children with more independence than day care can, while giving more supervision than a phone line can (Leigh, 1987).

Each of the above described types of care has both advantages and disadvantages. No one model will satisfy the needs of all children or all families in all communities (Long and Long, 1983). Each community will likely require a number of approaches to latchkey children in order to adequately respond to particular family needs and circumstances.

PUBLICATIONS

Kid Smarts for Working Parents

Targeting latchkey children and their working parents through written publications is still another strategy. *Kid Smarts for Working Parents*, subtitled *An After-School Food, Fun and Safety Guide*, was published several years ago by Rodale Press and underwritten by the Lipton Company. As the title implies, the premier issue of *Kid Smarts* contained articles for adults about children's health, nutrition, methods of encouraging children to complete their homework, recipes for snacks, and tips for accident-proofing a house. The "Bulletin Board" section described informational resources for latchkey parents and gave mailing addresses. The "Just for Kids" portion featured riddles, puzzles, brief stories, book reviews, and questions and answers concerning typical situations a child home alone might encounter (*Kid Smarts for Working Parents*, 1988).

Color Me Safe

Likewise, the Whirlpool Corporation has created several latchkey-oriented educational guides, including a booklet, *Color Me Safe*, which introduces young children to appliance safety, via brief text written in both English and Spanish and pictures to color and follow the dots to complete. *Color Me Safe* addresses safety precautions in cooking, storing poisonous flammable materials, and using electrical outlets. Whirlpool became interested in latchkey children several years ago after receiving a significant increase in the number of calls to its toll-free "Cool-Line" from children at home alone after school (Rothenberg, 1988; Whirlpool Corporation, 1984).

What If I'm Home Alone?

A third booklet, published by the Corporation for Public Broadcasting (CPB), is entitled *What If I'm Home Alone?: Your Family's Guide to Home and Personal Safety Skills* (Corporation for Public Broadcasting [CPB], 1987). This information and activities booklet gives latchkey children skills they need to feel more confident about taking care of themselves. Some of the inclusions in the 8 ½" by 11" publication are a "Getting Home Safely" maze, a "Play the Telephone Game" on letter recognition in the phone book, a "Safety in the Kitchen" picture (for which children are to find what's wrong), a page on which to list emergency telephone numbers and names and then cut out and post, and pages of cartoons with tips and advice on dealing with fires, babysitting, handling arguments, and first aid.

PROJECT HOME SAFE

Project Home Safe is the American Home Economics Association's (AHEA) national education and advocacy program on behalf of latchkey children and their families. Inaugurated on August 1, 1987, it is funded through October 31, 1991, by a grant from the Whirlpool Foundation. Operated by AHEA, the project promotes community-based solutions to the problem of children at home alone. Whirlpool's interest in latchkey children was prompted, at least in part, by telephone calls to the company's toll-free "Cool-Line" service from school-age children who had questions about operating home appliances (Koblinsky, Vaughn, and Schrage, 1990). Project Home Safe has earned national recognition for its efforts on behalf of children in self-care. The Chicago-based National Safety Council presented its first place award of honor for safety programs to AHEA for its development and operation of Project Home Safe.

Project Home Safe has four components. One is a national resource center on self-care and school-age child care that distributes materials free of charge. More than 4,000 people, including parents, researchers, educators, program developers, employers, elected officials, and others concerned with the latchkey issue, contacted the center during the first two years. Materials distributed include brochures on "Assessing Your Child's Readiness for Self Care" and "Preparing Your Child for Self Care," as well as bibliographies on a variety of self-care and school-age child care topics.

A second component is that of training and community involvement. Community representatives receive intensive preparation to become Project Home Safe trainers. Then they recruit and train volunteers to assess local child care needs and resources and provide at least 40 hours of community service implementing programs for children in self-care and their families.

Project Home Safe operates under the assumption that there is not just one solution to the problem of latchkey children: a range of strategies are required to meet the unique needs of many different communities (Koblinsky, Vaughn, and Schrage, 1990). In the past three years volunteer training programs have been hosted by 15 state home economics associations. Over 430 volunteer home economists have been trained in Arkansas, California, Colorado, Connecticut, the District of Columbia, Florida, Illinois, Kentucky, Michigan, New Mexico, North Carolina, Ohio, Oregon, Texas, and Wisconsin. In one year Project Home Safe volunteers contributed 7,700 hours of their time and reached over 450,000 people with information about self-care and school-age child care. Volunteer activities have included assisting in creating telephone reassurance lines during after-school hours, organizing a school-age child care task force in one county, writing a grant proposal that secured funding for a school-age child care facility in a public housing project, establishing "adopt-a-pal" programs between senior citizens and latchkey children, and developing "block parent programs"

(Koblinsky, Vaughn, and Schrage, 1990; Whirlpool Foundation and American Home Economics Association [AHEA], 1990).

Another volunteer activity of Project Home Safe took place in a public library in Maryland. That program is described in Chapter 7.

An initiative on school-age child care quality is a third component of Project Home Safe. Since there are no nationally recognized standards of quality for child care programs designed specifically for school-age children, Project Home Safe is focusing on identifying characteristics of high-quality programs rather than on minimum requirements. The results of the initiative are intended to serve as recommendations to assist in planning, self-assessment, and improvement activities. Because there is insufficient research on school-age child care to support research-based standards, guidelines being developed are based on the professional judgment of practitioners and experts about characteristics that comprise high-quality programs in child care for school-agers. Input for the guidelines was gained through a national panel at a conference on school-age child care in McLean, Virginia, in October 1989. In November 1989, Project Home Safe sponsored a working forum on school-age child care standards in conjunction with the National Association for the Education of Young Children Annual Conference in Atlanta.

Two documents will reflect the professional consensus arising from the McLean conference and the Atlanta forum: *Developmentally Appropriate Practice in School-Age Child Care Programs* and *Quality Criteria for School-Age Child Care Programs*. Although these documents describe high-quality practice, rather than baseline minimums, they can be useful in developing model legislation and accreditation, certification, and licensing requirements. They can also aid parents in evaluating the quality of available school-age child care programs (Whirlpool Foundation and American Home Economics Association [AHEA], 1990).

Research on self-care is the fourth component of Project Home Safe. Since high-quality research on latchkey children is limited, Project Home Safe awarded a professional grant supporting a study of "Predictors and Consequences of the Amount of Time Children Spend in Self Care" to Hyman Rodman. This study is described in more detail in Chapter 2. (Whirlpool Foundation and American Home Economics Association [AHEA], 1990).

REFERENCES

Addison Parks and Recreation Department. 1990. Flyer and registration form for Adventure Addison. Addison, Texas.

Austin, K. Letter to author, 20 September 1990.

Bachman, R.W. 1975. Elementary school children's perception of helpers and their characteristics. *Elementary School Guidance and Counseling* 10(December): 103–09.

Baker, N. 1990. *Strategies for school-age child care in Texas.* Austin: Texas Department of Community Affairs.

Barker, L. 1988. A place for apartment kids to be. *Dallas Morning News*, November 18, 1c+.

Baynham, P. 1990. Latchkey children in the public library. Paper presented at the Canadian Library Association Annual Conference, June 15, Ottawa, Ontario, Canada.

Blue, G.F. 1986. The value of pets in children's lives. *Childhood Education* 63(December): 84–90.

Bundy, M. and J. Boser. 1987. Helping latchkey children: A group guidance approach. *The School Counselor* 35(September): 58–65.

Camp Fire, Inc. n.d. What's the best thing about Camp Fire? Pamphlet. Kansas City, Missouri: Camp Fire, Inc.

Campbell, J. 1988. Meeting the needs in Tennessee. *Parks and Recreation* 23(February): 52–54.

Chambers, R. Letter to author, 5 May 1990.

Child-care patchwork. 1989. *Ladies Home Journal* (November): 199–203.

City University of New York (CUNY), Graduate School and University Center. 1990. Brochure of early adolescent helper program. Helper Program. New York.

Cole, C. and H. Rodman. 1987. When school-age children care for themselves: Issues for family life educators and parents. *Family Relations* 36(January): 92–96.

Coolsen, P., M. Seligson, and J. Garbarino. 1985. *When school's out and nobody's home.* Chicago: National Committee for Prevention of Child Abuse.

Corporate Child Development Fund for Texas (CCDFT). 1988. *Somebody cares: Model school-age programs for latchkey children in Texas.* Austin, Texas.

Corporation for Public Broadcasting (CPB). 1987. *What if I'm home alone?* Washington, D.C.

Dixon, J. Letter to author, 20 April and 5 September 1990a.

Dixon, J. Telephone conversation with author, 11 September 1990b.

EARTHNAUTS. 1990. A "kid's concept" of school and corporate child care programs for school-age kids. Proposal. Austin, Texas.

Fairfax County Office for Children. 1989. An introduction to the family day care check-in program: After-school care for children aged 10-14. Fairfax, Virginia.

Floria, B. and K. Effren. 1988. Easy cooking for latchkey kids. *Dallas Morning News*, February 3, 1F+.

Fosarelli, P. 1984. Latchkey children. *Developmental and Behavioral Pediatrics* 5(August): 173–77.

Gray, E. and P. Coolsen. 1987. How do kids really feel about being home alone? *Children Today* 16(July/August): 30–32.

Groves, S. 1990. Letter to author, 10 October 1990.

Guerney, L. and L. Moore. 1983. PhoneFriend: A prevention-oriented service for latchkey children. *Children Today* 12(July/August): 5–10.

Hawkeye Area Community Action Program. 1985. Shared heritage: An intergenerational child care program. ERIC Document ED 277 473. Cedar Rapids, Iowa.

Heath, D.T. and P. McKenry. 1989. Potential benefits of companion animals for self-care children. *Childhood Education* 65(5): 311–14.

Houston Independent School District (HISD). 1990. The lighted school house. Houston, Texas.

Jabs, C. 1989. Loving companions: Pets provide security, amusement, and affection. *Country Living* (December): 154.

Kid smarts for working parents. 1988. Englewood Cliffs, New Jersey: Thomas J. Lipton Company.

Kids with keys—Make sure your child is safe. 1986 *PTA Today* 2:4–5.

Koblinsky, S.A. and C.M. Todd. 1989. Teaching self care skills to latchkey children: A review of research. *Family Relations* 38(October): 431–35.

Koblinsky, S., G. Vaughn, and J. Schrage. 1990. Project home safe: A national initiative on behalf of children in self-care. *Journal of Home Economics* 82(Spring): 27–28+.

Larkin, K. 1989. I love you grandpa. *Family Circle* 102(November 7): 15–17.

Latchkey children. 1988. *Parks and Recreation* 23(February): 49–51.

Lee, J. 1990. CBS to televise segment on Murfreesboro school program. *The Tennessean*, January 12, 2B.

Leigh, S. 1987. Chicago's latchkey kids. *Today's Chicago Woman*, September 3, 1A+.

Liquoiri, W. Letter to author, 19 April 1990.

Long, L. and T. Long. 1983. *Handbook for latchkey children and their parents.* New York: Arbor House.

Long, L. and T. Long. 1988. Hotlines for children: What makes them effective? *Children Today* 17(March/April): 22–25.

May, P. A. 1989. The effect of a nursing intervention (basic aid training) on latchkey versus supervised children's stress and knowledge of first aid. *Dissertation Abstracts International* 49B(June) no.12: 12-B.

McHenry, J. Letter to author, 1 September 1990.

McKnight, J. and B. Shelsby. 1984. Checking-in: An alternative for latchkey kids. *Children Today* 13(May/June): 23–25.

Mock, L. n.d. On your own: 4-H curriculum enrichment project. College Station, Texas: Texas A&M University System, Texas Agricultural Extension Service.

Murfreesboro City School System. 1989. Success is spelled ESP—Extended school program. Videotape. Murfreesboro, Tennessee: Murfreesboro School System.

Murphey, J. and J. Viner. 1986. Police partners program provides "latch-key" outlet. *The Police Chief* 53(July): 68.

National Association of Elementary School Principals (NAESP). 1988. NAESP principals' opinion survey on before and after-school child care. *NAESP News.* January 28. Alexandria, Virginia.

Nichols, A. and R. Schilit. 1988. Telephone support for latchkey kids. *Child Welfare* 67(January/February): 49–59.

Ohio Cooperative Extension Service. 1985. Keys for kids: A learning packet for self-care/latchkey children and their parents. Columbus, Ohio: Ohio State University.

Peterson, L. 1984. Teaching home safety and survival skills to latchkey children: A comparison of two manuals and methods. *Journal of Applied Behavior Analysis* 17(Fall): 279–93.

Petrick, B. Telephone interview with author, 20 January 1990.

PhoneFriend. 1989. Mimeographed newsletter. 4(May): 1.

Press-Dawson, A. 1987. Unlock the latchkey problem? *Thrust for Educational Leadership* 16(May/June): 40–41.

Rickman, A. Letter to author, 14 March 1990.

Rosenthal, B. 1982. Help is just a call away. *Working Mother* (October): 142–44.

Rothenberg, R. 1988. Advertisers take aim at latchkey children. *Dallas Morning News*, May 10, 1C+.

Schine, J. 1989. Early adolescent helper program: Adolescents help themselves by helping others. *Children Today* 18(January/February): 10–15.

Schine, J. 1990. From the director. *Community Roles for Youth* 4 (March):1.

Seligson, M. and D. Fink. 1989. *No time to waste: An action agenda for school-age child care.* Wellesley, Massachusetts: School-Age Child Care Project, Wellesley College, Center for Research on Women.

Smith, S. 1989. The Houston "lighthouse" for unattended children. *Educational Leadership* 46(May): 79.

South, J. 1988. Service throws help line to children at home alone. *Dallas Times Herald*, May 25, 1B.

Strother, D.B. 1984. Latchkey children: The fastest growing special interest group in the school. *Phi Delta Kappan* 66(December): 290–93.

Sullam, S. 1990. Hawaii finds popular support for $15-million after-school care program. *The Baltimore Sun*, December 30, 5M.

Swan, H., S.M. Briggs, and M. Kelso. 1985. *I'm in charge: A self-care course for parents and children.* Topeka, Kansas: Kansas Committee for the Prevention of Child Abuse.

Todd, C., K. Albrecht, and M. Coleman. 1990. School-age child care: A continuum of options. *Journal of Home Economics* 82(Spring): 46–52.

Toenniessen, C.S., L.F. Little, and K.H. Rosen. 1985. Anybody home? Evaluation and intervention techniques with latchkey children. *Elementary School Guidance and Counseling* 20(December): 105–15.

Van Driel, S. 1990. Elementary school drama group builds pupils' self-esteem. *Port Orange Observer*, March 1, 1+.

Ventura-Merkel, C., D. Liederman, and J. Ossofsky. 1989. Exemplary intergenerational programs. *Journal of Children in Contemporary Society* 20: 173–80.

Watson, R. and K. Fitzgerald. 1989. 21st century school. *Parents* (October): 112–18.

Whirlpool Corporation. 1984. *Color me safe.* Benton Harbor, Michigan.

Whirlpool Foundation and American Home Economics Association (AHEA). 1990. Annual report: June, 1989 through May, 1990 on Project Home Safe. Alexandria, Virgina.

Wilks, P. Letter to author, 14 November 1990.

Wright, R. 1990. Who's watching the children? *McCall's* 117(January): 22–24+.

Wynn, R.L. 1987. Children's satisfaction with self care as a function of dog ownership and neighborhood safety. Paper presented at the Delta Society Conference, Vancouver, British Columbia, October.

Zigler, E. and P. Ennis. 1988. Child care: A new role for tomorrow's schools. *Principal* 68(September): 10–13.

Chapter 4
Recommendations for the Future

The escalating numbers of latchkey children and the variety of existing responses to the phenomenon make recommendations for future directions appropriate. What other strategies should be implemented on behalf of unattended children? Who might play a significant role in the implementation of these strategies?

RECOMMENDED LATCHKEY STRATEGIES

Recommended Strategies for Researchers

Young (1986) advocates study of the long- and short-term effects of various programs and services for latchkey children—particularly in regard to their effectiveness in reducing school failure and in increasing children's self-esteem and peer relationships. Such research is especially important because, as discussed in Chapter 2, the effect of self-care upon children is still largely unknown, and the response strategies described in Chapter 3 have been, for the most part, unevaluated other than quantitatively in terms of numbers served. Other research needs are discussed in Chapter 2.

Recommended Strategies for Organizations

Standards and guidelines for school-age child care programs need to be developed and the appropriate role of regulation needs to be determined (Young, 1986). Certainly in setting standards for school-age child care offered before and after the traditional school day, children's developmental needs should be paramount. These include the need to socialize with peers, to self-expression via arts and crafts, to have outlets for physical and emotional energies, to have a variety of choices from which to select activities, to have privacy, and to have homework help and tutoring (Young, 1986).

Some progress has been made toward the goal of developing standards; national and state conferences solely on the issues of latchkey children and school-age children have been held for several years by various organizations. For example, the mission statement of the Texas Association for School-Age Care (TASAC) speaks of "enhancing and facilitating developmentally appropriate care for school-age children outside the traditional school hours" (Corporate Child Development Fund for Texas [CCDFT], 1990). In September 1989 this group sponsored a conference in Austin entitled "The Latchkey Problem: Moving Toward Solutions," at which specific sessions, such as those entitled "School-Age Child Care: Why It's Worth Doing" and "Support and Guidance for Older Children: The Forgotten Latchkey Group," were presented. In October 1990 a second TASAC conference was held in San Antonio. At the national level, the American Child Care Foundation, Inc., held a conference in McLean, Virginia entitled "Perspectives on School-Age Child Care 1989," at which indicators of quality care and policy issues for school-age child care were discussed (American Child Care Foundation, Inc. [ACCF], 1989).

In addition, Project Home Safe, sponsored by Whirlpool Foundation and the American Home Economics Association is identifying characteristics of high-quality programs for school-age child care, based partially on existing accreditation criteria developed by the National Academy of Early Childhood Education (Whirlpool Foundation and American Home Economics Association [AHEA], 1990). Details on this endeavor are described in Chapter 3.

PTAs can play a major role in addressing the needs of children in self-care by developing a directory of school-age child care programs in the community and by establishing a block parent program and telephone warmline or reassurance line. This group could also encourage schools to offer survival skills training to all students as a regular part of their curriculum and conduct a safe babysitting campaign (National Parent Teacher's Association [PTA], 1985b).

Recommended Strategies for Communities

Since the self-care phenomenon is a community issue, several researchers have suggested that the first step in addressing it is to create a community task force comprised of parents, school personnel, day care providers, and representatives of youth service agencies. The next steps advocated are to conduct a community needs assessment survey; review existing school-age child care programs and develop program policies; promote networking among community agencies so that each shares some responsibility; arrange publicity; and evaluate via staff, parents, and children (Coleman, Rowland, and Robinson, 1989).

It is interesting to note that recommendations made 47 years ago are essentially identical to the proposed steps described above, and are still applicable today (Zucker, 1944). Zucker, the Secretary of the Emergency Child Care Committee of Cleveland and a member of the National Advisory Committee on Day Care of the Child Welfare League of America, urged that administrators of child care programs conduct extensive public education campaigns as to what constitutes good child care. In addition, Zucker advocated that schools either develop social services or a close relationship with social agencies.

Recommended Strategies for School Administrators

The public schools can play a variety of roles in relation to latchkey services for their students, starting with providing information to parents about options in the community for before- and after-school care. More active roles include encouraging the development of community-based programs by other agencies, coordinating transportation between the school site and child care providers, making space available to latchkey service providers in school buildings, and providing before- and after-school programs in the building on their own or in conjuction with other agencies. No single model to meet the need for supervision and care of school-age children before and after school is recommended, but common characteristics are shared by successful programs: tailoring to local needs, adaptation to local lifestyles, utilization of local resources, and meeting local expectations. The appropriate approach to providing latchkey services may be to borrow the theme of the Chicago Bears and "do whatever it takes" to meet the needs of children who do not have a parent at home after school (*When School Is Not in Session*, 1989).

Principals and other school officials can facilitate action for latchkey children by setting a positive tone at their institution, which can help intervention strategies succeed. School officials could begin by examining the degree to which their existing policies and procedures address the needs of latchkey children. Administrators can provide flexible scheduling for teachers and counselors, as well as funds for their travel to workshops and conferences, so that faculty can become knowledgeable about latchkey children (Robinson, Rowland, and Coleman, 1986a). They could even launch a latchkey conference on the school premises, and tap outside resources to form partnerships with the private and public sectors (Robinson, Rowland, and Coleman, 1986b).

The Longs (1989) list 10 suggestions administrators can implement to meet the needs of latchkey adolescents without jeopardizing the role of the schools as an educational institution. Highlights include:

1. Checking up on absent students. Following up calls home by calls to parents' worksites.
2. Sponsoring a telephone support service developed and staffed by high school students trained as peer counselors.
3. Instituting a phone-a-teacher service by which students who need homework help can reach an on-duty teacher during the afternoon or evening hours.
4. Providing a ride-home service. Coordinating public bus service with after-school activities, or developing a buddy system so that students who lack adequate transportation can be involved in after-school activities.
5. Increasing summer activities at schools. Helping students become involved in volunteer activities, or fostering summer job programs for students 15 years or younger, as alternatives to self-care when school is not in session.
6. Starting a guest house program for children who may be unattended overnight.

Recommended Strategies for School Physical Education Teachers and Recreation Leaders

Sponsoring a "latchkey intramural program" at the national level after the academic school day is an unusual recommendation from one source (Vannoy, 1988). The rationale for this is that many physical education teachers and recreation leaders are finding it difficult to locate jobs, school administrators may be purchasing expensive equipment yet overlooking students' physical and recreational needs, and physical education teachers and recreation leaders should proactively address the needs of latchkey youth. Stated goals of a latchkey intramural program are to improve the physical fitness of children, to reduce parental and child stress, to meet late afternoon supervision and recreational needs of children, to provide leadership opportunities for teens and adults, to help family life and wellness, and to enhance the schools' image due to interaction with the community. A sample five-day program schedule offering both active and inactive recreation could include table tennis, aerobics, painting, rope jumping, cheer leading, drama, model building, trivia games, juggling, wood crafts, crocheting, 4-H, and karate.

Recommended Strategies for Teachers

Teachers can play an instrumental role in facilitating the adjustment of latchkey children through classroom activities and through enlisting parental and community involvement. The following are specific strategies teachers could implement:

1. Provide children with opportunities to work through their feelings via painting, clay projects, flannel board stories, dramatic play, music and movement activities, and writing stories about their day.
2. Provide parents with opportunities to deal with the situation by having a "Latchkey Awareness" week or fair and inviting representatives from community agencies that serve children and families.
3. Provide opportunities to help children become more versatile by offering a course on minimal first aid or by developing a survival skills training program.
4. Involve parents and the community by forming "Parent Clusters" in which four or five families contract to assist each other over a period of time in providing caregiving needs.
5. Become involved in policy development by building coalitions with other groups to offer activities during school vacations and holidays.
6. Have children describe typical (actual or imaginary) emergency situations. Then role play these scenarios, incorporating first aid and safety procedures in the responses. Invite representatives from emergency services in the community (e.g., police,

firefighters, nurses) to class to observe and critique the responses (McGuire, 1989).

Recommended Strategies for School Librarians

Although before- and after-school care at school sites, or the extended day program, is becoming prevalent in public elementary schools to meet the needs of children who would otherwise be left in self-care for several hours each day, no examples were found by this author of the use of the school library facility or the school library materials collection, or involvement of the school librarian or library aides in such programs. This circumstance seems both remarkable and unfortunate, since space as well as print and nonprint materials are already in place in school libraries, and the reading ability of youth in general could stand improvement. The author recommends that schools having a manageable number of children participating in a before- and after-school program on the school premises, and a reasonable size library, pilot a before- and after-school program for children. This program should utilize school library materials in different ways. Adults (i.e., library aides, parent volunteers) should read and share books and stories with children; children should read or share books with other children; and/or book-related films or videos for children should be presented in the school library. This is an ideal way to foster what librarians and teachers want to achieve—a love of reading by children.

Recommended Strategies for School Counselors

School counselors are in a prime position to help make self-care less difficult for students. However, Bundy and Poppen (1989) note the unfortunate lack of relevant literature to guide counselors in their practice with this growing population of special youth. Nevertheless, school counselors can become referral sources to link parents and children with appropriate available community programs (Toenniessen, Little, and Rosen, 1985). Counselors, through the schools and PTAs can distribute literature on latchkey programs to students, teachers, parents, and administrators.

If existing resources are inadequate, counselors can become actively involved in planning and conducting latchkey education and remedial programs in their communities (Toenniessen, Little, and Rosen, 1985). For example, school counselors in two school systems in Tennessee implemented the "Being In Charge" guidance unit with third- to eighth-grade students, even though the counselors had attended only a brief orientation session using the program materials (Bundy and Boser, 1987). By leading parent workshops or speaking at PTA meetings to advise working parents regarding conflicts with children, counselors can help children in self-care. They can also conduct in-service training for teachers and administrators, focusing on problems of latchkey children and on offering practical suggestions for dealing with them. Organizing support groups and a "buddy system" are still other appropriate ways in which counselors can become involved (Toenniessen, Little, and Rosen, 1985).

At the professional level, Pitney (1989) urges counselors to attend conferences and workshops about latchkey children, lobby for more funding for schools to establish extended day programs, and write grant proposals for pilot latchkey programs in their school districts. Pitney concludes that a counselor's role should depend upon what makes the self-care experience a potentially negative one.

> If the reason is the environment in which a child lives, referral to adult care programs may be necessary. If the reason is lack of appropriate skills, the counselor's role may be to teach those skills in guidance units. If the reason lies within the child's or parent's feelings or attitudes, the counselor may need to do more individual or family counseling (Pitney, 1989).

To assess the state of self-care in their area, counselors could distribute surveys to parents and children that are tailored to the situation of each (Toenniessen, Little, and Rosen, 1985).

Recommended Strategies for Home Economists

Home economists can approach the issues of school-age child care and latchkey children in several ways: conducting community needs assessments, working to develop new child care resources or to improve the quality of existing programs, providing workshops and educational materials for parents, or helping communities influence public policy. If involved in community needs assessment, home economists should solicit input and seek assistance from a wide variety of service organizations, child care providers, public welfare groups, government agencies, employers, union officials, and media representatives (Todd, Albrecht, and Coleman, 1990). Certainly the volunteer efforts of economists involved in Project Home Safe (as described in chapters 3 and 7) are viable roles for home economists in working with latchkey children.

Recommended Strategies for Parents

The National Parent Teachers' Association (PTA) publication, "Kids with Keys...Parents with Jobs...Who's in Charge?" (1989) offers these recommendations for parents:

1. Talk to your employer about on-site or off-site child care centers for children, referral services, child care expense benefits, and a flex-time schedule.
2. Find out about block parent programs and "warmlines."
3. Teach responsibility to children. Help them make a schedule and allow them to help make house rules.
4. Offer children suggestions for constructive activities, such as reading a book or a children's magazine, starting a diary, or writing a pen pal.

The brochure "National PTA Takes Action" (National Parent Teacher's Association [PTA], 1985a) advocates these strategies for parents:

1. Work with the television and print media to encourage newspapers to write a feature article and TV stations to broadcast a news segment about latchkey children.
2. Develop a directory of school-age child care programs and other after-school activities available in your area.
3. Encourage the police department to establish an "Officer Friendly" program to provide classroom presentations and give safety tips for children in kindergarten to grade 3.
4. Obtain available books, newsletters, brochures, films, kits, and programs about latchkey children.
5. Schedule a PTA meeting with a panel of speakers representing community agencies to tell about after-school activities in the neighborhood.

Recommended Strategies for Employers

Employers should develop personnel policies that allow parents to work flexible hours or to take time off for any of these reasons: to care for a sick child, to attend a child care conference at the child's school or an after-school program, or to be with their child when there is no school due to early release or snow day. Personnel policies at work should also allow parents to receive calls from their children in an emergency or to ascertain their safety. Development of job opportunities that promote job-sharing or part-time employment, participation in a public education campaign to promote the need for more affordable school-age child care, and negotiations with union or employees to offer tuition assistance for school-age child care programs are other avenues by which employers can respond to the needs of latchkey children and their families (Parents United for Child Care and the Wellesley College Center for Research on Women, 1989).

Employers should also take the following steps, according to child care and employment experts interviewed by the Bureau of National Affairs:

1. Conduct a needs assessment to determine the type of help workers need for children
2. Train managers to be sensitive to latchkey children
3. Provide financial assistance to parents
4. Establish on-site child care programs
5. Support school-based child care programs (Bureau of National Affairs, 1988).

To support families in the workplace, and latchkey children in particular, these are other strategies employers could implement:

1. Encourage developers to include child care space in the work location rented
2. Organize a work and family committee or task force
3. Include positive family statements in company annual reports and strategic plans
4. Establish a working parent newsletter
5. Provide school vacation camps for children
6. Offer the work options of: telecommuting/working at home, a compressed work week, and flex-time ("Fifty Things Employers Can Do to Support Families in the Workplace," 1991).

Recommended Strategies for State and Federal Government

Each state should conduct a survey on the status of latchkey programs and every state legislature should pass laws or formulate policies mandating adult supervision for school-age children. These recommendations were made by researchers who conducted a national survey and wrote to the superintendent of schools in each state, as well as to the secretary of the education committee of the state legislatures in the 50 states, in order to obtain information on actual or pending latchkey programs and legislation. Results indicated that few programs were available to latchkey children and that only the state of Illinois had passed legislation for these children (Reynolds, 1985).

The Longs (1988) advocate the establishment of a national children's hotline center to assist local and state endeavors to develop hotlines and to provide technical assistance to ensure quality service. The center should include a hotline that children anywhere could call. A national help line would have a permanent staff, ensure equal access to all children, regardless of their location or residence, and maintain contact with local help lines throughout the country.

Recommended Strategies for Institutions of Higher Education

The Wellesley College Center for Research on Women, which has extensively researched and published on the topic of latchkey children, has stated 15 "Action Recommendations" for serving latchkey children and families in the forthcoming decades. One of their recommendations is that "universities, colleges and other training institutions, with the help of practitioners and professionals in related fields, need to create an agreed-upon body of knowledge and training curriculum [for providers of school-age child care programs] that can be widely adopted." The Center feels that staff training (both pre-service and in-service) must become widely available to caregivers and administrators of school-age child care (Seligson and Fink, 1989).

Recommendations from Public Librarians

In 1989 the author obtained recommendations from 10 librarians throughout the country as to what community programs or services (other than those specifically sponsored by the public library) would be desirable for latchkey children and/or their parents in their particular geographic area. This study is discussed in more detail in Chapter 6. Four of these librarians advocated better use of school buildings via extended day programs and summer enrichment activities. One mentioned that after-school care in school buildings should be a cooperative effort among volunteers, school staff, child development specialists, and park and recreation department staff. Sports programs, such as intramural athletics, were recommended by two librarians, with one noting that "the big need is for programs for 12 to 14 year old children, since they are too young to drive but too old to be in child care."

The creation of a clearinghouse hotline for after-school care in individual communities was advocated by one librarian. Since children frequently use the spending money parents give them on junk foods, one interviewee believed that an ideal service would be to provide students with a bag of healthy nutritional snacks when leaving school. Utilizing faculty from a university or staff from community agencies to present survival skills workshops for children on dealing with emergency situations was also suggested (Dowd, 1989).

REFERENCES

American Child Care Foundation, Inc. (ACCF). 1989. Perspectives on school-age child care 1989. Proceedings of Conference, October 13–15 in McLean, Virginia.

Bundy, M. and J. Boser. 1987. Helping latchkey children: A group guidance approach. *The School Counselor* 35(September): 58–65.

Bundy, M. and W. Poppen. 1989. Children in self care arrangements. *Journal of Counseling and Development* 10(June):592–93.

Bureau of National Affairs. 1988. *Latchkey children: A guide for employers.* National Report on Work and Family. Special Report #11. Washington, D.C.: Bureau of National Affairs, November.

Coleman, M., B. Rowland, and B. Robinson. 1989. School-age child care: The community leadership role of educators. *Childhood Education* 66(Winter): 78–82.

Corporate Child Development Fund for Texas (CCDFT). Letter to author, 19 February 1990.

Dowd, F.S. 1989. Serving latchkey children: Recommendations from librarians. *Public Libraries* 28(March/April): 101–06.

Fifty things employers can do to support families in the workplace. 1991. *Texas Child Care Resource Clearinghouse News.* Special Edition: 3.

Long, L. and T. Long. 1988. Hotlines for children: What makes them effective? *Children Today* 17(March/April): 22–25.

Long, L. and T. Long. 1989. Latchkey adolescents—How administrators can respond to their needs. *National Association of Elementary School Principals (NAESP) Bulletin* 73(February): 102–08.

McGuire, L. 1989. Who ya gonna call? Preparing kids to deal with emergencies. *Learning* (November/December): 38–40.

National Parent Teacher's Association (PTA). 1985a. National PTA takes action. Chicago, Illinois.

National Parent Teacher's Association (PTA). 1985b. *PTA Today* (April): 4–8.

National Parent Teacher's Association (PTA). 1989. Kids with keys...Parents with jobs...Who's in charge? Chicago, Illinois.

Parents United for Child Care and the Wellesley College Center for Research on Women. 1989. *Challenges facing Boston families: The need for school-age child care.* Parents United for Child Care, Boston. September.

Pitney, M. 1989. Children in self-care. In *Counseling young students at risk: Resources for elementary guidance counselors*, edited by J. Bluer and P. Schreibner. Ann Arbor, Michigan: ERIC Clearinghouse on Counseling and Personnel Services, ED 307 524.

Reynolds, R. 1985. Status of latch-key programs: A national survey. ERIC Document, ED 270 205.

Robinson, B., B. Rowland, and M. Coleman. 1986a. *Latchkey kids: Unlocking doors for children and their families.* Lexington, Massachusetts: Lexington Books.

Robinson, B., B. Rowland, and M. Coleman. 1986b. Taking action for latchkey children and their families. *Family Relations* 35(October): 473–78.

Seligson, M., and D. Fink. 1989. *No time to waste: An action agenda for school-age child care.* Wellesley, Massachusetts: School-Age Child Care Project, Wellesley College, Center for Research on Women.

Todd, C., K. Albrecht, and M. Coleman. 1990. School-age childcare: A continuum of options. *Journal of Home Economics* 82(Spring): 46–52.

Toenniessen, C., L. Little, and K. Rosen. 1985. Anybody home? Evaluation and intervention techniques with latchkey children. *Elementary School Guidance and Counseling* 20(December): 105–13.

Vannoy, W. 1988. Latchkey intramurals. *Journal of Physical Education, Recreation, and Dance* 59(April): 82–84.

When school is not in session: Report of the ad hoc committee on latchkey children of the Illinois Association of School Boards. 1989. Illinois Association of School Boards, Springfield. November.

Whirlpool Foundation and American Home Economics Association (AHEA). 1990. Progress report: January and March 1990 on Project Home Safe. Alexandria, Virginia.

Young, N. 1986. School-age child care: Concerns and challenges. *Young Children* 42(November): 3–10.

Zucker, H. 1944. Working parents and latchkey children. *Annals of the American Academy of Political and Social Science* 236: 43–50.

Part III
Latchkey Children in Public Libraries

Part III
Latchkey Children in Public Libraries

Chapter 5
Why Latchkey Children Present a Dilemma for Public Libraries

DEFINITIONS

A "library latchkey child" has been defined as one who on a regular basis (three or more times per week) is required by his/her parent or guardian to remain at the public library for extended periods of time after school (two or more hours per day) in lieu of day care (Stefansson, 1988). In the American Library Association's "position paper," *"Latchkey Children" in the Public Library* (American Library Association [ALA], 1988), the term "latchkey children" is used conditionally, and unattended children who use the public library for purposes other than materials selection, information, or cultural enrichment are described as falling into one of the following three categories:

1. "those who choose to frequent the public library because of personal, natural affinities for the library environment;
2. those who live nearby and go to the library because it is preferable to being at home alone after school;
3. those who are instructed to use the library as shelter by parents or guardians who are unable to provide alternative care for them."

The "position paper" further states that children in the first category create few (if any) problems for library staff and are, in fact, a source of great joy. But "it is the frequency and the length of visits to the library by children who fall into the latter categories that is of great concern." This is mainly because their presence "places additional burdens on the library in terms of staffing, resources and programming." But "worse still... rather than being a voluntary experience. . . .these children experience compulsion to be in a place not of their own choosing."

A former youth services coordinator states that library latchkey children "could be described as the temporary homeless. For two to three hours daily, these kids exist between home and school. During school breaks and vacations they might spend all day in the library. . .parents seek a reliable, affordable alternative for after-school care; kids want a secure relaxed refuge. And the way station of choice, a safe place, is often the library" (Strickland, 1988). Strickland also points out that latchkey children populate every community to some extent and are not restricted to any particular socioeconomic level.

THE NATURE OF THE PUBLIC LIBRARY DILEMMA

Library latchkey children are a prominent and significant group of children needing public library services. In fact, this clientele was the most frequently identified special population of children in the 1980s—in terms of atypical circumstances—mentioned by library respondents in a recent survey (Naylor, 1987). And "unsupervised children" who visit "libraries in larger numbers and for longer periods of time than ever before," are seen as "a critical issue facing public libraries" and as "another group that demands our attention" (Krull, 1991). To address the needs of this particular clientele, four staff development workshops, entitled "Coping with Latchkey Children" were conducted at Memphis/Shelby County Public Library and Information Center (Card, 1988).

However, library latchkey children are also a controversial issue among librarians and after-school library programming for this group, which is not restricted solely to metropolitan libraries, "has been the subject of much debate" (American Library Association [ALA], 1987; American Library Association [ALA], 1989). The presence of library latchkey children creates awkward choices, confusing dilemmas, and challenging opportunities for public libraries because service to this group seems both to coincide *and* to conflict with the very mission of these institutions. Traditionally, the professional ethics of public libraries have assured free public access to all patrons, and librarians have welcomed the use of library resources and materials by children. Yet most public librarians seem to agree that they are neither staffed nor trained, nor are their facilities equipped (or licensed), to function as child care centers.

Librarians also generally feel that their role should not be that of disciplinarian or babysitter (Dowd, 1990). Many librarians believe that service to other patrons will be impaired if their attention and time are spent supervising and/or entertaining unattended children (Chepesiuk, 1987). "In their role as child advocates, librarians find themselves between the two opposing factions, satisfying public needs and the demands of the organization" (Strickland, 1988). As one librarian remarked, "This ambivalent and contradictory attitude and approach might be accurately termed the 'come-to-me-but-stay-away-syndrome/dilemma'" (Stefansson, 1988).

The controversy surrounding public library service to children is best illustrated by the remarks of librarians themselves. Sager (1989), a prominent library administrator, states in his text on library management that latchkey children "represent an opportunity to work more effectively with schools and other youth supportive agencies to fill an important community need." He also writes that "when a large number of unsupervised children appear evident, the library administrator should exercise initiative...and launch new programs...", because "libraries have an important role" in this regard and "children are always welcome." Similarly, the ALA "position paper," *"Latchkey Children" in the Public Library* (1988), views latchkey children as an "unparalleled opportunity," and calls libraries that "are not part of the larger community solution...part of the problem."

Yet, not everyone agrees. A prominent library educator not only questioned the legitimacy of the ALA "position paper," but also sarcastically denied that latchkey children are even a legitimate clientele of public libraries:

> ...the manual...never deals with whether, only the how...It goes on to 'suggest programs to meet the needs of this clientele.' Clientele? Is the library's role the provision of shelter? It is if we simply assumed that we do for anyone what they came to have us do, that any professional decision-making by librarians is really incidental to a changing set of circumstances we do not control....Hospitals also serve children; why don't kids go there after school?...Because we have allowed ourselves to be so trivialized, the library can be seen simply as a handy place to come in out of the rain. It is of course possible, as the manual suggests, that such a new policy for the library might attract new converts to the opportunities that libraries offer. Possible, but I think not likely....I even have what may be the next clientele group to suggest....I understand there is a real shortage of golf courses, and waits for tee times, particularly on the weekend, can be many hours. Is there a potential role here for the library lawn? (White, 1990).

PHILOSOPHY OF PUBLIC LIBRARY SERVICE TO CHILDREN: A HISTORICAL VIEW

An understanding of the historical development of public library service to children, as influenced by societal factors, helps to clarify the philosophy of public library service to children that is adhered to today and upon which the ALA "position paper" is based. A historical perspective can also aid in understanding why latchkey children currently pose such a dilemma for public librarians who are often unprepared for working with them. In addition, the following excerpts reveal how amazingly similar the controversy over children in the public library which took place almost 100 years ago is to the current debate over public library service to latchkey children. Yet dedicated professionals surmounted that earlier controversy to offer young patrons remarkable service. Lastly, a historical look at the beginnings of public library service to children reveals the active traditional interaction between libraries and other community agencies—an interaction which must continue today to meet the challenge of latchkey children.

The public library emerged on the American scene as an adult service institution; children were not part of its initial patronage. But as children began to perceive the public library as a source of books, and their numbers among its patrons multiplied, librarians implemented methods of separating children from adult library users (Thomas, 1990).

These quotes from John Cotton Dana, the librarian of the Denver (Colorado) Public Library, and from others, describe the controversy about children in the public library:

> What to do with children in the free public library is one of the unsettled problems of library economy. For the comfort of the older reader it is certainly desirable that children should not come in large numbers into the main part of the library in which the public is given access to the shelves (Dana, 1896).

In the late nineteenth century the prime question of the day was whether or not children were the proper concern of public libraries which were beginning to arise across the land, offering free reading to everyone—except children under 12 or 14 or 16 years of age (Sayers, 1963).

> Children were denied entry. They were considered to be unequal to the ideal. Straightway, they made their own persistent and unorganized demands, knocking upon doors that were not open to them. They literally climbed upon window sills to peer in at their elders. . . . (Sayers, 1972).

The practice of separating juvenile from adult library patrons was probably begun by the staff at Brookline, Massachusetts, who in 1890 set aside a previously unoccupied basement room for children (Emery, 1917). But it "was not a children's room in any proper sense of the word" (Parsons, 1909); it was "merely a place to send the children to keep them quiet and out of the way of adults" (McNamara, 1986). Mary Wright Plummer wrote that the basement room "under the charge of the janitor" was opened because "the older people using the public library. . .complained that there were so many children underfoot" (Plummer, 1911). In 1894 Denver Public Library opened a children's room and this was followed by those in many cities.

But in 1897 Pratt Institute Free Library in New York opened not only the first children's room to be planned for in the architect's blueprint, but also the first to be supervised by a professional. That professional was Anne Carroll Moore, who began a full training course for children's librarians at Pratt in 1898 (McNamara, 1986). This training was essential as the young women assigned to the first children's rooms had no prior education or experience to prepare them to work with the new clientele of public libraries—children. As a result, they were forced to become innovators, improvisors, pioneers in a whole new area of being. . ., and molders of a philosophy of practice (Sayers, 1972). Because there had never been an institution quite like the free libraries for children, public libraries had a unique character, different from that of schools, kindergartens, and Sunday Schools, which also served children. Although children's libraries shared some aspects in common with the settlement houses and other social service institutions in large cities at the turn of the century, public libraries were education, in the broadest sense of the word (Sayers, 1963).

It is interesting to note that those who shaped services for children in public libraries initially did so with a broad vision. While emphasizing the library's traditional goal of providing quality materials, these pioneers reached out to schools, playgrounds, and recreational centers to the underserved and unserved in the role of information source in the community (Rollock, 1988).

Anne Carroll Moore can also be credited with establishing a philosophy of children's service in public libraries that is still in effect today. She focused on attractive, inviting rooms, qualified helpful staff, the fun of storytelling, and the recreational value of inspiring and promoting the love of lifelong reading (Dain, 1972). Moore was also among the first to endorse extending the librarians' work outside of the library and to initiate unique and innovative approaches of book-related programming for children.

Commenting at an American Library Association meeting on "how far the library should go in relating its work to that of other institutions," Moore advised that

> a firsthand knowledge of the aims, objects and method of work of all the forces in a given community and a perception of their interrelationship is essential if we wish to do away with the present tendency to duplicate work which is already being carried on by more effective agencies. . . .The aim should be to make [the library's] own work so clear to the community in which it is placed, that it will command the respect and support of every citizen (Rollock, 1988).

REFERENCES

American Library Association (ALA). 1987. *ALA Yearbook*. Chicago: American Library Association.

American Library Association (ALA). Association for Library Services to Children's Division. 1988. *"Latchkey children" in the public library*. Chicago: American Library Association.

American Library Association (ALA). 1989. *ALA Yearbook*. Chicago: American Library Association.

Card, J. 1988. Staff development at Memphis/Shelby County Public Library and Information Center. *Public Libraries* 27 (Summer): 103–05.

Chepesiuk, R. 1987. Reaching out: Greenville County Library's latchkey kids program. *Library Journal* 112(March 1): 46–48.

Dain, P. 1972. *The New York Public Library: A history of its founding and early years*. New York: New York Public Library.

Dana, J.C. 1896. The children in the public library. *The Outlook* 54(September 26): 555.

Dowd, F. 1990. Latchkey children: A community and public library phenomenon. *Public Library Quarterly* 10(1): 7–22.

Emery, J.W. 1917. *The library, the school and the child*. Toronto, Canada: Macmillan.

Krull, J. 1991. Social and demographic changes in "Critical issues facing public libraries" by Donald Sager. *Public Libraries* 30 (January/February): 13–20.

McNamara, S. 1986. Early public library work with children. *Top of the News* 43(Fall): 59–72.

Naylor, A. 1987. Reaching all children: A public library dilemma. *Library Trends* 35 (Winter): 369–81.

Parsons, J. 1909. First children's room. *Library Journal* 34(December): 552.

Plummer, M.W. 1911. Work with children in the libraries of greater New York. *The Survey* 27(October): 1058.

Rollock, B. 1988. *Public library service for children.* Hamden, Connecticut: Library Professional Publications.

Sager, D. 1989. *Managing the public library.* 2nd ed. Boston: G.K. Hall.

Sayers, F.C. 1963. The American origins of public library work with children. *Library Trends* 12(July): 6–13.

Sayers, F.C. 1972. *Anne Carroll Moore: A biography.* New York: Atheneum.

Stefansson, J. 1988. Kids with keys: San Marino Public Library—A case study. Presentation at the Public Library Association National Conference, 29 April, at Pittsburgh, Pennsylvania.

Strickland, C. 1988. Young users. *Wilson Library Bulletin* 62(June): 98–99.

Thomas, F. 1990. Early appearances of children's reading rooms in public libraries. *Journal of Youth Services in Libraries* 4(Fall): 81–90.

White, H. 1990. Pseudo-libraries and semi-teachers. *American Libraries* 21(February): 103–06.

Chapter 6
What National Research Tells Us About Library Latchkey Children

1988 NATIONAL SURVEY OF LATCHKEY CHILDREN IN PUBLIC LIBRARIES

Background and Need for Research

Prior to 1988 latchkey children in public libraries were largely unresearched. In fact, as of February 1988 only two short descriptive articles about the topic had been published in library literature (Chepesiuk, 1987; Mueller, 1987). The only other available information consisted of a few unpublished in-house memoranda from public libraries (San Marino Public Library and Los Angeles Public Library) and local newspaper articles from cities, both large and small, throughout the country (Los Angeles, Denton [Texas]), Dallas, Durham, Baltimore, Virginia Beach, New York) (Avery, 1986; Fairhall, 1987; Floria, 1988; "Latchkey Kids Called Top Problem," 1987; "Librarians Frustrated by Baby Sitter Role," 1987; Mitgang, 1988; Morris, 1987; Noble, 1988; "A Place to Go," 1986). However, such informal sources confirmed that latchkey children were spending their weekday afternoons in public libraries around the United States and that these institutions were grappling with this phenomenon, having defined neither their role nor their appropriate response to unattended children.

Consequently, in March 1988 the author began to explore latchkey children in public libraries throughout the nation, having received modest funding from Texas Woman's University. The goals of the research were to assist public libraries in clarifying their appropriate role in serving latchkey children and to develop recommendations for more effective service to this user group. A preliminary three-part questionnaire consisting of multiple choice and open-ended questions was constructed which addressed three aspects of service to latchkey children: description, magnitude of, and explanation for their existence in public libraries; content and extent of written or unwritten public library policies and procedures; and types of programs and services public libraries provided or recommended for this clientele.

Methodology

The preliminary questionnaire was pretested for appropriate wording, content validity, and reliability by utilizing a panel of nine librarians throughout the nation—children's coordinators, library directors, and salaried officials in the American Library Association—with expertise in children's services and/or research. After rewording to incorporate the recommendations of the majority, the final questionnaire was mailed, with assurance of anonymity, to a random sample of 125 of the 425 public library systems listed in the directory *Coordinators of Children's and Young Adult Services in Public Library Systems Serving at Least 100,000 People*, (American Library Association, 1984). (See Appendix A for a copy of the questionnaire.) The cover letter mailed with the questionnaire to the children's coordinators stated that the survey could be completed by the coordinator to represent the library system as a whole or could be forwarded to a particular children's librarian in the system who dealt with latchkey children on a regular basis.

The sample included 42 states and the District of Columbia, since eight states did not have public libraries serving over 100,000 people. Ninety-one usable questionnaires were received from each of the 43 geographic areas identified, with approximately one-third representing one facility and the remainder responding for between 2 and 86 facilities. The high response rate was partially due to the fact that follow up with nonrespondents via mail and finally via telephone continued through June. Data analysis for the multiple choice questions utilized the **SPSS-X** Statistical Package, which converted responses into frequencies and percentages. Open-ended questions were analyzed, and responses with similar meaning but different wording were categorized and then converted into frequencies and percentages.

Findings

Estimates and Impact of Latchkey Children in Public Libraries

The first question posed to respondents was: "Have you found that latchkey/unattended children are using your library for child care purposes after school on weekdays? On weekends?" A majority responded affirmatively; 76 percent reported unattended children after school on weekdays, and 50 percent reported latchkey children present on weekends. Sixty-one of the 91 participants completed at least some portion of a chart "estimating the number of latchkey children present in their public library during a typical week between 3:00 P.M. and 6:00 P.M." The number of children using the library regularly for child care purposes was found to increase with the age level of the child, until peaking for 10- to 12-year-olds, with an average of 21 children present at least three days per week during those hours.

For nine statements, participants were asked to select one of three phrases (i.e., "never," "sometimes," or "always") which most accurately described their library's situation in regard to latchkey children. Eight of the nine statements concerned adverse effects. The majority either "sometimes" or "always" encountered all but one of the eight adverse situations listed, including "some difficulty in performing regular library services effectively for other patrons," "uncertainty regarding how to best deal with unattended/latchkey children," and "vandalism/destruction of library property." "Disturbances due to inappropriate behaviors (as running, moving furniture, etc.)," "limited or unavailable seating," "delays or difficulty in closing the library when a child is left unattended," and "patron complaints" were also adverse situations the majority encountered. However, the majority (72 percent) did at least sometimes perceive the situation of latchkey children as a positive one that presented staff with "an opportunity to develop new methods of effective service."

Why Latchkey Children Use Public Libraries

Six questions dealt with respondents' opinions as to why latchkey children use the public library in lieu of after-school care, and asked participants to "check as many as apply." While the majority checked every option, participants almost unanimously felt that the reason was because "parents perceive the library as an appropriate facility where children can safely spend a few hours after school." However the majority also checked each of the other reasons (i.e., "parents can't afford child care," "parents lack child care information," "parents perceive library as educational," "library philosophy welcomes children," and "library near school."

Factors Aggravating the Library Latchkey Situation

As to possible factors which may aggravate the library latchkey situation, exactly half of the respondents perceived that the "architectural design and layout of the library building" exacerbated this, while 69 percent felt that limited personnel worsened the situation and a little over half believed limited seating or space was a factor. In regard to other factors which participants wrote-in and which were not listed on the questionnaire, 9 percent cited the location of the library as aggravating their latchkey children situation. In one case a branch was located in a public housing project; in several instances the library was in a park or across the street from a school. Two libraries were in areas where there were no playgrounds or backyards where children could play. Five percent of the respondents wrote that "other people"—i.e., "vagrants," "transients," "street people," "the deinstitutionalized," or "problem patrons"—were adverse influences.

Additional factors, each listed once, which librarians identified as negatively affecting latchkey/unattended children at the library included: "difficulty in communicating with children who don't speak English," "computer and telephone tie-ups by children," and "requests from hungry children for food or permission to eat snacks in the library."

Library's Main Challenge in Regard to Latchkey Children

In completion of the statement: "The main challenge that public libraries have in serving latchkey children is. . .," the response most frequently cited by participants (38 percent) referred to their attempts to achieve a balance between meeting the needs of latchkey children and maintaining an effective library climate and service to other patrons. Specifically, respondents referred to the challenge of providing latchkey children with normal and interesting library programs and experiences, helping them use their time in the library effectively, making them feel welcome, motivating them to read, and not turning them off to books and libraries—all without disturbing others through distracting behavior.

Fourteen percent expressed the library's main challenge primarily in terms of what they felt the library is *not* (i.e., not a day care center, not a drop-off center for children, and not a babysitting service). An equal percentage cited the library's main challenge as being able to deal with medical emergencies, children's safety and security, or the library's liability and legal responsibility. Eleven percent felt that coping with inadequate staff, insufficient training, or lack of funding was the main challenge. For 7 percent the challenge was building relationships with parents and/or with community agencies. Five percent mentioned finding alternatives to disruptive behavior besides sending children from the library, and an equal percentage wrote that the main challenge was providing after-school programs.

Library Policies and Procedures for Latchkey Children

In order to obtain an accurate description of current library policies and procedures for latchkey children, participants were asked to check the statement from a list of six alternatives which identified their library's situation. Less than one-third had written policies and procedures in effect, while 18 percent were developing them; an equal percentage recognized the need for them, and the same percentage followed unwritten policies and procedures.

The questionnaire listed six possible reasons why written library policies and procedures concerning latchkey children are or would be important and instructed participants to "check as many as apply" to their library's situation. Each of these reasons was cited by the majority, or between 65 and 83 percent of the respondents; "to standardize procedures for handling unattended children left at closing time" was the reason most often noted. "To maintain the appropriate and equitable use of the library" was cited least.

Libraries without policies and procedures for latchkey children were asked to skip the remainder of this section; therefore, the findings do not reflect data from 59 respondents. The majority of those who responded to this section had developed written policies and procedures for latchkey children "after experiencing a problem," while the minority developed them "before experiencing a problem," "after reviewing policies and procedures of other libraries," "after discussing the topic with persons from other community agencies," "or after a library committee/task force met to gather facts or make recommendations." Over two-thirds (69 percent) reported that their policies and procedures were adequate in meeting their needs, and 88 percent indicated that their policies and procedures "had been used/followed at least once."

Participants were given three options regarding potential methods in which the public might be informed of their library's policies and procedures for latchkey children and were asked to "check as many as apply." While none of the three methods—a sign, talks to community groups and schools, or printed material given to patrons—was utilized by the majority, most frequently a sign was posted in the library (35 percent).

The final questions in this section pertained to the actual content of the policies and procedures concerning latchkey children. Six specific statements or actions were listed and participants were instructed to "check as many as apply." The majority of library policy/procedure statements dealing with latchkey children included wording to the effect that "parents or guardians are responsible for the behavior of their child while in the library," and that "children under a specific age should not be left unattended in the library." Most policy/procedure statements also specified actions to be taken in situations where a child is unattended in the library at closing time or a child is disruptive in the library. The majority usually contained negative statements.

Library Programs and Services for Latchkey Children

All respondents—regardless of whether or not latchkey children were using their library, and regardless of whether or not their libraries had written policies and procedures for dealing with them—were instructed to complete the next section in its entirety. Participants were to indicate whether their library provided each of 12 programs/services for latchkey children, and whether they recommended that their library provide them. The service most frequently recommended (and the only one provided by a majority) was "information and referral services for parents regarding available licensed child care in the area." For almost all of the programs/services the percent of respondents recommending provision was higher than the percent actually providing the program/service. The service with the greatest discrepancy in this regard was "an on-line computer database community resource file listing activities for latchkey children and their parents." Conversely, in three instances a greater number of respondent libraries offered a service/program in comparison to the number who believed that it should be offered. This category included "after-school child care services"; "drop-in activity programs, such as arts and crafts projects"; and "special security guards or monitors to supervise unattended/latchkey children in the library."

Each of the final five items of the questionnaire was open-ended and was designed specifically to gather creative, positive, and effective methods for dealing with latchkey children in order to assist libraries experiencing similar situations. Participants were asked to complete this sentence: "An additional program/service which I would recommend public libraries provide for unattended/latchkey children is. . . ." Although no more than two respondents cited the same suggestion, among the inclusions were a free house phone for children's use in calling home, snacks or a break room for nutritional after-school foods, and additional staff or volunteers to allow more after-school programming.

Interactions Between Libraries and Community Agencies

A second open-ended question asked whether respondents felt that interaction between libraries and other community agencies in dealing with latchkey children was important. A clear majority—74 percent—indicated "yes," while 11 percent stated "no"; 3 percent partially agreed, and 11 percent left this blank. In clarification of their affirmative opinions, 9 percent stated that they felt libraries should serve as advocates for children, belong to or form coalitions for better child care, or network with other community agencies in behalf of children. A few cited children's welfare as their rationale: "It is important that children don't slip through the cracks." "Latchkey children could be facing other problems—neglect, unemployed parents, no shelter, and it's important that this be dealt with too." Additional reasons given for interaction between libraries and other community agencies were that no other agencies were addressing the situation, that it was too big a task for the library alone, and that lack of adequate library funding necessitated cooperation.

Although the consensus on cooperative ventures was certainly positive, librarians held quite varied opinions as to the extent and type of community involvement they felt was most appropriate for public libraries to assume in order to address latchkey children. For example, 11 percent felt that the library's cooperation with community agencies should pertain solely to knowing and disseminating information or to providing referrals. This involved providing parents with information about after-school programs in the community and serving as a clearinghouse for information about local agencies.

Three percent clearly believed that a greater extent of active participation on the part of the library was warranted. One respondent remarked that it is important to be in on the beginning of new programs. A second suggested that a cooperative scholarship financial assistance program be provided to families who cannot afford after-school care. The use of volunteers (grandparents, retired teachers, Big Brothers, Big Sisters, PTA members, and students majoring in education at local colleges) in programming for latchkey children was the type of cooperative activity most frequently mentioned.

The Library's Role in Regard to Latchkey Children

Respondents were asked to complete this statement: "The role of the public library in regard to latchkey/unattended children is. . ." Fifty-two percent of the participants indicated that the library's role is to provide normal effective service just as is given to any other user group. However, they qualified this by noting that this role was only feasible by working within the limits of funding and staffing so that other patrons' services are not adversely affected. An additional 4 percent carried the idea of assuring equitable service to latchkey children a step further, and expressed the opinion that this clientele deserved special attention: ". . .to serve them as patrons who spend more time in the library than other patrons. We should take advantage of that."

While 19 percent defined the library's role in negative terms, almost an equal percentage believed that role involved working with parents or community agencies. Seven percent stated their belief that the library had *no* role in regard to latchkey children, remarking that it was the responsibility of working parents or was handled by other agencies. Specific wording used to convey this viewpoint was: "ultimately not responsible" and "should absolve ourselves of the responsibility." Another 7 percent believed the library's role was unclear or undefined. One individual remarked: "Deal with it when it comes up....No resolution to the problem ever seems to come about." Ensuring children's safety was a role mentioned by 3 percent. Still another participant stated that the library's role was to be the best kind of library, and that in different areas that will mean different things.

Extent of and Reasons for Successful Library Service to Latchkey Children

Respondents were then asked: "Is your library successful in dealing with latchkey/unattended children?" Fifty-two percent stated "yes," 14 percent said "no," an equal percentage "partially agreed," and the remaining

20 percent left this blank. Although the majority did consider their library to be effectively serving this clientele, there was no consensus as to their reason for this estimation. Thirteen percent attributed their accomplishments with latchkey children to their staff—i.e., their positive attitude, constant supervision, personal contact, availability to introduce materials and services, and sufficient knowledge of specific children to handle problems and provide services appropriate to the circumstances.

Twelve percent noted community support or publicity as factors for success. More specifically, librarians described their contacts with children, schools, and parents. Often the interaction concerned making others aware of library policy or of children's misconduct. Participants explained that strong community support and interaction worked well for them. Another respondent explained that at the library they always establish eye contact, greet and talk to kids, and let them know they're friendly. But they do call parents whenever they feel there is a problem. In addition, their head of public services and head of the children's department meet with principals during the first week of school and discuss latchkey children, so that a groundwork for communication is built. They also meet and talk with parents and let them know their expectations from kids and them.

Eleven percent considered activities or programs to be responsible for their library's success in serving latchkey children. Film showings, craft activities, self-care survival skills workshops, after-school and special summer programs, playing with toys and games, and homework were among the activities described. One librarian wrote that she used a "task bowl" from which children draw tasks when disruptive.

In elaborating why their library was only "partially successful" in dealing with latchkey children, participants wrote that there was uncertainty and some frustration about serving latchkey children while maintaining other services. One expressed concern about controlling the situation without violating children's rights to use the library, which was believed to be very important. A most poignant remark was: "Our government and our society to a great extent view children as any expendable resource. Until this changes the library will not be able to deal with the problem."

Several Comments About Library Latchkey Children

In their general comments concerning latchkey children, participants discussed a variety of aspects, including policy development, differences between the terms "latchkey" and "unattended," concern about negative publicity from the media and restrictive library policies, and the need for better child care. The most frequently discussed aspect pertained to the pervasiveness and permanence of the library latchkey phenomenon: "It is a community/social problem and should be addressed as such." "This is part of a national crisis."

A topic discussed almost as frequently was that of children's safety and/or the library's liability and legal responsibility: "Thank goodness a child has not been lost, hurt or stolen!" "This questionnaire doesn't address the issue of accident or injury—a major concern that we have yet to confront." "Parents need to be educated. Most would not leave a young child unattended in a department store; yet many do not even remain in the library building with a child." "There are too many unanswered questions—What do we do with such children, no parents at home. Where do they rest? Do we wait for parents to retrieve children?"

Summary of the 1988 Survey of Public Libraries

This initial national survey made it evident that in 1988 latchkey children were using public libraries largely in lieu of child care and that librarians almost unanimously perceived the latchkey phenomenon as due to parental attitudes (i.e., parents' perception that libraries are safe and appropriate places for unattended children after school). Librarians felt that additional staff would lessen the negative effects of this situation, since the majority stated that inadequate staff was the most aggravating factor. Most were frustrated or ambivalent about how to handle latchkey children. The situation created "uncertainties" and "difficulties" for them in serving other patrons, yet at the same time offered "an opportunity" for developing new methods of effective service. Moreover, while librarians saw serving this clientele as part of their role, they also felt that fulfilling this role without negatively affecting service to other patrons was their "main challenge." It seems that public librarians needed assistance in serving latchkey children effectively, as only about half felt that their library was successfully dealing with the situation. Rather, in that the majority affirmed the importance of interacting with other community agencies, the libraries recognized they could not on their own effectively serve latchkey children.

It appeared that the majority of respondent librarians may not have considered written policies and procedures for latchkey children essential, since less than one-third had developed them. Most believed that written documents pertaining to latchkey children were as beneficial to staff as they were to these youth. Librarians have been reactive rather than proactive in developing written policies and procedures for latchkey children, and a majority have not devoted particular thought, time, or attention to the formulation of such policies. Developing policies and procedures for latchkey children seems well worth the time and effort, however, as almost all who did so used or followed them at least once, and the majority found them adequate for their needs.

Librarians were not in agreement as to the most effective method of informing the public about the content of their policies and procedures; no single technique was utilized by the majority. They were anxious to disclaim any potential liability for unattended children, as most incorporated in their policies and procedures specific statements which place responsibility for the behavior of children upon the parent or guardian. Adults may perceive most library policies and procedures for latchkey children as being restrictive, since many libraries expressed these official statements largely in negative terms. Apparently librarians recognized that their services and programs for latchkey children were inadequate, since traditional library information and referral services were more often recommended than provided—especially the online computer database community resource file listing activities for latchkey children and their parents. In contrast, they considered nontraditional services, such as having special monitors and providing child care services, inappropriate library activities, even though some did provide them (Dowd, 1989b).

Follow-up Interviews with Selected Librarians (1988)

As a follow-up to the 1988 national latchkey survey of public libraries, interviews were conducted by the author which resulted in recommendations for appropriate and effective service to latchkey children. Ten librarians identified from the questionnaire responses as having valuable and positive insights for service to this clientele were interviewed via telephone or in person. The librarians selected met two general criteria: they provided a great deal of information about their various actual or proposed services to latchkey children and they conveyed a willing and enthusiastic attitude regarding services to this group in the narrative section of the questionnaire (Dowd, 1989a).

The purposes of the interviews were to obtain in-depth, constructive recommendations from practicing librarians working with latchkey children and to highlight successful endeavors in various geographic areas that could assist public libraries in serving this clientele more effectively. Prior to the interview, participants received a schedule containing the four questions to be addressed. The responses given by selected librarians during these follow-up interviews are described in Chapter 8, in the section "Recommendations of Librarians (1988)."

1990 NATIONAL SURVEY OF LATCHKEY CHILDREN IN PUBLIC LIBRARIES

Background and Need for Research

The topic of library latchkey children continues to be of great interest to librarians. Since the completion of the author's initial survey, several articles and references to this clientele appeared in library literature. In 1988, 1989, and 1990, the American Library Association, the Public Library Association, state library associations (such as those of Oklahoma and Texas), and the Canadian Library Association scheduled sessions at their annual conferences about latchkey children. Since 1988 at least eight students at library schools around the country wrote theses or professional papers on the topic of latchkey children in completion of the requirements for their Master's Degree. And the National Commission on Libraries and Information Sciences (NCLIS) and ACTION awarded Intergenerational Library Assistance Grants, or Retired Senior Volunteer Projects (RSVP) to a dozen or so public libraries in 1988 and 1990 to address the needs of latchkey children with the help of retired senior citizen volunteers. (See Chapter 7 for more information on these awards.)

Despite those developments, no library research at the national level—other than the author's survey and follow-up interviews—had been undertaken. Consequently, in March 1990, the author began a second national survey regarding latchkey/unattended children in public libraries, again with modest funding from Texas Woman's University. The overall goals were identical to those in the first study: to assist public libraries in clarifying their appropriate role in serving latchkey children and to develop recommendations for more effective service to this user group. Three specific objectives were: to determine the current extent of latchkey children in public libraries as compared to that of 1988, their impact upon library service and the level of success of libraries in this regard; to determine the level of knowledge, sources of training, and additional training needs of librarians serving latchkey children; and to obtain descriptions of successful, innovative strategies public libraries were implementing (both independently and in cooperation with other community agencies) to address the needs of latchkey children and their families.

As in the prior survey, a preliminary three-part questionnaire was constructed which addressed three aspects of service to latchkey children: general description of the latchkey situation at public libraries; personnel training and experience; and library and community responses. While all three parts contained multiple choice questions, the third part also included five open-ended questions.

Methodology

The preliminary questionnaire was pretested for appropriate wording, content validity, and reliability by using a panel of nine validators (four of whom had served as validators in the first study) who had expertise in children's services and/or research. After rewording to incorporate the recommendations of the majority, the final questionnaire was mailed, with assurance of anonymity, to a random sample of 155 of the 425 public library systems listed in the directory *Coordinators of Children's and Young Adult Services in Public Libraries Serving at Least 100,000 People* (American Library Association, 1989). (See Appendix B for a copy of the questionnaire.) The library systems that had been mailed the 1988 questionnaire were deleted from this pool in order to obtain data from a new set of respondents. However, 12 exceptions were made for states with no other library system in the directory besides the one mailed to in the first survey. As before, the cover letter mailed with the questionnaire to children's coordinators stated that the survey could be completed by them to represent their library system as a whole or could be forwarded to a particular children's librarian in the system who dealt with latchkey children on a regular basis.

The sample included 42 states and Washington, D.C., since eight states did not have public libraries serving over 100,000 people. Of the 110 usable questionnaires received, 40 geographic regions were identified, with 36 percent responding for one facility, 52 percent responding for between 2 and 90 facilities, and the remainder uncommitted. (Since findings are reported in percentages rounded off into whole numbers rather than with decimals included, the sums do not always total 100 percent).

Findings

General Description and Impact of Latchkey Children at Libraries

For the first five items on the questionnaire librarians were asked to "check the response which most accurately describes the situation at your library," from the four options listed. The first statement was: "Latchkey/unattended children are using the library for child care purposes after school or on weekends." Affirmative responses were given almost unanimously. Fourteen percent of the 110 participants indicated that this was the case "to a great extent," and another 82 percent stated "somewhat."

"The impact of latchkey/unattended children upon the library's personnel and services" was noticeable in the majority (92 percent) of libraries surveyed—i.e., "high" in 20 percent of the participating libraries and "marginal" in 72 percent. In 6 percent there was no impact. The majority (58 percent) of librarians felt that they are meeting the needs of latchkey children at least partially; 6 percent "strongly agreed" and 52 percent "agreed somewhat." Twenty-one percent "disagreed" with the following statement: "In meeting the needs of latchkey/unattended children our library has met with success." Another 21 percent selected the option "don't know."

Participants were asked to select the phrase which most accurately completed the following statement: "In comparison with the situation two years ago, the number of latchkey/unattended children at the library is...." For the majority (64 percent) the number of latchkey children was "about the same," while for another 15 percent it was "higher." Fifteen percent checked "lower" and another 6 percent checked "don't know." For the majority of responding libraries (55 percent), "in comparison with the situation two years ago, the level of development of the library's policies and procedures dealing with latchkey/unattended children" is "the same," while for another 41 percent it is better (i.e., in 12 percent "much better" and in 29 percent "slightly better"). Four percent checked "don't know."

The next nine statements sought to determine the specific impact of latchkey/unattended children upon the library's personnel and services. Participants were asked to circle "yes" or "no" for each item. Only one of the eight circumstances listed (i.e., "delays in closing due to a child left alone") was experienced by the majority of libraries. Between 13 percent and 65 percent of the libraries were adversely affected in some way by latchkey children: "legal liability" (13 percent); "medical emergencies/accidents" (18 percent); "reallocation of staff to cover after-school hours" (20 percent); and "need for increased security measures" (34 percent).

However, for a minority of the libraries, latchkey children also created some opportunities, in terms of "increased recruitment of adult volunteers" (9 percent); "the need to develop new methods of service" (34 percent); and "closer interaction/cooperation with schools or representatives from other community agencies" (38 percent).

Personnel Training and Experience Regarding Latchkey Children

Part II of the questionnaire dealt with personnel: how they learned about serving latchkey children, what training was most valuable to them, how they would rate their level of knowledge, and what they would like to do to improve their understanding of this clientele. In order to determine how libraries had learned about services to latchkey children, respondents were asked to circle "yes" or "no" for 11 statements. Almost all of the responding librarians "gained an understanding of service to latchkey/unattended children" from "reading books and articles in library literature" as well as from "on the job experience." Two-thirds read the ALA "position paper" in particular. About half gained knowledge about latchkey children via personal contacts—i.e., "communicating (in writing or in person) with other librarians to pool ideas" (54 percent) and "interaction with representatives from community agencies" (45 percent). The minority learned about latchkey children from group activities—i.e., conferences or workshops, and in-service presentations. Only 7 percent indicated they received training in library school courses.

The majority (78 percent) felt competent in dealing with latchkey children in libraries. That is, while 6 percent termed their "level of knowledge of library service to latchkey/unattended children" as "high," 26 percent stated it was "good," and 46 percent perceived it as "satisfactory." Less than one-fifth (18 percent) termed it "inadequate." Five percent checked "don't know."

In order to obtain an indication as to which learning experience about latchkey/unattended children was most beneficial to them, the librarians participating were asked to complete this statement: "The most valuable method in which I learned about latchkey/unattended children was. . ." While the strategy respondents felt was most beneficial was "on the job experience," the least valuable was in-service training. No single method was considered to be most valuable by the majority. Reading library literature, discussing the topic with other librarians, attending conference programs, and interaction with community agencies were most valuable for less than 30 percent of the respondents.

The last item in Part II of the questionnaire sought to determine what training strategies librarians felt would be most helpful to them in learning more about this clientele in the future. Participants were asked to complete this statement: "Ideally I would like to increase my knowledge/understanding of latchkey/unattended children by doing the following. . . ." The preferred strategy would be attending conference sessions and workshops, with on-the-job experience least desirable. However, no single learning strategy mentioned represented the viewpoint of the majority.

Library Programs and Services for Latchkey Children

The third and final part of the questionnaire was designed to reveal the specific activities libraries were implementing to serve latchkey/unattended children, especially what was successful. Participants were instructed to indicate whether their library provided each of eight types of programs and services for this clientele. The most prevalent service or program provided (63 percent) was that of "information and referral for parents regarding available licensed child care." Slightly over half also offered "storyhours, clubs, and other traditional library programs specifically scheduled to meet the needs of latchkey children." "Drop-in activity programs, such as arts and crafts projects and films," as well as "volunteer opportunities for children after school at the library," were available at 47 and 43 percent of the libraries, respectively. The remaining four services or programs were available in less than one-third of the libraries, with a "'warm-line' telephone service for children to ask self-care questions" an extremely rare library service.

In Part III of the questionnaire there were also five open-ended statements requiring narrative responses. Two of these were included to identify successful, innovative strategies public libraries were undertaking to serve latchkey children effectively. The first one was: "Please describe any successful strategies (in terms of special services, programs, activities, etc.) which 'work' at your library in meeting the needs of latchkey/unattended children or their families." Another open-ended item requested participants to "describe specifically any cooperative activities with other agencies/institutions in the community which you are involved in on behalf of latchkey children."

The author telephoned libraries whose responses to either of these questions seemed innovative and substantial. Telephone follow-ups were conducted to obtain more thorough, accurate, and current information regarding "workable" activities and strategies libraries were implementing to serve latchkey children, so that ultimately other practitioners would be able to replicate these ideas in addressing this clientele more effectively. Since the information obtained from those interviews explains services actually "in place" at various libraries, the descriptions are contained in Chapter 7, which highlights individual library efforts on behalf of latchkey children. However, the following is a summarized general overview of those strategies and activities.

Successful Strategies in Serving Latchkey Children

In regard to the first narrative item, "successful strategies," the most popular (noted by 28 respondents) was provision of after-school programs—both informal drop-in programs as well as formal activities advertised at a specific time. They ranged from film showings and arts and crafts projects to puppet shows and game days. Homework help and tutoring by senior citizens and local teen volunteers followed in frequency of occurrence.

Providing latchkey children with opportunities to use materials and equipment, informally and individually, reportedly worked well in 16 libraries surveyed. This usually involved either making computers accessible to children (along with programs and activity sheets) or providing puzzles, toys, games, activity books, paper, pencils, crayons, and scissors so that children could work quietly and independently on simple educational projects. A few stated that they made puppets and a puppet stage available, as well as audiovisual equipment, such as records, audio and video cassettes, and filmstrips.

A scant number mentioned strategies which might be categorized under "personnel"—i.e., scheduling staff in the children's department from 3:00 P.M. to 6:00 P.M., and providing in-service training and discussion opportunities for librarians about child care and latchkey children. Two other effective approaches might be categorized as "administrative matters" and "public relations." Four respondents felt that developing written policies and procedures concerning latchkey children was successful. Public relations strategies primarily consisted of communication of librarians with principals at local elementary schools and with parents of latchkey children to discuss the library's appropriate role, safety concerns, and how each could work together on behalf of children; or cooperation of libraries with community agencies.

Cooperative Activities of Libraries and Other Agencies in Serving Latchkey Children

Responses to the second narrative item, "cooperative activities," revealed that a significant number of libraries participated with a wide variety of neighborhood agencies and institutions on behalf of latchkey children, and that this interaction took various forms. Respondents mentioned cooperative endeavors with each of the following agencies and institutions: senior citizens; Girls Scouts; Social Services; elementary schools; day care centers; local governmental departments such as fire, police, health, parks and recreation, and youth bureau and probation; American Red Cross; Humane Society; Cooperative Extension Service; YMCA and YWCA; Salvation Army; Camp Fire Boys and Girls; 4-H Clubs; and United Way.

Most often (in 11 instances) a librarian went to another agency, (such as an extended day care center provided by the YMCA at a public school) to tell stories and show films. Or, if bookmobile service was available, materials were also circulated. Conversely, sometimes children from other agencies, such as Camp Fire Girls or an extended day program at a school, came as a group to the library for these purposes. Other reciprocal arrangements between the library and community agencies included workshops by librarians for child care agencies regarding literature and library resources; child care agencies supplying libraries with information to include in a grant proposal submission; libraries supplying latchkey centers with books checked out on a long-term basis; and programs presented at the library by other agencies (Camp Fire Boys and Girls, parks and recreation, American Red Cross, and university students).

Two additional open-ended items at the conclusion of the questionnaire required descriptive responses and focused on librarians' recommendations for serving latchkey children. Participants were asked to "state the most important positive words of advice you would give to a library which has a substantial number of latchkey/unattended children" and to "describe specifically what IDEALLY, (BUDGET PERMITTING) public libraries should 'do' for latchkey/unattended children." Since the data obtained from participants' responses to these two items are really recommendations for library services to latchkey children rather than, necessarily, strategies actually implemented at a particular library, the information is described in Chapter 8.

Because the author wanted to determine librarians' level of awareness of efforts in their geographic area pertaining to latchkey children, a fifth and final narrative item was listed on the questionnaire. This item asked participants to "describe any specific nonlibrary-sponsored activities, services or programs in your community which addressed the needs of latchkey/unattended children." By far the most prevalent program was that of extended day care both before and after the school day, or school-age child care. Most often this was at school sites, but respondents also mentioned that it was offered at the YMCA, parks and recreation department, local community centers, churches, and Jewish community centers.

Each of these activities was noted several times: telephone "warm line" services, such as PhoneFriend or ones provided by United Way or Camp Fire; homework hotlines; Boys and Girls Club and Salvation Army programs; and self-help survival skills training programs by the County Extension Services, American Red Cross, Camp Fire Boys and Girls, Girl Scouts, or local hospitals. Programs or services provided by senior citizen groups; tutoring from college students, retired teachers, and parent volunteers; art classes at the museum; and child care referrals made by community child care organizations were each listed once.

Summary of the 1990 Survey of Public Libraries

This second national survey made it evident that almost all public libraries are experiencing the phenomenon of latchkey children, and that this situation impacts personnel and services. For most libraries it causes delays in closing because often children are left unattended. For a minority, having latchkey children is negative in terms of legal liability, medical emergencies and accidents, security needs, and adjustments in staffing patterns. However, for more than one-third of the libraries, latchkey children may be an asset, since their prevalence is causing increased cooperation between librarians and other community agencies as well as the realization that libraries need to develop new methods of service.

Although the majority of librarians feel that they are at least partially successful in meeting the needs of this clientele, approximately one-fifth feel ineffective. In comparison to two years before, most librarians see little change in numbers of library latchkey children or in the level of their library's policy and procedure development regarding latchkey children, although two-fifths feel that the latter is better than it had been.

Four-fifths of the participating librarians term their level of knowledge in serving latchkey children as at least "satisfactory," and about one-fifth describe it as "inadequate." Almost all learn about service to latchkey children from reading and on-the-job experience, which are considered more valuable than other learning strategies, especially in-service training. Rarely did librarians learn about service to latchkey children in library school. To increase their knowledge in working with this group, librarians prefer to attend conferences, workshops, and in-service presentations, and to communicate with other librarians who have experienced this situation. Reading library literature and interacting with representatives from other community agencies were also considered desirable learning strategies. Learning on-the-job was the least desirable method cited to improve knowledge of latchkey children.

Almost two-thirds of the libraries provide information and referral services for parents regarding available licensed child care. Approximately half successfully offer drop-in activity programs, storyhours, clubs, or other traditional library programs in the after-school hours. Tutoring in homework and reading as well as self-help survival skills training are provided at slightly over one-fourth of the libraries.

Librarians are not only familiar with a variety of community services and activities for latchkey children but many also cooperate with institutions and agencies providing such programs. The most important words of advice librarians offer their peers about latchkey children are to consider this group as an opportunity to recruit library users and to work with parents and community agencies in devising solutions for the challenges raised by this audience.

REFERENCES

American Library Association. Association for Library Service to Children Division. 1984. *Coordinators of children's and young adult services in public library systems serving at least 100,000 people.* Chicago, Illinois.

American Library Association. Association for Library Service to Children Division. 1989. *Coordinators of children's and young adult services in public library systems serving at least 100,000 people.* Chicago, Illinois.

Avery, S. 1986. Libraries cope with latchkey children. *Los Angeles Times*, January 1, Part IX, 1+.

Chepesiuk, R. 1987. Reaching out: Greenville County Library's latchkey kids program. *Library Journal* 112(March): 46–48.

Dowd, F.S. 1989a. Serving latchkey children: Recommendations from librarians. *Public Libraries* 28(March/April): 101–06.

Dowd, F.S. 1989b. Unlocking doors for children: The public library and the latchkey problem: A survey. *School Library Journal* 35(July): 19–24.

Fairhall, J. 1987. Lawmakers champion child care plan. *Baltimore Evening Sun*, November 20, 10A.

Floria, B. 1988. Help is just a phone call away on Kidtalk Line. *Dallas Morning News*, February 3, 1F+.

Latchkey kids called top problem. *Dallas Morning News*, September 3, 1987, 1A+.

Librarians frustrated by baby sitter role. *The Beacon* (Virginia Beach, Virginia), June 30/July 1, 1987, 7.

Mitgang, L. 1988. Libraries new haven for latchkey children. *Denton Record Chronicle*, February 21, 4F.

Morris, J. 1987. Latchkey kids are borrowing library time. *Dallas Times Herald*, September 10, 1A+.

Mueller, W. 1987. Kid stuff: A policy that works for two cities. *Library Journal* (March 1): 48–51.

Noble, K. 1988. Library as daycare: New curbs and concerns. *New York Times*, February 15, 1A+.

A place to go. *Durham Morning News*, November 30, 1986, 1E+.

Chapter 7
Library Responses

OVERVIEW

This chapter describes the innovative and successful strategies public libraries and other related institutions are undertaking to address the needs of latchkey children in the after-school hours. It describes how libraries are utilizing this situation as an opportunity to develop in unattended children a love of the library, books, and reading.

Some of the individual library efforts in working with latchkey children involve a service, such as offering homework help after school, or a program, such as creating a Teen Scene Club. Still other libraries are focusing upon policy development, the layout and function of the building, staff attitudes, or effective communication with and education of parents concerning the library's appropriate role in regard to unattended children. Organizations are also assisting librarians in serving latchkey children. The American Library Association published a "position paper" on this issue. The Metropolitan Cooperative Library System (California) provides a National Clearinghouse on Library Latchkey Children. The United States National Commission on Libraries and Information Science (NCLIS), together with ACTION, has awarded grants since 1987 to enable senior citizen volunteers to assist public libraries with many unattended children after school. And graduate students in library and information science have conducted research about this clientele, such as content analysis of materials directed toward latchkey children. Efforts of nonlibrary organizations, such as Project Home Safe: Children in Self Care, the national undertaking of the Whirlpool Foundation and the American Home Economics Association (AHEA), have impacted public library service to latchkey children in a Maryland suburb. Details about all of the above efforts are discussed in the following pages.

THE RESPONSE OF ORGANIZATIONS WORKING WITH LIBRARIES

ACTION and NCLIS' RSVP Intergenerational Library Assistance Project

In 1987 ACTION, the federal domestic volunteer agency, in cooperation with the United States National Commission on Libraries and Information Science (NCLIS) initiated a library project aimed at after-school youth—the RSVP Intergenerational Library Assistance Project. The project provides volunteer services to public libraries having unattended children after school, via nonrenewable grants of up to $5,000. Grants are awarded to participating RSVP projects at selected sites where interested library personnel and RSVP projects are co-located.

The RSVP Intergenerational Library Assistance projects were "designed to provide a new volunteer opportunity to Retired Senior Volunteer Program volunteers to serve children." The RSVP volunteers address "the growing needs of public libraries to provide book, literacy and information-related activities to children and youth who are using the library after school in increasing numbers" (ACTION, 1988). The "problem" the RSVP projects impact is latchkey children—i.e., "children coming directly to their libraries after school because their parents are working and there is no one at home." The stated need for RSVP volunteers is "to assist library staff in presenting programs and activities which enhance and enrich children's education and appreciation of library resources, to relieve library staff overload, and to promote intergenerational relationships between children and RSVP volunteers" (ACTION, 1988).

Intergenerational grants address two demographic trends: an increasing percentage of children whose parents work, and an increasing percentage of senior citizens in the population (Waters, 1990; Willett, 1985). Since both trends represent pressing service issues for libraries, RSVP grants enable librarians to advantageously utilize the experience and spare time of retired persons while providing programs for children who would otherwise be regularly left on their own during the after-school hours.

In 1987 four RSVP Intergenerational Library Assistance Grants were funded, and volunteers operated in public libraries in Los Angeles, Chicago, Dallas, and Ogden, Utah. In fiscal year 1988, 13 more awards were made to public libraries in Connecticut, Rhode Island, New York, Maryland, Pennsylvania, Tennessee, Iowa, and California. Awards in 1989 went for the first time to public libraries in New Jersey, North Carolina, Minnesota, West Virginia, Montana, Nebraska, and Oregon. Through April 1991, 15 demonstration projects funded in fiscal year 1989 are being monitored by ACTION (Burns, 1990). This chapter describes RSVP programs implemented at several libraries. Evaluation of the RSVP Intergenerational Library Assistance Grant projects included the completion of questionnaires by RSVP project directors, RSVP volunteers, and librarians at demonstration sites. Responses from the questionnaires confirm "that the service of RSVP volunteers does impact on the need of public libraries to provide activities and services to children and youth who are using libraries after school in increasing numbers" (Burns, 1990).

One important recommendation made by the majority of the 11 RSVP project directors who responded to the 1989 survey was that the Intergenerational Library Assistance Project "be carefully planned with the library staff before volunteers are placed with the children" (Burns, 1990). More specifically, the RSVP project directors would like assurance that the library staff wants to work with volunteers and the children; understands that the initiative will take library staff time; designates a library staff member who will be available for planning, coordination and supervision; and is knowledgeable about the program. Data from the 11 directors' questionnaires also revealed that 10 of the libraries recognized the RSVP volunteers with banquets, receptions with library officials, a cook-out at a state park, or awarding of certificates.

Forty-seven of the 283 RSVP volunteers in 1989 completed their survey, which covered the five areas of training, activities, benefits to children, benefits to volunteers, and volunteer satisfaction. Training, which was planned and provided by the library staff and the RSVP coordinator, included orientation to the library and to computers to locate books, effective techniques for reading aloud and for holding children's interest, appropriate books for children of various ages, operation of filmstrip projectors and video equipment, basic discipline, and understanding children and their needs. Although varying with the age of the children, activities included listening to children's problems, storytelling, acting out stories, crafts and ceramics, assisting in homework and reading, introducing children to good literature, and board games. Among the benefits RSVP volunteers noted on their surveys were making new friends, receiving compliments from parents, learning new skills, taking part in enjoyable activities with children, and satisfaction of knowing children are safe and happy while parents are not at home. The benefits they perceived children received were learning respect for elders, understanding of older persons, an improved perception of the library, having a safe place for activities, and one-to-one help.

Of the 15 librarians who completed their questionnaire, seven stated that more children are visiting the library since RSVP volunteers are serving there (Burns, 1990).

Metropolitan Cooperative Library System's National Clearinghouse on Library Latchkey Children

The National Clearinghouse on Library Latchkey Children was established in 1988 by the Metropolitan Cooperative Library System, an association of public libraries in the greater Los Angeles area which cooperate to improve library service to the residents of all participating jurisdictions. The purpose of the Clearinghouse is to collect and disseminate information on the phenomenon of children using libraries as surrogate day-care facilities. The Clearinghouse does not endorse any one policy, procedure, or management philosophy, but rather urges libraries to consider their community objectives and the opinions of their governing bodies in determining the best action in regard to latchkey children. Examination of the American Library Association's "position paper" is also advocated. The Clearinghouse has available a sample packet of policies, a list of their entire collection of policies from libraries, and a bibliography of articles and books about library latchkey children (Metropolitan Cooperative Library System [MCLS], 1988).

Whirlpool and AHEA's Project Home Safe at Prince George's County Memorial Library (Maryland)

Whirlpool and the American Home Economics Association (AHEA) can be credited with the effective service to latchkey children at the Hillcrest Heights Branch of the Prince George's County Memorial Library System in Hyattsville, Maryland. (A description of Project Home Safe is contained in Chapter 3.) For several months in 1988 the library experienced problems with children 6 to 12 years old coming to the library after school from about 2:15 P.M. to 4:00 P.M., and "hanging out." The children were disruptive and extremely energetic. From talking with the children the librarians learned that most walked to the library after school, had no parent home in the after-school hours, and were told by their parents to go to the library and stay there until they were picked up or until a certain time when they could go home. The librarians tried to entertain the children, to read them books, to show them films, and to talk to the parents. But their strategies were not very successful and sometimes they had to ask children to leave the library. The library's goal was to develop a plan for the fall school year which would provide appropriate behavior and planned activities for this group.

Then Louise Frazier, a certified home economist who had completed the comprehensive Project Home Safe training course sponsored by the American Home Economics Association, started her practicum at Hillcrest Heights Branch Library in September 1988 as part of the Home Safe course. The goals of the Home Safe program at the library were to offer unattended children one enjoyable hour three days per week (Mondays, Tuesdays, and Wednesdays from 3:15 P.M. to 4:15 P.M.) from September to December. During this hour children could learn skills to help them cope with being home alone, as well as to help them learn to appreciate reading and library materials. Parent participation in the program was encouraged. The library sent a flyer to parents explaining its cosponsorship of Project Home Safe with AHEA and that the program was about tips for activities for children in the after-school hours. Parents were invited to come to the library to learn about Project Home Safe in more detail and to find out what they could do to help. On the bottom portion of a flyer parents were asked to write their address and telephone number, indicate whether they would come, whether their child could participate, and if he/she could eat the nutritional snacks served each day.

The content of the latchkey program at Hillcrest Heights Branch Library emphasized survival skills for children who must stay home alone. In addition, each session had a book-related activity planned by a librarian. Louise Frazier, the Project Home Safe volunteer, coordinated the program with the librarian. At the beginning of each session children received a nutritious snack of pure fruit juice, peanut butter on saltine crackers, and carrot sticks, provided with money donated by Giant Foods and Safeway Corporation. The program covered sharing feelings about and dealing with fear, loneliness, and boredom; developing schedules for effective time management; personal home safety; and food and eating habits. In the first session Louise Frazier showed the videotape, "Alone at Home," and then discussed with children the importance of knowing how to lock and unlock their house door, designating a place to put their house key for safe-keeping, making a list of important phone numbers, knowing what to do if they smelled smoke, and being able to deal with feelings of loneliness and fear.

At each session one librarian sat in on the Project Home Safe volunteer's presentation, gave booktalks, and demonstrated a book-related activity. For example, the librarian supervised the children's performance of the play, "The King with the Terrible Temper," from the book, *With a Deep Sea Smile* by Virginia Tashjian. She also helped children with poetry readings of *Honey I Love* by Eloise Greenfield, and demonstrated arts and crafts activities. Community resource personnel, including representatives from the 4-H Club, the fire department, and the American Red Cross, served as guest speakers.

The number of children attending each Project Home Safe session at Hillcrest Heights Branch Library varied from 2 to 13, with the total attendance from September 1988 through June 1989 at 528. Children participating received an award signed by Louise Frazier and by the librarians at the branch. All involved with the project felt that it was very beneficial to the children and to the library. Not only did children learn survival skills to take care of themselves but they also learned to use books in the library through book-related activities (Frazier, 1989; American Library Association [ALA], 1989). The program was discontinued for the summer of 1989 because the number of latchkey children declined when school was not in session.

Although the Project Home Safe latchkey program at Hillcrest Heights Branch Library did not have the skillful guidance of Louise Frazier in the academic year 1989–90, it resumed in September 1989 through June 1990 with three library staff members sharing responsibility for planning and conducting the individual sessions. Each librarian planned and presented a program one day a week in her own unique way. Programs were held Mondays, Tuesdays, and Wednesdays for one hour, with children ages 6 to 12 attending. For the most part, programs were book-related and the librarian read to the children. On occasion filmstrips were shown and then discussed afterwards. Several librarians used the "Mini-Page" from the Sunday's *Washington Post* newspaper. Some of the subjects were dinosaurs, the Titanic, and famous biographies. *Highlights* was another source for activities, because the Wordsearch puzzles and "find the hidden picture" were popular with the group. One librarian worked on poetry and rhymes with children, another assisted them in writing creative mystery stories, and a third utilized the Project Home Safe curriculum (Uebelacker, 1990a).

The objective of the after-school program at Hillcrest Heights Branch Library, developed in fall 1990 by Ida Lewis, After School Program Coordinator/Librarian, was "to help students be more effective and comfortable caring for themselves for short periods before and after school." To achieve this objective, the library offered programs that focused on the following skills: survival skills (preparing food, traffic safety, walking to school, conduct with strangers, etc.); library skills (reading improvement, homework, good study skills, etc.); social skills (good manners, cooperation, respect for others, parties and holiday celebrations, etc.); and enrichment skills (music, cooking, crafts, etc.). Specific programs addressing those skills highlighted Fire Prevention Week (October 7–13); Child Safety and Protection Month (November); National Young Reader's Day (November 14); Kwanzaa (December 26–January 1); and National Hobby Month (January). During Fire Prevention Week children discussed what to do in case of a fire, drew maps of the route they'd take to get out of their home in an emergency, learned how to call the fire department, and enjoyed the presentation of a firefighter from the department who demonstrated his equipment and helped children try on his jacket, boots, hat, mask, and tank. More children are joining the sessions each week, and are very enthusiastic about the after-school activities at Hillcrest Heights Branch Library (Uebelacker, 1990b).

ALA's "Latchkey Children" in the Public Library

In 1988 the American Library Association responded to the phenomenon of library latchkey children by publishing *"Latchkey Children" in the Public Library*, which was prepared by the Services to Children Committee of the Public Library Association Division in collaboration with the Library Service to Children with Special Needs Committee of the Association for Library Service to Children Division. The document refers to the situation of library latchkey children as a concern that has become "one of the most rapidly developing public library policy arenas." The authors state that this work is "intended to assist those librarians coping with latchkey children to find solutions that do not dilute one of the strongest historical commitments of the public library as an institution—service to children" (American Library Association [ALA], 1988).

The philosophical position taken in the paper is, first, that latchkey children are not just a library problem, but a community problem, and consequently a solution must be sought within the entire community. Second, "insofar as public libraries are not part of the larger community solution to the problem of latchkey children, they are part of the problem." Third, latchkey children "should not be blamed for circumstances not of their own making and over which they have no control." Fourth, "latchkey children in the library and at home offer many as yet unexplored opportunities for public libraries to carry out their historic mission." And lastly, latchkey children "offer an unparalleled opportunity for public libraries to become part of their community services network as they engage in activities that advocate community attention to the welfare of children" (American Library Association [ALA], 1988).

Emphasis in ALA's publication is mainly upon policy development, which is advocated as a good way to communicate the library's concern for child safety and welfare to the community; to maintain orderly, appropriate, and equitable use of the library; to reduce potential liability; to standardize and clarify staff response; and to increase staff confidence (American Library Association [ALA], 1988). *"Latchkey Children" in the Public Library* describes the four components a good latchkey policy should contain: an introduction/needs statement; a statement of the policy itself; a clear problem definition; and procedures for staff.

The introduction/needs statement of a library policy about latchkey children is a means of explaining why the library is instituting the policy and of clarifying why the library exists without overtly proclaiming in negatives that it is not a babysitting or a free day care service. The authors of the ALA document note that "it is interesting how many libraries confuse policies and procedures and do not state a policy at all." A second component of a policy is a statement of the policy itself, something in which library latchkey policies often fall short. Unfortunately, as the authors state, many policy statements about latchkey children which have been developed in libraries intend only to absolve the library of any responsibility for children on their own after school or at closing, and therefore the policies may be perceived as punitive.

A clear problem definition, the third component of a library latchkey policy, explains terms, such as "unattended children," "disruptive behavior," "inappropriate behaviors," and "regular basis." In the problem definition, each of these aspects should be addressed separately: children not picked up at closing time; supervision of preschool children; disruptive behavior; and appropriate use of the library. The fourth policy component, that of staff procedures, should be derived from the prior three elements. The authors of the "position paper" state that procedural directions should be unequivocal and should strike a balance between permissive and punitive. Procedures should also take into account the age of the child and the general safety of the library's neighborhood, and should be written in terms of levels (so that a call to the police is not the first and only solution, for example).

Staff training in regard to policies and procedures, a plan to publicize the policy, and pre- and post-policy documentation as a means of validating the need for a policy, are also discussed in the ALA "position paper." However, in concluding the section on policy, *"Latchkey Children" in the Public Library* states that policy development is not the only way to cope with this situation, but rather a first step, with community networking probably the most effective way of developing creative solutions.

No one strategy of addressing library latchkey children is fostered in the document. Instead, librarians are urged to study their community and its organizations in order to determine the most appropriate role in relation to their particular circumstances. In order to provide readers with a range of alternatives in meeting the needs of latchkey children, another section of the "position paper" briefly cites various services or programs for children and for their parents/caregivers, as well as advocacy/networking strategies which various public libraries offer (American Library Association [ALA], 1988).

Library Science Research: A Content Analysis of Children's Materials Directed Toward the Latchkey Child

Because latchkey children present a golden opportunity for the profession to develop in these youth a lifelong love of reading and a library habit, it is imperative that librarians not only know the available materials about and for children in self-care, but also that they know which materials are appropriate, in terms of presenting an accurate portrayal of latchkey children. Recently a graduate student at the Palmer School of Library and Information Science of Long Island University conducted a study to accomplish the above goals. Specific research questions of the study were directed toward determining whether identifiable characteristics of latchkey children are present in fiction and nonfiction (including print and audiovisual materials) about or for latchkey children; whether a stereotypic latchkey child was presented in the literature; and whether the materials meet both the evaluative criteria of quality literature as well as the physical and emotional concerns of latchkey children (Kart, 1989).

Kart applied evaluative criteria she developed about the latchkey child as well as literary evaluative criteria to a total of 26 titles—13 fiction, 8 nonfiction, and 5 audiovisual materials—identified in various bibliographies as presenting a latchkey child as a central character. These evaluative criteria are listed below. Based upon her content analysis of the materials, Kart made the following conclusions:

1. Some of the portrayals of latchkey children in the materials were stereotyped.
2. Many of the materials in the study did not represent a realistic depiction of the family of the latchkey child in comparison to the latest census data.
3. The data on psychological factors of the latchkey child showed the child to be overwhelmingly at risk.
4. The majority of nonfiction materials lacked comprehensive coverage.
5. The majority of materials met evaluative criteria both for good literature and evaluative criteria appropriate to the latchkey child.

Among the recommendations Kart offered were:

1. Materials for latchkey children need to be unbiased, realistic, and meet established evaluative criteria.
2. Further research needs to be done on a national level which utilizes the census data generated in 1990 in order to assess the development of new characteristics of the latchkey child.

Kart's Evaluative Criteria for Fiction

1. *Setting:* Is the setting a new one to the child? A new home, or a new school? Is the setting depicted in a biased way?
2. *Point of View:* Is the child telling the story about his or her feelings? If a third person account, is it didactic or morally biased in any way?
3. *Characters:* Who else, besides the latchkey child, is presented? Are all characters fully developed individuals? Are there any stereotypes revealed? How are the child's feelings handled?
4. *Plot:* Is there a plot? Or is it a moralistic lesson? Is what happens forced, or plausible? Is the action fast-moving, or boring?
5. *Theme:* Is there a message? Is it determinable or null? Is the theme positive or negative towards self-care?

6. *Styles and Presentation:* Is there a lively style? Does it make the material come alive? Is the prose simple and sincere? What is the author's purpose? Does the book have literary merit?

Kart's Evaluative Criteria for Nonfiction

1. *Scope and Content:* Will the contents contribute to the child's increased knowledge and understanding? Do the contents fit the needs and interests of the age group intended? Will the child gain new insight into his or her own personal situation? May the child experience vicariously the situation of others like him or herself? Do the contents portray a realistic depiction or a stereotyped latchkey child?
2. *Treatment:* Does the author display any bias? If so, is the bias clearly stated? Is the information factual, accurate, and complete?
3. *Physical Characteristics:* Is the size, shape and appearance of the book jacket appropriate to the reader? Is the size of the print appropriate to the age group? Is the book illustrated? If so, are the illustrations appropriate to the contents on that page? Is there color?Are the illustrations cartoonish, or realistic? How is the white space used? Is the vocabulary level suitable?
4. *Special Features:* Are there any photographs? Is there a glossary?Is there an index? Is there a table of contents? Is there space for emergency phone numbers?
5. *Other:* Does the author deal with safety and survival skills, such as self-care activities, dealing with strangers, handling emergencies, looking after younger children? Is a manual used by parents and children?

THE RESPONSE OF LIBRARIES: INDIVIDUAL CASE STUDIES

Huntsville-Madison County Public Library (Alabama)

A three-pronged approach is used to cope with the large numbers of unattended children who frequent the Huntsville-Madison County Public Library (HMCPL) particularly due to its convenient location. It is in close proximity to a low-cost housing project and a recreation center and there are no major streets children need to cross to reach the library from those centers (Fuqua, 1988). First, HMCPL relocated loungers to a more visible area near the librarian's station where disruptive problems could be confronted head on. Secondly, the library works with a coalition of local community agencies designed to deal with the growing phenomenon of latchkey children.

Thirdly and most importantly HMCPL adopted the philosophy that staff must "get involved" and become "very engaged with children" entering the library. Rather than saying "here are the books, find one, sit down and read it," the staff asks children if they have read a particular book or would like to work on a puzzle or game. The "engagement policy" may even involve assisting children with homework. The Head of Children's Services, Sally Barnett, believes that the extra time and attention is an investment that will pay off in the long run, as these youth will return to use the library properly in the years ahead. If one can judge the effectiveness of these strategies by the changes witnessed, Barnett may be right, for driving by the housing project she noticed four young children out on the porch reading books!

County of Los Angeles Public Library (California)

The sustained efforts of Penny Markey, Coordinator of Youth Services, made the County of Los Angeles Public Library one of the first systems to recognize the need to work with the community in funding alternatives for latchkey children. This clientele initially caught Markey's attention in 1984 when she received a telephone call from a librarian in the system who needed assistance in addressing children staying at the library after school until a parent picked them up (Markey, 1988).

One of the initial approaches Markey implemented regarding this situation was a December 1984 survey of the 92 libraries in the County of Los Angeles Public Library System. The findings revealed that the phenomenon of unattended children was widespread; 396 children were identified as spending their after-school hours at 42 sites on a full-time basis four of five days per week. This was occurring both in branch libraries in inner city locations as well as in affluent suburbs. In June 1985 a second expanded study, which included 25 other independent city libraries in the area, revealed similar findings, indicating the problem existed in all areas of the county.

The County of Los Angeles Public Library decided upon a two-pronged approach to this situation. At the system level, the library developed written policy and procedures, and brought the problem to the attention of the public and policy makers so that the library could participate in the process of legislated solutions. At the local level, each branch library compiled a listing of child care referral agencies and after-school child care alternatives. Each library also examined its community in regard to resources, and then networked toward solutions. For example, under the auspices of the United Way one branch worked closely with a scouting organization to develop a pilot after-school program that met three days a week in the library's meeting room. Many branches organized latchkey youth into formal volunteer groups giving them responsibility for decorating the children's room and helping to plan after-school programs.

Networking involved contacting local schools and agencies to inform them of the situation and to seek their help and support. One example of success was in the city of Carson, which now provides after-school child care in local parks, relieving pressure on the library. Another example is Huntington Park Library, where approximately 100–125 children per day were identified as latchkey children. As a result of the library's cooperative efforts with neighborhood schools, the schools allocated funds to staff and keep a playground open after 3:00 P.M.

Markey's advocacy efforts have included presentations about latchkey children in public libraries to the Interagency Council on Child Abuse and Neglect, testimony before the child care fact-finding hearing conducted by Senator Alan Cranston, and a presentation to the League of Women Voters studying child care issues. The latter subsequently broadened their scope to include library latchkey children. She also met with United Way personnel and served on two of their task forces. One task force developed after-school child care models to present to corporations; the second created a support network for child care providers.

Long Beach Public Library and Information Center (California)

The Long Beach Public Library and Information Center provides a form letter from the director for staff to use as needed. This letter is addressed to "parents, guardians, and care givers." The letter disavows any "wish to discourage anyone from using the library," but frankly states that "unattended children who are misbehaving create problems for library patrons and staff." Parents, guardians, and care givers are asked "not to leave your child unattended in the library" as it "is not a day care facility and our staff is not qualified to provide day care services." The letter concludes by stating that "for your children's comfort and safety, it is in their best interest to make other after-school and/or day care arrangements. We want everyone to have a positive library experience, and by working together...we can provide the best service possible for our community" (Long Beach Public Library and Information Center, 1988).

A California State Library grant-funded program called "Partnerships for Change," developed in conjunction with and supported by a number of community groups, is also in place at the Long Beach Public Library and Information Center. The program provides fifth graders in specific schools with homework materials and assistance at an After School Study Center in a branch library. Although the Center is intended to assist Cambodian students whose non-English-speaking parents cannot help them with their school work, it does also meet the needs of some latchkey children (Messineo, 1990).

Los Angeles Public Library (California)

In 1988 Los Angeles Public Library initiated "GAB"—Grandparents and Books—to meet two important needs: the need of L.A.'s elderly population, nearly one-third of whom live alone, to find meaningful contact with others; the need to promote the love of reading in over 200,000 children who have no one to care for them after school and who have among the lowest reading scores in the state (Wade and Patron, 1990). By bringing the two groups together and training older adults to read to younger children, it was hoped that reading skills would be bolstered and intergenerational understanding and appreciation would be enhanced. The stated purpose of "GAB" was "to use books to link older adults and children in after-school activities that facilitate the sharing of cultural traditions and cross-cultural understanding while increasing the reading skills and usage of both" (Wade, 1990).

Through a 1988 LSCA grant a pilot demonstration program was offered in three branches whose service populations reflected some of the ethnic diversity in L.A. The specific objectives of "GAB" include provision of after-school programming; promotion of interagency cooperation (with RSVP/ACTION, senior centers, etc.); and the offering of a multilingual literature-rich program that recognizes non-English language proficiency among older community members and children.

Older adults are recruited for "Grandparents and Books" through presentations to community groups; children are recruited through flyers and letters announcing the program sent to principals, and through school visit announcements. Senior volunteers or "grandparents" work 2 to 10 hours per week for a six-month commitment after they attend three workshops that cover the values of reading to children, flannel board techniques, selecting appropriate books for various age levels, using hand puppets, and genres and types of children's books. Flannel board techniques are demonstrated by either a flannel board and puppet specialist or library staff at the workshops. Volunteers participate in step-by-step hands-on experience making flannel figures and basic puppets. Volunteers are also trained through monthly meetings. They receive certificates at the completion of their involvement in "GAB" (Los Angeles Public Library, 1990).

Some of the "grandparents" are former teachers and have prior experience using flannel boards and puppets. Although bilingual language skills are not essential requirements, they are an asset for "GAB" volunteers. Some of the "library grandparents" are Hispanic, Chinese, Korean, and Russian. They read to children in their native language when applicable.

Evaluation of Los Angeles Public Library's "Grandparents and Books" has been wonderfully positive. The total number of children read to tripled the projected figures. Between January and December 1989, 46 "library grandparents" read to over 7,000 children for a total of more than 2,000 hours. Questionnaires administered to "grandparents" indicated that they liked learning about puppets and flannel boards, working with children, and making friends with children and other senior citizen "grandparents." Most found that reading to children and listening to them read were very rewarding experiences that exceeded their expectations. Other rewards "GAB" volunteers noted were being recognized and asked for by name by the children and meeting childrens' parents. In general, "GAB" helped alleviate "grandparents'" loneliness and enabled them to share a life-long love of reading.

Children's evaluations of "GAB" were also obtained via oral questions, such as "What would you tell a friend about 'GAB'?" Children's typical answer was that "Grandparents and Books" was fun and someone would read and listen to you. One child remarked, "It's like having my own Grandparent there!" Judging from the number of children reached and the number repeatedly coming back, as well as from the smiles on their faces, "GAB" has been extremely successful (Los Angeles Public Library, 1990). "Grandparents" were significant reading motivators in the library's summer reading club, keeping children in the club by reading to them. In general, children said that "GAB" was fun, improved their reading, and that they enjoyed and appreciated the feeling of being cared for that the program provided.

Currently, "Grandparents and Books" is implemented at 30 Los Angeles Public Libraries (LAPL) and uses the help of 200 volunteers. Because of its success, "GAB" has been refunded a third year to accomplish the following goals:

1. To conduct a systemwide workshop for libraries at LAPL on strategies to use when introducing "GAB" to multicultural communities;
2. To establish a Grandparent Support Group at all 30 participating branches;
3. To publish a supplement of the last two chapters of the trainer's manual; and
4. To initiate contacts with senior citizen centers to establish community partners for 27 expansion sites (Wade, 1990).

"Grandparents and Books" has the potential for being a model for volunteer-driven, community-based library programs for children. While benefits are somewhat intangible, they are perceived by all participants. Benefits that have not been fully exploited by library staff include the political and public relations impact of the program and the recognition that this is an opportunity for children's librarians to gain supervisory experience (Wade, 1990).

Sacramento Public Library (California)

The Martin Luther King Regional Library in the Sacramento Public Library System is underused by children and adults in its service area. Students in the vicinity have a higher than average use of drugs, and gang activity and time spent watching television are very high. The librarian informally deals with latchkey children by providing games for children to play with in the library, such as checkers, chess, and Chutes and Ladders, provided they have a library card. The same rule applies to use of the puppets and puppet stage, another unstructured activity. Children know they must keep the noise level low and that no more than two persons are allowed behind the stage at the same time. With puppets children may act out books read or stories heard (Ryall, 1990).

A more formal activity at the Martin Luther King Regional Library in the Sacramento Public Library System was a two-year LSCA grant funded program, "The Reading Connection," which began in 1988. "The Reading Connection" targeted "at risk" students in seven public elementary schools within a radius of five miles from the library. Students who were the focus of "The Reading Connection" are predominantly minority children, and have the lowest third- and sixth-grade reading scores in the Sacramento City Unified School District. The primary goal of the program was to build on the library's limited outreach to "at risk" students and families by establishing links between the public and the school libraries.

Other goals of "The Reading Connection" were to increase student reading and appreciation of literature; help disadvantaged parents become partners in their children's reading growth; and promote public awareness of the positive impact of public library use and effective school library programs on student reading (Sacramento Public Library, 1990). Specific objectives of Sacramento Public Library's "Reading Connection" were to issue a public library card to every student in the project schools; to issue 500 new cards to project parents and other family members; to circulate six items from the King Library per person for 50 percent of the project students; to increase student participation in the King Library's Summer Reading Club by at least 50 percent; to increase attendance by project students at King Library after-school programs by 50 percent; and to increase statewide CMLEA (California Media and Library Educator's Association) Reading Interest Survey scores for fifth-grade students by 30 percent from the beginning to the end of the project.

The CMLEA Reading Survey is a multiple choice instrument which evaluates students' interest in reading, time spent in reading, and attitudes about literature and reading. On the basis of the CMLEA Reading Survey administered as a pretest to fifth graders in January 1989 and administered as a posttest in June 1989, these findings were evident: television watching at three of the six participating schools decreased significantly; at four of the schools children were more likely to read books that their teacher or librarian recommended; at four of the schools children started sharing books they had read with a friend (Chekon, 1990).

The "Reading Connection" project extended and improved outreach to students in seven elementary schools. "Reading Connection" staff visited individual classes (either in the classroom or in the school library) on a bi- or tri-weekly basis, depending on the size of the school. They created presentations that could reach a wide range of ability levels and appeal to children of diverse cultural backgrounds. Although entertainment was a criterion, the staff were primarily interested in being a catalyst for enjoyment and further pursuit of reading. Presentations included the following categories: read-alouds, non-fiction, reader's theatre, poetry, storytelling, and booktalks (Chekon, 1990).

"Reading Connection" staff also initiated and established contact with school-age child care programs in the project service area, and they provided workshops for child care staff on using resources at the library, children's literature, and techniques for sharing materials. As a result, child care staff now recognize the value of contacts with the public library, and the positive outlet that library and literature-based activities provide their children (Chekon, 1990).

Since lack of transportation is a barrier to public library use in disadvantaged neighborhoods, the project funded regional transit bus passes in the second year, which were used to bring child care children to the library's weekly summer programs (Chekon, 1990).

The final evaluation of the impact of the "Reading Connection" indicated that children in the grant project schools are reading more, are reading a greater variety of literary genres, feel more positive about reading and visiting their school library, are visiting the public library more frequently, are sharing books they read with friends, and are watching television less (Sacramento Public Library, 1990). It has also been observed that teachers are coming into the library more frequently to check out materials after they have seen the "Reading Connection" presentations, and those materials are always similar to what has been presented. Moreover, children in the project schools have more recognition of the variety of materials the library offers, and are better able to use the library independently to find what they need (Chekon, 1990). Other project successes include initiation and establishment of contacts with child care facilities and supportive relationships and interaction between the schools, the public library, and the community through representation on the Advisory Board (Sacramento Public Library, 1990).

Two tangible by-products of "The Reading Connection" are a videotape and a curriculum guide, and both are available for purchase. The 38-minute video, "Teaching Children the Art of Storytelling," presents successful techniques for teaching children how to tell stories. For example, the video shows children making a comic strip of a story, telling the story on audiotape, listening to the tape to learn it, telling the story with the comic strip, and finally telling the story without aids. The book, *Reading Motiva-*

tors: Kindergarten through Grade Six, emphasizes multicultural, cross-curriculum, and whole language materials, and contains over 100 pages of literature-based group presentations and activities developed by the staff of "The Reading Connection" (Sacramento Public Library, 1990).

San Marino Public Library (California)

Since San Marino Public Library was one of the first public libraries to address latchkey children and to publicize its efforts, it presents an ideal case study of a latchkey success story. In 1987, when it became evident that large numbers of latchkey children were using the library in lieu of day care, the Children's Librarian, Jody Stefansson, met with representatives from community agencies and institutions in her service area to cooperatively decide upon strategies for coping with the situation. She helped plan, served as a panelist, and represented the library at a day-long workshop entitled, "Kids with Keys," which was co-sponsored by the California Library Association, the Graduate School of Library and Information Science at UCLA, and the 29 independent local public libraries who are members of the Metropolitan Cooperative Library System in California. At the workshop, participants (a child psychologist; a state senator; child care employees; and representatives from the police department, the local public school district, and the YMCA) explored alternative services for latchkey children in the community (Prince, 1987). As a result, the recreation department and the YMCA instituted an after-school program in the area for latchkey children.

Stefansson described her community involvement in a second presentation entitled "Kids with Keys," which she gave at the Public Library Association National Conference in Pittsburgh in April 1988. She worked closely with teachers, principals, and parents at each of the schools in her service area. Every fall she and her library director sent a letter, a copy of the library policy, and a listing of the library's hours of service to parents or guardians having students enrolled in the public schools. After the parent or guardian signed the letter, it was kept on file. In the letter the two librarians reaffirmed their interest in fostering children's life-long learning and exposure to books, and their eagerness to be involved in children's education. They stated that they were available to assist children in this regard, and urged parents and students to use the library after school and to take advantage of its resources. At the same time they explained that continued utilization of the library as a day care facility in the after-school hours would no longer be tolerated. Parents were asked to help librarians by discussing the library policies with their children (San Marino Public Library, 1987; Stefansson, 1988).

Although Stefansson is no longer the children's librarian, students from the local schools continue to use the San Marino Public Library after school for about two hours per day, and most are well behaved. But because so many use the facility at the same time, the noise and activity level impact the entire library. Currently, library management plans to continue to work closely with the schools, recreation department, and other local agencies to provide a positive library experience for the students and all other library patrons. Future plans being considered include a youth volunteer corps; a Junior Friends group; book-related programs after school; craft programs; and extension of library hours in order to open at 10:00 A.M. and allow adults more time to use the facility when students are not there (Crain, 1990).

Santa Clara County Free Library (California)

At the Santa Clara County Free Library System, bookmobile service meets the library needs of previously unserved latchkey children in the primary grades. In 1988 the system targeted latchkey children for bookmobile service in the after-school hours because the area has a large population of families with two working parents. Now Santa Clara County Free Library reaches by bookmobile after school approximately 520 students enrolled in seven private facilities providing after-school day care (including those operated by the YMCA, Kinder Care, and commercial establishments). The bookmobile also stops at five public elementary schools, each of which have between 300 and 700 students enrolled in school-age child care. Since many of the children served do not go to their local library, bookmobile service is their only experience with public libraries. Many elect to borrow recreational reading; others want homework assignment materials. Most of the after-school day care center staff come on board with children. For some day care centers the Santa Clara County Free Library preselects materials and drops them off on a bi-weekly basis, which is a very popular service. After-school day care centers continue to be priority sites for afternoon openings in the bookmobile schedule (Yee, 1990).

Washington, D.C. Public Library (District of Columbia)

An informal after-school "tutorial" has been successful for the past two years in serving unattended children at one branch of the Washington D.C.

Public Library. The Friends initiated the tutorial, which the library facilitates. About 20 volunteers, many of whom are senior citizens, read to young patrons, listen to them read, help them with homework, or simply chat. Volunteers commit to being there one or two hours per week and are available on a drop-in basis in the children's section of the branch.

The Children's Coordinator, Maria Salvadore, believes that an appropriate role of the library in regard to latchkey children is to facilitate community organizations to work with this clientele. With this as a goal the Washington D.C. Public Library was involved in planning a city-wide training summit for nonprofit centers, sponsored by the Mayor's Advisory Committee on Early Childhood Development. The event provided professionals working with children the opportunity to exchange information and resources, and to network concerning programs and services for children. At the summit the library was promoted as a source of information on after-school programs, and as a result it has conducted some parent workshops (Salvadore, 1990).

Volusia County Public Library (Florida)

Three separate programs—"Movies and More," "Three O'Clock Club," and the "Youth Homework Tutoring Center"—are all effectively meeting the needs of latchkey children at the Volusia County Public Library in Daytona Beach, Florida. "Movies and More," initiated in 1984 at one of the regional libraries, now serves children after school at three library sites. Hour-long programs are held year-round every Wednesday at 3:30 P.M. with an average of 11 children ages 6 to 10 attending. Two of the libraries invite day care centers to bring their children to "Movies and More," while one library holds its programs for walk-in children only. "Movies and More" consists of a short film, usually followed by a related craft. For example, a paper airplane-making session may take place after children watch a film called "Wings and Things" about model airplanes and flight, with a contest to see whose paper airplane flies the farthest, the highest, the loopiest, etc., as a concluding activity (Manson, 1990).

"The Three O'Clock Club," funded by an LSCA grant, was initiated in October 1989 because the Volusia County Public Library found that its weekly after-school programs were no longer adequate and that children needed supervision and more structured activities. A survey of county libraries indicated that an average of 12 unattended children were at each library during the after-school hours each day. Although the library was pleased with a "ready-made" clientele, it lacked the staff and materials to serve them adequately. Data obtained from a County Government Study revealed that after-school care and summer care were expenses that many parents could not afford, and that many parents were using the public library as a "safe haven" to send children between the close of school and the end of the working day (Manson, 1990).

"The Three O'Clock Club" was designed to help the library become part of the network of community agencies serving children, to provide activities for latchkey children, and to serve as a source of child care information for parents. Six specific library objectives of the club are as follows: to develop written guidelines and policies pertaining to unattended children for staff to follow; to increase staff awareness of the needs of latchkey children by providing a workshop; to become part of the community's child care agency network by providing latchkey program information to United Way and other agencies serving families; to provide families of library latchkey children with informational packets describing the library's policies, hours of service, services offered, programs and activities; to provide throughout the school year daily, supervised after-school activities, including one program per week; and to incorporate and extend the summer library program activities with the latchkey project. In addition to these strategies, the library purchased 100 arts and crafts kits, a furnished doll house, 15 recordings, 10 video cassettes, 5 educational and recreational software packages, 15 puzzles, and 10 games for latchkey children to use during the daily activity times.

Children in "The Three O'Clock Club" are invited to assist in planning activities and are required to complete registration information, which includes their name, age, grade, school, address, and a parent's or guardian's phone number to reach in case of an emergency. Only children who register are eligible to participate in the library's activities and programs which are provided four afternoons per week and include a homework time. Some programs geared to the needs of latchkey children in self-care focus upon home safety and are presented by local community personnel, such as the police and fire departments. Daily library activities include booktalks, arts and crafts projects, and storytelling (Manson, 1990).

The "Youth Homework Tutoring Center" offers established homework centers and tutorial programs in 13 libraries throughout Volusia County. Junior and senior high school students needing homework assistance are tutored by local recruits, the majority of whom are their peers. The Homework Center contains computers, CD-ROMs, and basic reference books about using the library and preparing term papers. The goals of the Youth Homework Tutoring Center are to promote better cooperation between the schools and the library, and to lower the dropout rate in Volusia County (Manson, 1990).

Atlanta-Fulton Public Library (Georgia)

Eleven Atlanta-Fulton Public Library branches, designated as Homework Help Centers, emphasize homework and research paper assistance to elementary, middle, and high school students. In this structured after-school environment, students are able to avail themselves of resources and information in the library to help them complete their assignments. Librarians help direct students to proper resources, and through individual consultations, encourage teachers and media specialists to incorporate library resources in their curriculum planning.

Occasionally, one of the Homework Center sites may offer a free workshop to instruct parents on ways to help their children with school assignments. The workshop offers suggestions and techniques for organizing the home environment, making acquaintances with school support staff, and utilizing community resources, such as libraries and homework hotlines (Pickens, 1990).

DeKalb County Public Library (Georgia)

The DeKalb County Public Library in Georgia addresses latchkey children by sending letters to parents regarding youngsters left unattended at their branches, and by providing two homework libraries (Bruce Street and Tobie Grant), as well as after-school programs and "desk top activities." In the letter the librarians ask for "help in making library visits for your children as safe and pleasant as possible," and offer suggestions for parents of older children who will be visiting the library. These suggestions include: "assess whether your children are comfortable being at the library for long periods. If going directly from school, do they need something to eat or some kind of physical or social outlet first? Always pick up your children at least 30 minutes before closing time. In case you are delayed, give your children an alternative plan, such as calling a neighbor for a ride home." The letter further states that "these guidelines are designed to protect children, not discourage them from using the library, as children are always welcome at all DeKalb County Public Libraries" (DeKalb County Public Library, 1990).

Through a federal grant the Tobie Grant Homework Library, which was previously underused, was converted into a Homework Library complete with computers and educational software to support and encourage the educational advancement of young students. The branch has become a model for similar services in many states throughout the nation. Hours of operation are from 3:00 P.M. to 8:00 P.M. Monday through Thursday. Services include computer orientation classes Monday afternoons, programs for school-age children Thursday afternoons, and computer diskette day Wednesday afternoons. After-school programs for the school age at 4:00 P.M. have consisted of movies, face painting, and Halloween crafts, with "Wonderful Wednesday Specials," including a "Back to School Survival Kit" program, and a program on nutrition. Homework Help Sessions are available daily from 4:00 P.M. until closing, in math, reading, English, etc. (DeKalb County Public Library, 1990). Typewriters, magazines, Apple II computers, learning games, readalong books, stations to listen to audio tapes, and study carrels are among the materials available. In 1983 the library received the County Achievement Award from the National Association of Counties, and in 1984 it earned the Outstanding Southeastern Library Program Award from the Southeastern Library Association. In 1991 DeKalb County Public Library will be opening an additional homework library at the Gresham Branch, which will be similar in concept to the Bruce Street and Tobie Grant branches, with special materials and equipment to assist children with their education (Rogers, 1990).

DeKalb also offers after-school programs and "aftercare" programs in the summer. Since two of the libraries are housed in the same facility with recreational centers, cooperative programming is planned. Latchkey children can participate in "desk top" activities—simple crafts with easy directions which children can do independently at a desk or table. For example, a child might be given scissors, crayons, paper, and a book about art, drawing, or optical illusions. Each week at the librarian's desk, where these materials and books are kept, children can get and use a book and supplies on a different topic (Des Enfants, 1990).

Rolling Meadows Library (Illinois)

At the Rolling Meadows Library, G.A.S.P. (Great After School Program), initiated as a pilot project in fall 1987, continues every school year serving first through fifth graders who might otherwise be latchkey children

(Davis, 1988). Participants—school children (many of whom are foreign-born), their teachers, librarians, and two high school students who are fluent in English and Spanish—all meet at the library once a week for an hour of games and crafts. G.A.S.P. originated because of a need for an after-school activity that would enrich students' lives as well as serve as a bridge to the library.

The object of G.A.S.P. is to offer creative after-school recreation, allowing children to choose among a variety of activities. G.A.S.P. represents a cooperative effort between the library and the local school district in order to introduce grade school children of many nationalities to the local public library in a "recreational" way. Library staff prepare the sessions, select the themes, provide snacks, and offer a pleasant surrounding. The school district provides transportation for the students to the library from school, and after the session takes the children from the library to their homes. Expenses for snacks and for extra pay of school staff are also covered by the school district. Direct costs for a typical 12-week session include $380 for bus transportation, $180 for salary of school staff, and $60 for snacks. Indirect costs to the library are staff time for planning and conducting the sessions. Both the library and the school district agree that the combined costs are very affordable in light of the great benefits of welcoming young students to the public library, where they have fun while learning new skills (Ryan, 1990).

Instead of replacing the more "structured" classroom visit to the library which emphasizes teaching library skills, G.A.S.P. provides the opportunity for those children who would not normally be able to do so to come to the library by themselves (Ryan, 1990). In the first year of G.A.S.P., three high school volunteers assisted mainly to interpret activities for Spanish-speaking students. In 1990, sixth-grade students assisted the library staff, as well as a Spanish-speaking classroom teacher (Ryan, 1990).

Once per week, immediately after school lets out, a school bus transports as many as 50 children to the Rolling Meadows Library from Willow Bend Elementary School, which is in a Chicago suburb about five miles away. From about 3:45 P.M., the first and second graders enjoy refreshments in the program room while they watch a film about making new friends, assemble an "I Love My Library" pennant in their school's colors to take home, play a variation of "Pin the Tail on the Donkey," communicate with puppets, or complete a puzzle. The third, fourth, and fifth graders start with games and crafts, then watch a movie while eating a snack, and may listen to a booktalk.

Each one-hour weekly G.A.S.P. session has a special theme. Many sessions focus on topics non-English-speaking children welcome, such as, "Me," "Birthdays," "Friendship," "American holidays," and "Mexican fiestas," although snakes, space, and sandwiches have also been themes. Emphasis is on making the experience an enjoyable one for children and on allowing them to see first-hand all of the things that are available at the library, such as the Homework Center, study area, play area, and well-maintained collections which include audiovisual materials and computers.

G.A.S.P. is a successful program at Rolling Meadows Library because it sparks curiosity, promotes the fun of learning new things, and involves teamwork and careful planning between the library and schools. The high school students are an invaluable link between Spanish-speaking youngsters and their English-speaking counterparts. The program demonstrates that a library can provide many activities, supply materials for study as well as for entertainment, and successfully offer services for latchkey children after school. For children who have recently arrived from other countries, G.A.S.P. provides an opportunity to visit a library outside of their school media center.

St. Joseph County Public Library (Indiana)

Strategies implemented by St. Joseph County Public Library in Indiana to address the needs of children in the after-school hours have included craft programs, "Brain Busters," self-guided activity sheets, and tutoring students (Gilbert, 1990). On Thursdays from 4:00 P.M. to 5:00 P.M. during the 1987–88 school year as children worked on crafts the librarian read aloud a short novel, summarizing previous chapters for anyone who might have missed the week before. Since most children in attendance during October were second and third graders, *Zucchini* by Barbara Dana was a very appropriate and popular choice. Related art projects undertaken by the children included fall murals for the library's bulletin boards; felt banners decorated with yarn, ribbon, sequins, and cloth scraps; and costumes and masks. In November the children selected *One Fine Day* by Nonny Hogrogian to perform as a puppet show. By adding a fox chorus all 14 children attending had a part. Each child created his or her own puppet. The foxes were sock puppets with button eyes and felt ears, and the chicken and the cow were rod puppets, which the younger children easily made. For one week children made scenery on poster board and during another two weeks they made the puppets. Rehearsals lasted a week, and performances for younger children took place the next week.

In February the children's librarian read *The Midnight Fox*, by Betsy Byars, while children made snow scenes with ivory soap mixture on paper, and decorated their silhouettes as Valentine presents for their parents. During March the group entered the Caldecott Banner Contest, and created their own "wild things" to attach to a "Where the Wild Things Are" banner.

A successful craft program at St. Joseph County Public Library during the summer was "Bug Buddies," in which children glued together wooden bug cages and left them to dry while they practiced reading with a partner poems from *Joyful Noise* by Paul Fleischman. For another program called "Dream Visions," students read Native American legends about special visionary experiences and decorated wooden bracelets with authentic Native American symbols. Bracelets were tongue depressors that had been soaked in water, carefully curved, and left to dry in drinking glasses so they would hold their shape. Children drew symbols on the tongue depressors with magic markers and painted them with a clear nail polish. For "Dino Diorama" children made a shoebox diorama, and for "Make a Fossil" they created a plaster of Paris cast of shells and leaves. Both of the latter craft projects were made while the librarian read dinosaur stories and poems. For "Clown Day" children painted each others' faces with grease paint, made balloon animals, and created clown faces on styrofoam balls placed on straws. In December the group made Christmas crackers, sang "The Twelve Days of Christmas," and read a Christmas play (Moore, 1990).

"Brain Busters" was scheduled for 3:30 P.M. to 4:00 P.M. on Thursdays after school was out at the Virginia Tutt Branch of the St. Joseph County Public Library. Using "Trivial Pursuit," "Junior Trivial Pursuit," riddle books, and other trivia titles, boys usually played against the girls. The program ran for eight weeks, involved about 12 children per week, and was so successful that children have asked for it again. The two goals of "Brain Busters" were to occupy latchkey children and to relieve after-school "chaos," since the branch which offered this is within walking distance of five elementary schools (Hernandez, 1990).

During October 1990, middle grade children participated at all the system's branches in after-school mystery games which require completion of questions or puzzles on self-guided activity sheets as well as research in the use of the library. For example, two questions were "What are two names (pseudonyms) of the author of *The Velveteen Rabbit?*" and "What is the call number for *Alfred Hitchcock's Daring Detectives?*" Five correct answers earn a child the right to paste his/her name on the "Honor Role for Detective of the Day." In a second detective game called "Awful Arnold," children can track a bank robber who left secret messages in various places of the library in code, giving clues to his whereabouts. The trail involves six locations and successful sleuths are awarded a small plastic magnifying glass (Gilbert, 1990).

Free tutoring at the Western Branch of the St. Joseph County Public Library began in fall 1989 and still continues. Through the Neighborhood Study Help Program, students enrolled at either Notre Dame University or St. Mary's College tutored youngsters needing help in school subjects on Mondays and Wednesdays from 4:30 P.M. to 5:30 P.M. during the academic year. An average of 12 tutors, mainly the same college students, although substitute tutors participated as needed, assisted any child who came and requested help. Depending upon turnout, tutors worked with one to three children at a time. The same tutor and tutee(s) were paired throughout a particular semester, either fall 1989 or spring 1990. The program proved highly successful, especially in reaching "at risk" or culturally disadvantaged elementary and secondary school students (Raymer, 1990).

Baltimore County Public Library (Maryland)

Parents and caregivers of latchkey children may need information about parenting in general as well as child care and after-school activities for children (American Library Association [ALA], 1988). Libraries can meet the first need by establishing parenting collections, by cosponsoring an annual parenting open house at the library at which vendors display their products or services of interest to parents/providers, and via printed methods such as newspaper columns, bibliographies, and brochures. Librarians can address the second need by providing information and referral options to parents. For example, since 1985 the Baltimore County Public Library has operated LOCATE: Child Care Referral Service. Every month the library receives approximately 6,500 calls, about 12 percent of which concern children needing before- and after-school care (Bath, 1990).

LOCATE works like this: when a parent calls, a clerical counselor or library associate on LOCATE's staff discusses with the parent the type of care preferred, where the care is needed, the age and special needs of the child, options available, and licensing regulations. Names of centers are offered over the phone or by mail. Although not specifically targeting latchkey children, LOCATE is available through Baltimore County Public

Library as a resource and referral service for parents and providers desiring information about licensing and child care training. Although LOCATE was originally funded from a grant from the Maryland State Department of Education through LSCA funds, maintenance of the database, which includes 300 centers and 1,300 family day care providers, has been absorbed by the library (Bath, 1990).

Charles County Public Library (Maryland)

Several years ago the "Teen Scene Club" was offered in Charles County Public Library in Maryland as an alternative for kids to "hang out" in order to create something for them to do after school that's fun, and to enable students to learn a little about the library (Denney, 1988). The club, which met twice a week after school for one hour, provided informally structured activities for middle school latchkey youth who had been congregating in or around the Charles County Public Library (Wolfram, 1990). Activities were planned in four-, six-, or eight-week cycles, for Mondays and Wednesdays from 3:00 P.M. to 4:00 P.M.

Some of the most successful events were library trivia games using different reference materials as resources; a 30-minute reader's theatre presentation for family and friends emphasizing literature rather than the dramatics of presenting a full-scale performance; and using etiquette sources to plan and host an afternoon tea for the library trustees, principals, teachers, family, and friends. Programs have also been offered on preparing a good science project, skin care and make up, and making the most of your money. One afternoon, Teen Scene Club members performed their version of a chapter of A.A. Milne's "The World of Winnie the Pooh," for about 20 young children (Denney, 1988). Often community resource persons, such as a science teacher or 4-H extension agent, presented the programs. The teens in the club also helped decorate the library for Christmas, Hanukkah, Thanksgiving, and Halloween, and in doing so learned how to cooperate among themselves to get the task completed. And, in planning and preparing for the tea and trivia games, young adults learned how to do library research, a skill which carried over to their school assignments (Knott, 1990).

Charles County Public Library's Teen Scene Club members were also responsible for planning, writing, and publishing "Teeny Mag," a bi-annual newsletter consisting of stories, poetry, book reviews, and cartoons created entirely by and for teens, primarily to publicize the types of activities available at the library (Denney, 1988; Ryan, 1990). One issue of "Teeny

Mag" contained short biographical sketches of new club members, original limericks, and questions and answers about the library from an interview of the Young Adult Librarian, Mrs. Donna Wolfram, by a Teen Scene Club member.

Muskegon County Library (Michigan)

At the Norton Shores Branch, the largest of the nine branches in the Muskegon County Library System, "Wednesday After School Specials" are offered from 3:45 P.M. to 5:00 P.M. during the school year. While these are basically storyhours, they are specifically directed toward elementary-age children, and involve longer more sophisticated stories as well as group games. Average attendance for a six-week session in March and April 1990 was 12, with predominantly first graders participating. One game was "Trivial Book Pursuit," in which a child teamed up with a friend to make a team, and then both became the pieces of a lifesize game board, and moved themselves around by answering trivia questions about the books they had read. For the scheduled play-off games the top three teams played against teams from other libraries. Teams had to register beforehand. Books upon which the questions were asked were listed at the library desk so that children could read in preparation for the event (McDonald, 1990).

Various Libraries (Missouri)

Drop-in programs at libraries can reach latchkey children in an informal setting and provide them with hours of enjoyment at very little expense in terms of time and staff for the library. The Children's Services Round Table of the Missouri Library Association has published a booklet, which includes descriptions of "drop-in programs" for children from all over the state (although the names of specific libraries are not identified). Drop-in programs are defined as those intended for children "who have just a little extra time to spend in the library after they have selected their books." They may consist of "an activity that can be enjoyed by just one child or by a small group," "is self-directing with a minimum of supervision," and "does not have a specific starting or ending time" (Missouri Library Association, 1985). The introduction to the booklet, *Drop-In Delights*, emphasizes that the programs described are not intended to be a babysitting service, since most of the ideas can be completed in 10 minutes or less. The rationale given for providing drop-in programs is that they can highlight the collection, provide hands-on experiences, reach children not participating in other scheduled programs, result in fun for all with a minimum budget, and keep children interested and involved.

One drop-in program described in the booklet is a "Children's Book Swap" in which the library's hard and paperback books (perhaps donated ones not used in the collection) are exchanged one-for-one for copies children bring in. Under the category of "Creative Writing" are the following drop-in activities: "Author Pen Pals," in which sample letters written by authors are displayed, and addresses and paper are available for children to write their favorite authors; and "Riddle Me This," which involves children in writing their own riddles, and posting them so that a flap must be lifted to reveal the answer for others to read. The "Quizzes and Contests" section of *Drop-In Delights* describes a "Stack Stalk: Scavenger Hunt." On cards an adult makes up questions for children which are designed to get them into many areas of the library and to demonstrate the ways of finding information—i.e., spine labels, catalog, booklists. Each child draws a card and tries to answer the question. If the answer is correct the child signs the card and puts it into a drawing for the big prize. Everyone who tries receives a small prize, regardless of the answer.

Under "Arts and Crafts" the activity of "Greeting Cards" is suggested. For this children are provided with paper, scissors, glue, crayons, and decorative scrap materials with which to make their own cards for various holidays. However, this author suggests a literature-based variation of that activity. That is, encourage children to create greeting cards for any occasion, (such as a birthday, new baby, sympathy, accident, hospital stay, new home, wedding, etc.) to "send" to book characters, as appropriate to their particular literary situation and to the plot of a particular picture book story. For example, after reading *Curious George Goes to the Hospital* by Hans Augusto Rey, a get-well card could be made, with a verse, illustration, and a note to the monkey character. Mother Goose rhymes could be used as a basis for this activity, too. For example, Humpty Dumpty's experience would merit a sympathy card. Sample cards could be displayed as incentives along with relevant books for children to read before making a card.

A related but similar "drop-in program" for creative writing might be called "The _____ Library Gazette" (filling in the name of the particular public library at which this is available). Children could write "newspaper accounts" for various book and literary characters, and include them in the appropriate section or column of this literary newspaper. For the "Lost and

Found" section of the Classified Ads the story of *Cinderella* might serve as a basis. A "Sports" column could be based on *The Tortoise and the Hare*. For the "Foods/Cooking" section of the paper try *Stone Soup*; as an "Obituary" use *Henny Penny*. *The Three Little Pigs* could be made into a "Real Estate" item, while *Hansel and Gretel* would make a good "Dear Abby" or "Advice" piece.

Still another creative writing drop-in program could be used with wordless picture books and might be termed "Write It Out." Children could write their version of picture books without text, such as Tomie DePaola's *Pancakes for Breakfast*, Peter Spier's *Noah's Ark*; or Chris Van Allsburg's *Mysteries of Hans Burdick*.

Harve-Hill County Library (Montana)

The Hill County Retired Senior Volunteer Program (RSVP) and the Harve-Hill County Library began a joint venture in October 1989 via funding through ACTION, in order to provide additional services to youngsters in the hours after school. Senior volunteers were recruited and then trained in five two-hour segments, which focused upon working with minority children building language skills and self-esteem. Then the 16 RSVP volunteers were placed in the library during peak hours identified by staff.

Some worked with the librarian to help youngsters locate resource material and recreational reading selections. Some assisted students in completing homework assignments. Two worked with children on special activities—a writing project initiated by a retired newspaper editor with the intention of preparing a quarterly newsletter for the library, and coin-collecting begun by a long-time hobbyist (Williamson, 1990). The March 1990 issue of the Harve-Hill County Library newsletter contained a short discussion of what a library is, biographical information about the nine library staff members and their positions, and a list of books about Montana which the library owns.

The ACTION grant that funded this program at the Harve-Hill County Library continued through Feburary 1991. A board consisting of three members from the Friends of the Library and three members from the RSVP Advisory Committee keep the program in place and plan for continued monies and supportive promotional ideas. Although the intergenerational program at the library took many months to achieve recognizable results, the library feels that its goals were achieved, i.e., bringing senior citizens and young patrons together in the evening after school and on Saturday afternoon, bridging the gap between the generations, providing a safe place for children, and giving older Americans the opportunity to make a difference (Williamson, 1990).

Crawford Public Library (Nebraska)

The Crawford Public Library and the Crawford Retired Senior Volunteer Program (RSVP), funded through a $5,000 grant from ACTION, provided after-school programs for latchkey children in their Nebraska community every Monday and Wednesday from 4:00 P.M. to 6:00 P.M., and Saturday afternoons from 2:00 P.M. to 4:00 P.M. Since this small library is only open 20 hours per week, the librarians are very limited as to the days and times they can offer a program. Nevertheless, the following schedule was worked out to accommodate all grade levels of latchkey children: first, second, and third graders may come on Monday afternoons; students in grades four, five, and six may come Wednesday afternoons; and children of all ages may come on Saturday afternoons. Eight senior volunteers show videos to approximately 50 children, help them make a craft, or read a book to them.

The videos, which the library rents from the Nebraska Library Commission, are based on a book, so that children are encouraged to read afterward. For example, one day children watched a video about magic tricks and tried the tricks as they watched the movie. Another day they watched a video about drawing pictures, and afterward the librarian featured a display of drawing books which children used to practice their artistic talents. Through the RSVP program senior volunteers and latchkey children have developed friendships, and children who spent much time alone in the library's service area now read books and participate in fun activities with volunteers interested in helping (Dodd, 1990).

The same schedule is followed and volunteers' assistance is vital for the informal craft activities and the summer reading club. To provide constructive opportunities for latchkey children a "craft table" is arranged with various art supplies geared to the age level child at the library that particular day. Senior volunteers assist children needing help. During the month of June children of all ages came to the library to play games, make a craft, and watch videos (Dodd, 1990). In the future the Crawford Public Library hopes to have volunteers make audio tapes of stories and package them with books so that children could check out a book and tape together.

Omaha Public Library (Nebraska)

Many children come to the Charles E. Washington Branch of the Omaha Public Library "directly after school and remain until dinner time." "Not all are truly latchkey children as they have grandparents at home," but they did want "constant attention" which the small staff was unable to provide (Price, 1990b). So the library contacted their local Retired Senior Volunteer Program for help. Now older citizens assist these youth by supervising an arts and craft table set up in the library with materials for younger children to make projects.

Another unique strategy the Washington Branch Library has implemented which effectively impacts latchkey children is a 4-H Club. For the past two years the 4-H Club has met at the library once a week and membership has become very large. The library assists children working on projects for the county fair, and the County Extension Office provides instruction in nutrition through a series of classes after school on weekdays (Price, 1990b). About 50 students were involved in 4-H projects, such as rug braiding, cookie making, and t-shirt painting. All who entered their projects in the state fair received free admission and ribbons. There is no charge for participating in the 4-H Club activities, as the materials children use to make their projects are either purchased by the library or received as donations. Some children become members of the 4-H Club, while others don't, but still participate.

In addition, the 4-H organization makes available pre-packaged programs from the County Extension Office for use by the library, or by any other club. For example, "Bread in a Bag" comes with materials, such as grains and a loaf of bread. Children take the bread home and bake it to learn about this food (Price, 1990b). Another pre-packaged program is an incubator with 12 eggs which was set up at the Washington Branch Library and became an interesting attraction for patrons checking on the progress of the hatching chicks. The 4-H Club also provides everything needed for a model rocket project which the library would like to try (Price, 1990b).

Currently this branch of the Omaha Public Library System has about 19 children from 6 years of age to teenage enrolled in 4-H activities. Moreover, the Girl Scouts of America plans to offer scouting on a different basis from the usual troop concept. Since all programs at the public library must be open to anyone who wishes to attend, the Girl Scouts and Boy's Club are co-facilitating programs available to both boys and girls two afternoons a week (Price, 1990b).

Presently, the Office on Aging in Omaha also has an RSVP grant and the library is assisting with it, too. A half-time coordinator hired by the Office on Aging recruits tutors from the schools to listen to children read, and to help with art projects, such as decorating the library. In the future the library would like to offer aerobics and other active physical opportunities for latchkey children (Price, 1990a).

The librarians at the Washington Branch of the Omaha Public Library have noticed a number of benefits of the 4-H Club, tutoring, and crafts programs:

1. They were able to involve many school-age children who they had been trying to reach for many years.
2. New families got library cards, participated in programs, and encouraged others in the community to use the library.
3. Local organizations became involved in library activities.
4. The atmosphere of the library has become more lively and people stop there as a part of their family activities.
5. The RSVP volunteers enjoy the children's books and talk to children to recommend titles.
6. The personal touch of the library and volunteer staff has made children feel that the library belongs to them.

In summary, "before the 4-H program the children were weary of reading and homework after school with still an hour to wait at the library for parents to pick them up. Now it is a pleasure to see the faces of children light up when staff and volunteers show an interest in them" (Gilbert, 1990).

Montclair Free Public Library (New Jersey)

Every weekday at 3:00 P.M. hordes of children from the 12 elementary schools and high schools surrounding the Montclair Free Public Library in New Jersey gravitate to this facility where parents pick them up at the end of the workday. Until about 6:00 P.M. the library overflows with young children. Consequently, Mary Ruskind, assistant to the manager of youth services, and Deidre O'Hagan, the manager, created a Homework Helper Program (Adamec, 1990). Volunteers were recruited from the Literacy Volunteers of America (LVA) to come to the library after school to help children on a one-to-one basis with their homework.

The specific objectives of the Homework Helper Program were to provide homework assistance and to reinforce good study habits in the library setting. The general goals were to support the wise use of children's time, to encourage positive adult/child rapport outside the school setting, and to help create an awareness of the valuable resources of the library. Volunteers were required to have strong basic math and reading skills, as well as the ability to relate to children and early adolescents. The time commitment of volunteers was at least two hours per week, either on a weekday after school, or on a Saturday or Sunday. Responsibilities included offering homework assistance, encouraging reading by reading aloud and discussing books with children, and helping the librarian with displays and program preparation (Riskind, 1990).

Training consisted of three two-hour sessions. The first dealt with identifying slow readers, building self-esteem during the study process, and establishing correlations between math and reading study skills. The second session taught "know-how." Volunteers toured the children's section to become familiar with the library's software, watched a demonstration of the online catalog and of the Dewey Decimal Classification system, and were oriented to basic reference tools. The final training session defined the duties of the librarian and the tutor.

The Homework Helpers program is not funded by anyone, as the cost is low, tutors are not paid, and materials from the LVA program and the library's collection are used. The program is successful and tutors have made connections with children. Parents are calling asking for their children to be tutored and more volunteers are joining. "Homework Helpers is the answer to a need that had to be met," says one volunteer. "If I could be one link in the chain that might help turn that need around a little bit, even for a few kids, it would be really neat" (Adamec, 1990).

Durham County Library (North Carolina)

Three programs specifically for latchkey children are offered at the Stanford L. Warren Branch of the Durham County Library System. They are a Homework Hotline or Walk-In, a Retired Senior Volunteer Program (RSVP) funded through a $5,000 grant from ACTION, and "Teen Issues Made Easy" (T.I.M.E.). The first is a service sponsored jointly by the library and the Durham City Schools through their Community Education Office. The library provides space and reference materials, while the school system provides text books, tutors, and a telephone, primarily in the four basic skill areas of mathematics, science, social studies, and language arts. Homework Hotline or Walk-In operates from October to mid-May, Monday through Thursday during the academic year, from 3:00 P.M. to 7:30 P.M., and is available to students in kindergarten through twelfth grade, as well as to their parents. Individuals may either telephone or come to the library for assistance on homework assignments. Those who are served in person at the library register for service, indicating in which of the four skill areas they would like to receive tutoring, as well as their name, school, and grade (Taylor, 1990).

The Intergenerational Library Assistance Project involves 12 retired senior volunteers who work with about 40 latchkey children per day by reading to them, listening to the children read, or helping them construct art projects. Senior citizens also instruct children in piano, puppet making, storytelling, book making, and singing songs. Events take place Monday through Friday from 3:00 P.M. to 5:30 P.M. for children ages 5 to 11. The library provides all the materials and supplies, while the RSVP recruits the volunteers, who bring many specialized skills to help latchkey children. Grant monies are used primarily to coordinate the program and to reimburse volunteers for transportation to and from the Stanford L. Warren Branch.

T.I.M.E. ("Teen Issues Made Easy"), is an information forum available at this same branch in the Durham County Library System. Geared toward 12- to 17-year-olds, its goal is to make issues perceived as overwhelming somehow manageable and understandable. T.I.M.E., offered each Wednesday from 3:30 P.M. to 5:00 P.M., has included sessions on careers, child abuse, self-esteem, drugs, peer pressure, suicide, money, diseases, law enforcement, family relationships, adolescence, teen pregnancy, and citizenship. Community resource personnel who are professionals in the particular topic serve as presenters. The format of each session is as follows: presentation of information and facts by the professional, discussion, questions and answers, and video or some other incentive for attendance.

Cleveland Heights-University Heights Public Library (Ohio)

Policy development and cooperation with community agencies were key factors in resolving the "latchkey problem" at the Cleveland Heights-University Heights Public Library, where more than 50 children per day used the library as an after-school oasis to wait for an adult to pick them up.

After the library identified latchkey children as a community issue, it worked with eight schools in the area, the city council, and PTAs to set guidelines as to what it could and could not provide for this clientele. As a result, the local YMCA expanded its after-school program. Cleveland Heights-University Heights Public Library developed a brochure, "Guide for Parents of Young Library Users," which makes clear that parents are responsible for supervising their children, encourages appropriate use of the library, and describes alternatives for after-school care. The guide is distributed to new patrons, to persons attending children's programs, to parents at PTA meetings, and to new teachers via their informational packets (Rome, 1990).

Cleveland Public Library (Ohio)

Between July 1988 and June 1989 Cleveland Public Library implemented an LSCA Title I grant program entitled the "Preteen Project," aimed at meeting the needs of young people for after-school activities. Special programs were offered which utilized the talents of community leaders, professional and skilled musicians, storytellers, puppeteers, and entertainers. Ethnic craft sessions encouraged positive human relations and hobby clubs assisted youth in developing self-esteem.

Among the objectives of the "Preteen Project" were:

1. To provide 1,700 high-interest books and materials for preteens.
2. To provide two sessions in each of four branches on the importance of eating nutritional breakfasts and snacks.
3. To provide two sessions in each branch introducing youngsters to accomplished musicians.
4. To provide four sessions on ethnic history (Cleveland Public Library, 1988–1989).

Programs offered weekday afternoons included crafts, camera club, a charm club for girls, an American Indian Pow-Wow Program, cooking by the Cooperative Extension Agency, gardening, stamp collecting, and guitar and violin musical programs (Cleveland Public Library, 1988–1989).

Geauga County Public Library System (Ohio)

An unofficial solution to the influx of the after-school crowd on weekdays at the Middlefield Public Library Branch of the Geauga County

Public Library System is monthly programs for teens accompanied with opening up of the meeting room for a social interaction area. A television is available and minimal rules of behavior are posted.

The Geauga West Library, a new facility located in an exurban area next to public schools, has employed several unusual strategies (i.e., the layout and function of the building, a monitor, vending machines, and bus transportation) in addressing the special needs of unattended children after school. Geauga West Library's "experiment" in providing library service stems from the library's concept that one appropriate role of the public library is to function as a social interaction center or community hub (Rome, 1990).

The nontraditional design of the Geauga West Library was meant to accommodate different groups of people for varied purposes simultaneously without disturbances. The library's layout is divided into two areas: the lobby or commons area, which serves as a social interaction space for youth (as well as for adults) to meet at the library; and the quiet area for traditional library functions, such as reference and study. The commons area accommodates noisier activities, and includes the circulation desk, rest rooms, water fountain, public lockers, public meeting rooms, vending machines, and tables and chairs, so that students can work together on group projects without worrying that their voices are too loud. In the quieter library proper there are three individual study rooms with two seats each, as well as a variety of other seating arrangements. Cynthia Orr, Library Manager at Geauga West Library, points out that "the big word here is alternatives. Instead of asking someone to change their activity or go outside, we can merely ask that they move to another part of the building" (Orr, 1990).

Money from the vending machines helps pay for a substitute teacher who was hired as a monitor of the lobby area to maintain decorum. The monitor, who works three hours per day after school, serves as someone who sets appropriate limits, supervises the vending machines, and even helps with homework. Orr explained that the monitor is

> able to maintain order without antagonizing anyone. Some libraries hire security guards, but these have a negative connotation. In our case hiring a substitute teacher was perfect. A benefit that I did not foresee is that she knows the students by name, knows their reputation at school and is a known quantity herself. If there is a serious problem we call the police. But by helping with homework, she gives children a positive image of the library. Sometimes she will walk a child to the reference desk and introduce the student to the reference librarian, overcoming the reluctance a child may

have to approach library staff for help. The emphasis here is on the positive. One of our goals is assuring a positive image with all library users.

At the Geauga West Library children are actually *encouraged* to come to the library after school. In fact, starting in the 1989–90 school year, the library facilitated students coming to the library by cooperative busing from school. Three public library representatives, the principals of the two local public elementary schools and the one parochial school, and the director of transportation from the school system met to arrange bus transportation from the school to the library for fourth and fifth graders who are later picked up by their parents. Orr states that "much of the credit should go to school personnel who recognized that in a community such as ours children cannot get to the library easily, but that the library is a desirable place for them to go." Logistics were worked out based upon bus capacity and the recognition that parents and school personnel had to be sure where a child was going at the end of a day. This problem was addressed by designating Mondays and Wednesdays for fourth graders and Tuesdays and Thursdays for fifth graders. There is no bus on Friday because the library closes at 5:00 P.M. and staff did not want students stranded if their parents could not pick them up before closing. On the other nights the library is open until 9:00 P.M.

The school requires a permission slip for children to be bused to the library, but the library neither takes attendance nor accepts any responsibility for making sure children come from the bus to the library. Usually students stay one to two hours, and most parents pick up their children before 6:30 P.M. About 30 fifth graders and approximately 12 fourth graders participate in the library busing program per day. Since the middle school and high school buildings are not far away, these students can come daily on their own to the library. Another reason why busing is not available five days a week is that the library and the schools decided that the former should not serve as an after-school day care alternative. The Geauga West Library does not offer organized programs after school for unattended children because it has been the library's experience that children do not want more organization after a whole day of school.

Not surprisingly, many of the children participating in the busing program are at the library because "their parents don't want them home alone to let themselves in with a 'latchkey'." But the library has found that "it is not just working parents who allow their children to be bused to the library. In this sprawling community, it is very convenient not to have to drive the child back to the library after he or she arrives home on the bus if the child has homework or just wants a good book" (Orr, 1990).

How successful is the busing, as well as the employment of a monitor? The monitor has noticed that because of increased accessibility, usage of the library has increased, and many students have learned library procedures, such as working with the computerized catalog. Students are making new friendships, as they come together in the library from two public elementary schools and the parochial school (which enrolls K to eighth graders), thus giving them a chance to meet some of their prospective middle school classmates (Orr, 1990).

In 1991 Geauga West Library, budget permitting, will try to have a personal computer on a moveable cart, which can be used in the commons area after school (and elsewhere in the library during other times). Software programs, including an electronic encyclopedia, would be available to support studying for the SAT and choosing a career. This would be supervised by the monitor (Orr, 1990).

Free Library of Philadelphia (Pennsylvania)

Between September 1989 and April 1990, with a grant of $235,000 from the William Penn Foundation, the Free Library of Philadelphia implemented Project LEAP: Learn, Enjoy, and Play at the Library, in order to meet the needs of children 7 to 12 years of age during the after-school hours. Through Project LEAP the library offered 1,144 sessions of after-school activities, provided homework help to 9,600 students, and presented special book and library-related activities to 13,978 participants. At 63 Family Programs in the evenings, 3,773 adults and children came together to hear about LEAP and to enjoy musicians, magicians, storytellers, and other talented performers. To reinforce the concept of the library and books as information sources, 19 different titles of paperback reference books were given away to children to form the nucleus of their home libraries (Free Library of Philadelphia, 1990).

LEAP was implemented in order to allow time for librarians to spend with individual children, to ensure that children knew how to use materials, to give children encouragement, and to provide after-school public programs which would stimulate creative library use. The project was offered from 3:00 P.M. to 5:00 P.M. three afternoons a week at 15 of the system's 49 branches. The first hour of Project LEAP was spent helping students to complete their homework and providing reference assistance. Then in the meeting room, book-oriented activities were shared. Sites for LEAP were selected using four criteria: geographic distribution throughout the city; already existing heavy after-school use; a children's librarian on the staff at the agency; and a meeting room which could be used for activities.

The library hired leaders for LEAP who were experienced in working with children and books. Several were retired children's librarians from the system, and a few were teachers or librarians in the city's public schools. Some branches also had senior citizen volunteers from the Retired Senior Volunteer Program (RSVP) helping. With grant funds the library hired a coordinator to oversee the project. Each children's librarian was responsible for hiring two high school students to be aides. Each aide worked three hours a day, three days a week. Their responsibilities included assisting children with homework; reading to young children; helping leaders prepare for craft programs; setting up tables, chairs, and refreshments for Family Nights; and assisting in distributing the paperback giveaways. For many children the aides became a surrogate "someone to come home to."

LEAP's activities after school varied from branch to branch and reflected the personalities and interests of the children's librarians and leaders, so that there was wonderful diversity. The leaders, children's librarians, and branch manager agreed upon the specific schedule and activities for each branch, since needs of the children varied in different neighborhoods, and adults who worked with the children represented a variety of talents. Storytelling, creative dramatics, pantomime, poetry writing, film and video programs, board games, puppetry, drawing, crafts, weaving, singing, and dancing were among the activities scheduled.

LEAP's arts and crafts projects linked to books were extremely popular with children and leaders alike. For example, at the Cobbs Creek Branch, the leader utilized her artistic talents to work with children in flower arranging, jewelry making, mask making, origami, dolls, and potato prints. The children's librarian's interest in drama was reflected in the presentation of "Santa Claus for President," which children performed for an audience of 130 people attending the Family Holiday Program.

At the Katharine Drexel Branch the leader enjoyed word and thinking games and taught the children "Name That Book," "Balderdash" (a word game), "Scruples," and several others. Activity centers were set up with different board games, including "Hangman," "States," "Battleship," Leggos, and checkers, at the McPherson Square Branch. Some games were fun and educational while others dealt with manual dexterity and creativity. Aides supervised the game area while the leader involved other children in crafts, puppetry, and storytelling.

At the South Philadelphia Branch the leader and children's librarian agreed to focus upon homework help since many of the children in that service area were new to this country and were struggling with English. So the special activities there were designed to acculturate children to American life in a way that maximized their opportunities to verbalize informally. For instance, the children as a group wrote a "fractured fairy tale" for the "One-Eyed Giant" and acted it out.

Still other daily LEAP activities at the Free Library of Philadelphia's branches were a crocheting project; cooking, with math skills used in measuring; a birthday party for Benjamin Franklin at which children ate cake, recreated Ben's science experiments, and listened to readings from *Poor Richard's Almanac*; and a talent show in which children danced and sang raps they had composed. At one branch the leader told open-ended stories and children supplied the endings. At another facility children played "Monster Ring," a game which explored feelings caused by being picked on by a bully.

Project LEAP included paperback reference book giveaways to children during Family Night Programs as a means of reinforcing the library skills they had learned. Among the books distributed were dictionaries, almanacs, atlases, *The Guiness Book of World Records*, *Roget's Thesaurus*, *Pocket Factfinder*, *Great Negroes Past and Present*, first aid books, and insect and mammal field guides. Books were also distributed at special after-school sessions on their use, as prizes for treasure hunts that featured correct use of the library, as incentives to return to LEAP another day, as prizes for spelling bees (in the case of dictionaries), and as tokens of appreciation for working diligently on homework. LEAP staff used the giveaway books to assist with homework and in special arts and crafts activities. For example, children who had a geography assignment could receive an atlas and children could draw pictures of anything they thought would be appropriate for the *Guiness Book*, such as a car with the most wheels.

Every branch library participating in LEAP hosted a Family Night Program at the inception and again at the conclusion of LEAP, as a means of introducing parents to its goals and activities, and of showing proud parents what their children had done. This was followed by entertainment which included dramatic, folksinger, storytelling, and puppet presentations. A blind folksinger not only entertained but also talked about her disability and guide dog. Other public programs presented after school utilized the talents of magicians, crafts people, storytellers, and members of the Green

Circle Program, which teaches tolerance for people different from ourselves. Conrail presented a session on safety near railroads and the SPCA demonstrated pet care. The programs and refreshments were funded with grant monies allocated as honoraria for entertainers and speakers.

Some of the grant monies were used to purchase five cassette players per branch (along with earphones and batteries) and 20 book/cassette titles, so that children could listen to the book and read along as they listened, or could read a book later. This was a great help to children who were learning English as a second language. Some book/cassette pairs were classic titles (such as *The Phantom Tollbooth* by Juster and *Pippi Longstocking* by Lindgren) while others were contemporary stories (such as *Freckle Juice* by Blume and *How to Eat Fried Worms* by Rockwell).

Public relations played an important part in Project LEAP. A city-wide media announcement was held at the Southwark Branch with Chris Davis of the School Age Child Care Coalition as guest. *The Philadelphia Inquirer* ran a feature article on LEAP, and interviews of LEAP personnel appeared on cable television. Children's librarians contacted principals of schools within a half mile radius of the branch and the LEAP Project Coordinator sent announcements to the principals of schools in LEAP neighborhoods. The Free Library's Graphic Arts Department created a LEAP logo which was used on the flyers to publicize events. Pencils and buttons were given away as publicity strategies also, but the very best publicity came from the children themselves via word of mouth.

All involved in the Free Library of Philadelphia's Project LEAP—the LEAP coordinator, children's librarians, leaders, branch managers, high school aides, and the children themselves—believed the impact of the program was extremely positive. Below are some of their comments.

> The book give-away made the library a very popular place...lots of children checked out books when they came for the free ones.

> LEAP made it possible to expose our less privileged children to a variety of live performances which their parents could never provide for them.

> More adults became aware of the library.

> LEAP has definitely improved the quality of children's time spent in the library.

> Many of the children definitely needed the one-on-one homework assistance. Creating a home reference library was definitely an outstanding idea.

One child (Den Nguyen, age 10) wrote a touching and candid letter of appreciation to the William Penn Foundation which funded LEAP. Here is an excerpt from it:

> Dear William Penn Foundation,
>
> We thank you for give us moneys to do the things and we enjoy it. . . from my heart I am very thanks to you leap and Mrs. Paula for teaching us all the wonderful things. . . .
>
> (Free Library of Philadelphia, 1990).

In November 1990 the Free Library of Philadelphia announced the refunding of Project LEAP for two more years, with this stated goal: "to continue. . .the project which has positively demonstrated that it enhances the development of basic learning skills in children ages seven to twelve through creative, informative, and enjoyable supervised after-school activities in Free Library branches" (Hall, 1990).

Greenville County Library (South Carolina)

In 1985, as a part of a $10,000 LSCA Title I Grant, Greenville County Library in Greenville, South Carolina, implemented a program especially designed to reach approximately 1,500 latchkey children who were left on their own after school, primarily because of working parents. The "Latchkey Kids Program" was implemented at nine neighborhood centers to provide assistance to this target group in the form of books, brochures, films, filmstrips, and speakers and community resource people. Activity workshops were conducted by library staff about babysitting, storytelling, leisure activities, and creating a "Master Emergency Telephone List." On the list children wrote telephone numbers for their parent's workplace, the sheriff's department, a neighbor, and the fire department. Resource people presented the following sessions: first aid by Red Cross personnel, drawing by a local artist, games and activities by parks and recreation personnel, growing a box garden and easy cooking by extension personnel, dental care by dental professionals, and pet care by veterinarians.

The "Latchkey Kids Program" was the brainchild of Gay Nell Duckett, Coordinator of the Extension Department, who noticed when she worked in the library's reference department in the early 1980s that children would come to the library and stay until closing. She felt the library needed to provide some type of special service to help these children survive and adapt to society when they were locked outside the house. The library's administration liked Duckett's idea and decided to apply to the South Carolina State Library for an LSCA Title I grant (Chepesiuk, 1987). Carolyn Cody-Fuller planned, conducted, and expanded the latchkey program (Clark, 1990).

As part of its "Latchkey Kids Program," Greenville County Library left bookcases in each of the neighborhood centers. Each bookcase contained about 130 books, covering such topics as dental care, preparing easy meals, general safety, pet care, and babysitting.

In 1989 the Greenville County Library provided a workshop entitled "Responding to the Challenge of Training Latchkey Children," to which parents and children were invited. Topics covered were national/local statistics; causes of "latchkey" children; problems latchkey children confront; how to help fearful children; viewing of the training film, "In Charge at Home"; and materials and resources about and for latchkey children. Another aspect of the project was the publication of a brochure entitled "Latchkey Kids Program: Helpful Hints," which contains tips on what to do in crisis situations—lockouts, blackouts, plumbing problems—as well as a bibliography of books in the "latchkey collection."

Salt Lake County Library (Utah)

The South Jordan Library of the Salt Lake County Library System is surrounded by four elementary schools participating in a year-round school program. To meet the needs of latchkey children in the off-school hours, special activities are offered for one hour two mornings per week during a three-week period, rather than after 3:00 P.M. on a continuous basis, as is the situation in areas not having year-round school. The reason for the three-week series is that children in the year-round school program have a three-week vacation and there are four different "tracks" in the schools. Consequently, the library arranges "off-track" programs designed to provide information and fun activities for kindergarten through sixth-grade students every Tuesday and Thursday from 10:00 A.M. to 11:00 A.M., in three-week intervals. Programs are repeated four times so that each child has the same programs, consisting of six individual presentations (Julian, 1990).

"Off-track" programming was initiated in September 1989 by the PTAs of the local elementary schools, who used the library as a site for activities which they planned and implemented. In January 1990 the administration of the Salt Lake County Library System began arranging and sponsoring the "off track" programs. Presenters, who are asked to make a commitment to come to the library four times, have included local business people, (such as an individual from a video store, who presented a program on Nintendo, and another from Domino's Pizza, who presented "Say 'No' To Drugs"), as well as public service employees (such as a fireman and an animal control officer, who spoke about fire safety and raising rabbits, respectively). Earthquake preparedness, scuba diving, dental hygiene, nutrition, baseball card collecting, microwave cooking, and model airplanes have been topics of other "off-track" programs, although the most successful ones have been puppet and magic shows.

The Salt Lake County Library feels the "off-track" programs have grown into a habit and have been successful for a small branch (which circulates about 14,200 items per month). For example, before the library offered the "off-track" programs circulation averaged 474 items on Tuesdays and Thursdays, but since then the average daily circulation for those two days has been about 650. The staff has also perceived an increase in patrons during the hour the programs are presented. In terms of attendance at "off-track" programs, as publicity became more aggressive and as the activities were consistently offered, the number of "regulars" increased. Now an average of 45 children attend per program, although this fluctuates from 150 to 6 children, depending upon the topic.

Publicity for the "off track" programs includes flyers distributed to schools, listing of the programs in the library's monthly brochure and in the school's newspaper to inform parents, and in-house posters to attract library users. A three-week foreign language series is being considered as a future program, although it would require a three-week commitment from a child. The library also plans to develop a resource file of potential speakers by conducting a parent survey that would be distributed to children in schools to take home to their parents to complete. The survey would ask for descriptions of topics the library could present and the parents' preference of dates for those "off track" programs (Julian, 1990). Other potential topics for programs include the NASA space shot, gymnastics, and first aid information from paramedics (Nelson, 1990).

Weber County Library (Utah)

In December 1989 the Weber County Library in Ogden, Utah, initiated "Homework Help," a strategy addressing latchkey children which has "definitively made a solid transition" from "the hoards of elementary students who ran up and down the stairs and rode the elevators." Now programming "more closely matches the library's service capabilities with the needs of children" and "the elementary children who participate are in the library to study and to develop helping relationships with older students." The library feels that this program "could be replicated at other libraries and has not created an extra workload for librarians" (Gonzales, 1990).

Weber County Library was selected in 1988 as one of the first library sites to pilot an Intergenerational Library Assistance Project after-school program, with a $5,000 grant from ACTION to the local RSVP office. But the library was not pleased with the results because the one program offered per week did "not begin to meet the needs of local latchkey children" and it "actually created a programming and service nightmare for the staff, not only in the children's department but throughout the library" (Gonzales, 1990).

Consequently, the Weber County librarians met with principals of two local elementary schools and decided to initiate a "Homework Help" program which would "blend more realistically with the library's mission." Realizing the limitations of staffing, the library wrote job descriptions for two volunteer positions—a coordinator and an assistant coordinator—and advertised for those positions through their community volunteer agency. A former school teacher was hired as the coordinator and a high school student was hired as her assistant. The coordinator contacted school principals and the Key Club of a local high school and recruited students who were willing to devote two to three hours per week in working with elementary children.

The high school students who applied for volunteer positions completed a form listing prior experience in working with children as well as their preference in regard to days and times of the week, grade level, and the sex of the children they would help. It was emphasized that students must provide their own transportation to and from the library. Parental support was sought in that parents needed to make a commitment to have their children meet their assigned volunteer on the scheduled day. Simultaneously with the recruitment of high school student helpers, forms were sent home with each elementary student inviting them to participate in the program.

Between December 1989 and May 1990 nine high school students helped 17 elementary children at the Weber County Library for a total of 186 hours of "Homework Help." Since the volunteers were not specifically trained as tutors, the program was not advertised as tutoring but rather as homework assistance. Elementary students who signed up for the program brought their regular assignments to the library and completed them with the assistance of the high school volunteers. The library also made available a small reference section of donated elementary math and reading texts, math games, and flash cards, which the volunteers used to help students (Gonzales, 1990). The Homework Help program continues to be offered at the Weber County Library, utilizing high school students as volunteers to coordinate the program and do the actual work, while the librarians assist and supervise.

Weber County Library librarians are currently in contact with the Weber State University teacher education program in order to establish the public library as a site for a senior practicum project. It is hoped that these aspiring teachers may be able to gain experience in working one-to-one with small groups of students in the Homework Help program.

The most recent venture of Weber County Library's youth services librarians and volunteers on behalf of latchkey children is their participation in a pilot latchkey program sponsored by the city recreation department, but which takes place at a local elementary school. Weber County librarians are conducting story hour programs twice a month at the school as an outreach project (Gonzales, 1990).

Seattle Public Library (Washington)

The most innovative and well-planned program, and perhaps the most successful, seems to be "Seattle Public Library's After School Happenings"—S.P.L.A.S.H., which is available at the Beacon Hill, High Point, Holly Park, and Madrona-Sally Goldmark branches of this Washington system. Children's services librarians use S.P.L.A.S.H. to provide after-school activities for children who are on their own after school, Monday through Friday from 4:00 P.M. until 7:00 P.M. S.P.L.A.S.H. was initially funded with $247,500 from the Library's operation budget, but currently is financed from city funds. S.P.L.A.S.H addresses urgent city priorities to serve children at risk, support education, and support neighborhoods (McNeil, 1990).

S.P.L.A.S.H. goals are:

1. To develop literate children by providing an environment where they can become comfortable with reading, books, and learning.
2. To promote learning as a life-long activity.

3. To provide activities which will aid in the development of self-esteem, self-worth, and creativity.
4. To coordinate with other community agencies, groups, and community councils in serving families of children who have been identified as "at risk" or from low-income and single-parent families.
5. To provide activities which are positive alternatives to street life.
6. To establish services for new Asian immigrants.
7. To provide help with homework by using volunteers in libraries to facilitate homework questions.
8. To supply materials that can be used in answering homework questions.
9. To provide reader's assistance and reference services.
10. To provide a safe and friendly space with established and consistent behavior expectations (Seattle Public Library, 1990).

S.P.L.A.S.H. has been in full operation at all four Seattle Public Library sites since May 1989. Each of the very small (1,000 to 13,000 square feet) branches has a full-time librarian, as well as volunteer college students working with S.P.L.A.S.H. While S.P.L.A.S.H. librarians meet to share ideas, each independently plans and offers programs tailored to the needs of the children in his or her community. In a clubhouse atmosphere at High Point Library, children from diverse cultures and ethnicities participate in crafts, games, and story times/sing-a-longs, with emphasis on social skills/ getting along with others, and/or appreciation of books. At Holly Park Library, "Black, White, Asian, Pacific Islander, Native American, and biracial children who are all economically deprived" design aquarium scenes after looking at fish books, tape their readings of poems and stories, and make puppets for folk tales while learning courteous behavior. At the Beacon Hill Library, a 73-year-old volunteer, Yuki Takagi, helps a child do straw-weaving in what she calls "the best government program to help kids I've ever heard of." A major equipment addition at Beacon Hill is a VCR for viewing videos, which has worked better than a noisy film projector. Although the initial emphasis was upon arts and crafts, films, and games, this has evolved to a homework/reading and crafts program for a regular group of 15–20 children per day.

Madrona-Sally Goldmark Library, a very small facility with a seating capacity of 49, is located in an old fire station across the street from one elementary school and within a few blocks of another. Due to its location, and because the neighborhood lacks other after-school alternatives for children, the library is extremely overcrowded in the afternoon hours with children involved in reading, crafts, or other activities. This causes disturbances and creates difficulties in serving other patrons. Strategies staff have undertaken to alleviate the situation have included sending letters to parents through the school describing what the library could and could not offer, assisting the school district in applying for a grant to establish before- and after-school child care programs, and meeting with representatives of the parks department to explore funding for recreation programs.

Yet despite this difficulty, the library tries to accommodate the 64–84 children at Madrona-Sally Goldmark Library who may pass daily through its doors between 3:00 P.M. and 6:00 P.M. Because the area is so small and can only fit 20 or so chairs, the librarian offers several activities each afternoon. Some children do homework, some play games, others "visit" and read (if they can find a secluded space); all enjoy a snack, which may be cookies children bake there. Self-directed "side" activities are available, such as working on mazes and making paper airplanes. Major activities involve making dollhouse furniture and maintaining the library's flower beds. Some children play with the dress-up clothes, puppet stage, or other literary props.

Although a formal evaluation of S.P.L.A.S.H. is in the process of being conducted through March 1991, Seattle Public Library's informal evaluation, based on reports from the librarians at the four program sites, as well as from discussion with staff and library users, indicate that it has been successful in meeting its goals (McNeil, 1990). Indicators of that success include:

- Between May 1989 and June 1990, 717 programs were offered, with a total attendance of 15,816 (averaging 22 persons per program).
- Between May 1989 and June 1990 total circulation at the four S.P.L.A.S.H. sites increased by 10 percent.
- Every one of the regular summer S.P.L.A.S.H. attendees finished the Summer Reading Club.
- Librarians have frequent, sustained interactions with children and their parents, in contrast to the prior situation in which community interaction was minimal.
- Children who regularly attend S.P.L.A.S.H. have increased their confidence and improved their academic achievement.

The editor and staff of *Seattle's Child* magazine designated the librarians at S.P.L.A.S.H., "who view latchkey children as an opportunity instead of a burden," as the winner of their "Best Unsung Heroines and Heroes" Award (*Seattle's Child*, 1990).

In spite of its success, "Seattle Public Library's After School Happenings" is not without problems, and does contain aspects upon which the library and the local community disagree. One issue concerns entertainment versus literary activities, or exactly how much of each are appropriate for the library to provide for latchkey youth after school. Secondly, there is disagreement regarding the library's role. Consequently, the Madrona-Sally Goldmark Library has had to reclarify its responsibilities and reemphasize that it is not a day care center. A third problem is balancing the needs of all library users, since S.P.L.A.S.H. programs often dominate the small library sites during peak after-school hours. This has been most severe at Madrona-Sally Goldmark. However, this is really a matter of scarce resources and inadequate facilities. Four other issues Seattle staff are dealing with are obtaining private donations for new child-appropriate furnishings, equipment, and educational toys and games; getting and keeping volunteers to provide one-to-one interaction with children, to listen to them read, and to assist with activities; preventing staff burn-out; and conducting formal evaluations (McNeil, 1990).

Librarians involved in S.P.L.A.S.H. are very committed to the program and emphasize three important points. First, the program not only fills a need in providing library services, but also provides a "safe place" for "kids-at-risk." Secondly, since S.P.L.A.S.H. creates a "ripple-effect" in reaching not only school-age children, but also preschoolers, parents, and grandparents, the library ultimately impacts the academic and social lives of many. Thirdly, "this library experience is unique and offered only by the library. Daycares, churches, schools, and playgrounds don't have what we have. The children who aren't plugged into those agencies are depending upon us to be there" (McNeil, 1990).

Seattle Public Library initiated still another venture in April 1990 to meet the needs of children in self-care after school—The KEY/H.E.L.P. Project, a cooperative program between the library and the Department of Parks and Recreation. KEY (which stands for "latchkey" but is shortened to signify service to *some* latchkey youth) and H.E.L.P. ("Homework Enrichment Library Project") meet children's needs for homework assistance, nutritional snacks, and physical exercise. H.E.L.P. and KEY are both free and open to students in grades three to seven (Winfield, 1990). H.E.L.P. is scheduled Monday through Thursday during library hours at four branches—Douglass-Truth, Lake City, Rainier Beach, and Southwest—while KEY operates 3:30 P.M. to 7:00 P.M. weekdays at three community centers. Registration is required because KEY can serve only 20 children per site. While the Parks and Recreation Department provided $32,000 for the year for KEY, the Seattle Public Library system allotted $30,000 for H.E.L.P.

Most KEY/H.E.L.P. programs begin with children eating snacks at the community center. Afterward they may play ping-pong video or other games. Around 4:30 P.M. KEY staff escort children to nearby libraries where librarians help them with homework and to use the computers and microfilm machines. The KEY project satisfies parents' "requests for an after-school program which emphasizes homework as well as recreational activities," and serves "children who would otherwise be alone," as it "takes the place of mom and dad" (Winfield, 1990). Through KEY/H.E.L.P., children who don't have access to school libraries after class are transported from the community center to the library where they can use a telefax connection with the downtown library, books and media on curriculum topics, a public access microcomputer with software and printer, and *The Magazine Collection* (over 300 journals on microfilm). Then they are transported back to the community center by the Parks Department.

Toward the end of 1989 Seattle Public Library revised its mission statement and added not only "goals" but "organizational values." The wording of these official statements meshes with the library's recent efforts in behalf of latchkey children. Part of the "mission" states: "we strive to inform, enrich, and empower every citizen. . .by supporting lifelong learning and love of reading. . . .We. . .serve. . .and reach out to all members of our community." Among Seattle's written "goals" are "a close working relationship with. . .community agencies and organizations that fosters collaboration. . .," and "services that. . . result in library use from the broadest possible spectrum of citizens." But it is Seattle Public Library's "organizational values" which perhaps best exemplify the library's commitment to the latchkey segment of the community, as the following excerpts reveal: "Those who need us most should be our highest priority." "We are a learning organization that is. . .risk-taking." "We constantly reassess our services and methods to adapt to the changing needs of our community." Each of the above is an "organizational value" essential in working with latchkey youth, as is the final one listed: "staff and patrons are encouraged to laugh often and out loud" (Seattle Public Library, 1989)!

Fort Erie Public Library (Ontario, Canada)

At the Fort Erie Public Library, a pilot cooperative interagency organizational project was initiated in September 1990 and specifically directed toward 10- to 12-year-olds in self-care. Funded with $25,000 from the Ministry of Community and Social Services and coordinated and supported by the Boys and Girls Clubs of Ontario, the Creative Afterschool Recreation and Enrichment (C.A.R.E.) project features before-school (7:00 A.M. to 9:00 A.M.) and after-school (3:00 P.M. to 6:00 P.M.) activities at two library sites, transportation of children from schools to the library, nutritional snacks prepared by the children, use of the pool and recreational facilities at the YMCA, and field trips to historical sites, such as Old Fort Erie. C.A.R.E., a cooperative venture between the library, the YMCA, local school boards, and parents, currently serves 28 children, and is expected to involve about 40 at a later date.

The Fort Erie Public Library provides office space, administrative assistance, programming expertise, and provision of two sites for children to attend morning and afternoon programs. The YMCA provides recreational expertise and programming assistance for alternative activities (such as swimming). The school board provides transportation for the children from predetermined child care sites to schools in the morning and from schools to designated child care sites in the afternoon (Rossnagel, 1990a). The children design a menu they want for the week, with the guidance of a coordinator. They have made their own pizza and decorated cupcakes and cookies ("C.A.R.E.," Is for Kids, 1990).

Guest speakers, compact disc listening areas, craft activities, computers, homework help, and reading clubs are available. Personnel consists of one salaried program staff member per site, as well as community and secondary school student volunteers as needed. A community-based advisory Board of Directors, composed of representatives from the Fort Erie Public Library, the YMCA, the public and parochial school board, and parents, oversees the program. However the majority of administrative responsibilities rests with the Library Board and its Chief Executive Officer, Elizabeth Rossnagel. The fee structure is competitive and financial assistance for low-income families is being sought from local service clubs (Baynham, 1990).

Evaluation will involve feedback from parents via representation on the Board of Directors and via regularly distributed evaluation forms. C.A.R.E. anticipates the following library benefits: increased usage of library resources; increased child and adult memberships from those who may not otherwise use the library; an opportunity to introduce library services to low income families and reluctant readers; good relationships between library and community organizations, including the local board of education; and the development of the library's image as not just a "book place" (Rossnagel, 1990b).

As the Fort Erie Public Library enters the second half of the project year, there are a number of issues which the administration feels must be addressed in regard to C.A.R.E.:

1. Will the program be able to sustain itself in future years by program fees only or will other funding be required? If the latter applies, from where will these funds be derived and who will be responsible for fundraising?
2. With the economic downturn and an increasing number of layoffs in the Greater Fort Erie area, will the demand for the program diminish in the coming years? If so, what will the impact be on the program's feasibility?
3. What, if any, funding will be available from the provincial government for the operation of such programs?
4. What should the library's future role be in this program? Should some other organization(s) take on the task of administering the program? (Rossnagel, 1990b).

The C.A.R.E. project at the Fort Erie Public Library is one of four C.A.R.E. pilot programs in Ontario offered to address the unique after-school needs of 10- to 12-year-olds in self-care. Other C.A.R.E. programs, which do not involve libraries, are discussed in Chapter 3.

REFERENCES

ACTION. 1988. Retired Senior Volunteer Program. Guidelines for intergenerational library assistance project. Washington, D.C.

Adamec, J. 1990. Homework helpers: Making study time quality time. *Wilson Library Bulletin* 65(September): 31–32.

American Library Association (ALA). Association for Library Services to Children Division of ALA. 1988. *"Latchkey children" in the public library.* Chicago: American Library Association.

American Library Association (ALA). 1989. Libraries respond to latchkeys. *Library Video Magazine* 3(2).

Bath, S. Letter to author, 3 October 1990.

Baynham, P. 1990. Latchkey children in the public library. Paper presented at the Canadian Library Association Annual Conference, June 15, Ottawa, Ontario, Canada.

Burns, C. Letter to Dr. Young, Executive Director, U.S. National Commission on Libraries and Information Science, 2 November 1990.

C.A.R.E is for kids. 1990. *Times-Review* (Fort Erie, Ontario, Canada) October 20, 9.

Chekon, T. Letters to author, 13 June 1990 and 6 November 1990.

Chepesiuk, R. 1987. Reaching out: The Greenville County Library's latchkey kid's program. *Library Journal* 112 (March 1): 46–47.

Clark, R. Letter and enclosures to author, 4 April 1990.

Cleveland Public Library. 1988–1989. LSCA Title I Project grant reports. Cleveland, Ohio.

Crain, C. Letter to author, 4 June 1990.

Davis, V. 1988. GASP! Afterschool fun! *School Library Journal* 34(October): 48.

DeKalb County Public Library. 1990. Dear parent form letter and brochures. Decatur, Georgia.

Denney, M. 1988. Teen Scene performs Pooh. *Times-Crescent* (LaPlata, Maryland) March 23, 6.

Des Enfants, S. Telephone conversation with author, 17 April 1990.

Dodd, J. Letter to author, 28 March 1990.

Frazier, L. Letter to author, 1 November 1989.

Free Library of Philadelphia. 1990. Final report on LEAP. Philadelphia, Pennsylvania.

Fuqua, C. 1988. Unattended children: An engagement policy that works. *Wilson Library Bulletin* 62(June): 88–90.

Gilbert, M. Letters to author, 18 June 1990 and 30 October 1990.

Gonzales, B. Letters to author, 14 May 1990 and 25 August 1990.

Hall L. Letter to author, 7 November 1990.

Hernandez, M. Letter to author, 18 June 1990.

Julian, S. Letter to author, 10 May 1990.

Kart, M. 1989. A content analysis of children's materials directed towards the latchkey child. Master's Paper. Palmer School of Library and Information Science of Long Island University, Brookville, New York.

Knott, D. Letter to author, 15 October 1990.

Long Beach Public Library and Information Center. 1988. Letter to parents, guardians and care givers. Long Beach, California.

Los Angeles Public Library. 1990. Report on Grandparents and Books. Los Angeles, California.

Manson, E. Letter to author, 6 June 1990.

Markey, P. 1988. The library latchkey phenomenon. What is it? What can we do about it? Paper presented at Librarians for Social Responsibility Round Table, at the Illinois Library Association Conference, May 12, Chicago, Illinois.

McDonald, A. Letter to author, 12 April 1990.

McNeil, D. Memorandum to Liz Stroup, City Librarian, Seattle Public Library, 8 August 1990.

Messineo, N. Telephone conversation with author, 11 April 1990.

Metropolitan Cooperative Library System (MCLS). 1988. National clearinghouse for library latchkey policies news release. Altadena, California.

Missouri Library Association. Children's Services Round Table. 1985. *Drop-in delights.* Waynesville, Missouri.

Moore, M.A. Letter to author, 18 June 1990.

Nelson, R. Letter to author, 14 November 1990.

Orr, C. Letters to author, 18 May 1990 and 14 November 1990.

Pickens, L. Letters to author, 12 June 1990, 5 September 1990, and 11 November 1990.

Price, G. Telephone conversation with author, 17 April 1990a.

Price, G. Letter to author, 13 October 1990b.

Prince, L. 1987. How the latchkey situation affects children and the implications for our community and for the library system. Paper presented at "Kids with Keys" Conference at the University of California, March 27, Los Angeles, California.

Raymer, A. Letter to author, 18 June 1990.

Riskind, M. Letter to author, 11 December 1990.

Rogers, B. Letter to author, 1 October 1990.

Rome, L. 1990. Services to latchkey kids and the public library: Dealing with the real issues. *Wilson Library Bulletin* 64(April): 34–37+.

Rossnagel, E. Telephone conversation with author, 24 October 1990a.

Rossnagel, E. Letters to author, 1 and 22 November, 1990b.

Ryall, G. 1990. Telephone conversation with author, 25 April 1990.

Ryan, M. Letter to author, 1 June 1990.

Sacramento Public Library. 1990. Quarterly report narrative on LSCA grant and final report. Sacramento, California.

Salvadore, M. Letter to author, 16 April 1990.

San Marino Public Library. 1987. Letter to parents and guidelines for San Marino Public Library. San Marino, California.

Seattle Public Library. 1989. Mission goals and organizational values. Seattle, Washington.

Seattle Public Library. 1990. S.P.L.A.S.H. flyer. Seattle, Washington.

Seattle's Child. 1990. Best unsung heroines and heroes. (August):10

Stefansson, J. 1988. Kids with keys: San Marino Public Library—A case study. Presentation at the Public Library Association National Conference, April 29, Pittsburgh, Pennsylvania.

Taylor, K. Letter to author, 22 June 1990.

Uebelacker, S. Telephone conversation with author, 6 June 1990a.

Uebelacker, S. Letters to author, 11 July 1990 and 24 October 1990b.

Wade, M. Letters to author, 15 October 1990 and 15 November 1990.

Wade, M. and S. Patron. 1990. *Grandparents and books: Trainer's manual.* Los Angeles Public Library. Los Angeles, California.

Waters, R. 1990. Editorial. *Public Library Quarterly* 10(1): 1–5.

Willett, H. 1985. Current issues in public library services for children. *Public Libraries* 24(Winter): 137–40.

Williamson, B. Letter to author, 10 July 1990.

Winfield, P. 1990. Teamwork: Program helps latchkey kids. *Seattle Times*, April 16, 3 B.

Wolfram, D. Letter to author, 12 June 1990.

Yee, J. Letter to author, 7 May 1990.

Chapter 8
Recommendations for Future Library Service

A former youth services coordinator advocates that public librarians take the following measures to meet the challenge of latchkey children. She emphasizes the importance of these strategies, even if the presence of latchkey children is not yet noticeable, stating that eventually these youth will surface (Strickland, 1988). Begin by systematically evaluating and analyzing the impact of latchkey children in your community. Talk to children and their parents about why they visit the library and whether the library makes them feel welcome. Next, survey existing community agencies and resources available for these children and talk to local educators about starting or expanding after-school programs, especially within walking distance to the library.

Then prepare a "child friendly management plan," which involves both developing guidelines or policies regarding unattended or latchkey children that avoid negative, unfair, and restrictive language and providing service alternatives that invite this clientele into the library. This may mean that your library would cooperatively sponsor programs with other community agencies, such as the YMCA, Camp Fire, Scouts, 4-H, local churches, etc. It may mean recruiting teen and senior volunteers to assist in program presentation. Implementation of homework centers, read-aloud times, special programs presented by volunteer hosts, or offsite referrals to other community resources are also options.

One librarian at the Mid-Continent Public Library in Independence, Missouri, wrote the author that librarians who welcome and concern themselves with latchkey children can really affect those children's lives. At her first library job in the early 1970s she had worked with a "latchkey" child who showed up so regularly that she gave her work cutting out storytime name tags and straightening picture books. In 1989 at the American Library

Association's Annual Conference in Dallas that "latchkey" youth looked up the librarian to say "thank you" for being a positive role model and encouraging her to get an education, because she is very happy as a reference librarian at a college in Virginia (Steele, 1990)!

RECOMMENDATIONS OF LIBRARIANS (1988)

Recommendations regarding appropriate and effective library service to latchkey children were obtained during the summer of 1988 from 10 selected public librarians throughout the country, via in-person and telephone interviews conducted by the author as a follow-up to her initial survey research. (This research is described in Chapter 6.) Librarians participating in the interviews represented the following institutions: Boston Public Library; Brooklyn Public Library; East Central Georgia Regional Library; Enoch Pratt Free Library (Baltimore, Maryland); Harford County Library (Maryland); Hennepin County Library (Minnesota); Huntsville-Madison County Public Library (Alabama); Los Angeles Public Library; Pierce County Library (Washington); and Weber County Library (Utah). Interviewees offered a variety of noteworthy recommendations in response to the following question: "Ideally, with adequate funding and staff, how could/should public libraries most effectively and appropriately respond presently or in the future years to the needs of unattended/latchkey children who use public libraries as a substitute for child care—in terms of: services/ programs? personnel? physical facility? materials? policy/procedures?"

Programs/Services

Gretchen Wronka, Coordinator of Children's Service at Hennepin County Library (Minnesota), advocated that "libraries adopt a mail-a-book program specifically for latchkey children in which books would be mailed to children at home alone or having no means of transportation to the library, just as is done for physically handicapped patrons." A program which has been very popular with school-age children at the Pierce County Library in Tacoma, according to Kathy Crosby, Coordinator of Children's Services, is the "Cinema Sandwich." It is a one-hour film event offered in the afternoon hours on weekdays and during spring break to which students bring a sack lunch which they eat while watching movies. Crosby also suggested informal book discussion groups, noting that because unattended children are a "captive audience," some programs that might not otherwise achieve success are effective because latchkey children often need activities to occupy the great deal of time they spend in the library each week. Selma Levi, Head of the Children's Department at Enoch Pratt Free Library (Baltimore), recommended starting an after-school book club for children, using a "fun name" and mascot, and having children create wall murals or string figures to depict books read. Brooklyn Public Library, according to Ellen Loughran, Assistant Coordinator of Collection Development, sponsors library treasure hunts to teach reference skills, impromptu read-aloud and pop-up book-sharing times, film showings, art and drawing activities, and game and toy periods from 3:00 P.M. to 5:00 P.M. at several branches.

Volunteers to provide homework or reading assistance for children was a service recommended in 4 of the 10 interviews. Christine Schnick, Manager of the Wallace Branch Homework Center of the East Central Georgia Regional Library, described a strategy that she has found to be successful. Children receive tutoring in math and reading, as well as homework assistance, since nonreaders often find libraries frustrating. Working parents express their appreciation for the extra time afforded them in the evenings and for the assurance that their children have completed school assignments. Although applicants for tutoring at the Wallace Branch outnumber tutors three to one, many of those who do obtain homework assistance have improved their standardized test scores at school. Levi suggested identifying latchkey pairs and matching younger children with older ones who will read to them or help them with craft activities. At the Weber County Library in Ogden, Utah, retired seniors volunteered to tutor children in homework, identified community personnel to present programs, and published a monthly almanac of community activities for children after school. These volunteers participated, through ACTION, in an RSVP Intergenerational Library Assistance Grant.

Frequently, interviewees noted involvement with other community agencies in programming. Schnick related her positive experiences with events that the library cosponsored with the police department, fire department, and medical professionals. These personnel presented sessions on nutrition, sexual abuse, sex education, and teenage pregnancy. Crosby suggested involving Friends groups, contacting persons from the community to present special programs, and brainstorming with other local agencies to gather ideas. Rocky Weaver, General Library, Children's Services, Boston Public Library, remarked that librarians should cooperate with day care agencies by scheduling caregivers to bring groups of children to the library for booktalks, storyhours, film showings, browsing, or quiet reading experiences. Sally Barnett, Head of Youth Services, Huntsville-Madison County Public Library (Alabama), utilized teen volunteers in an LSCA grant which involved cooperation with schools. She took deposit collections and conducted programs at sites where school-age youth were supervised in the after-school hours.

Materials

In terms of materials, two persons interviewed felt that, ideally, libraries should have arts and crafts materials available for children to use independently or with others after school. Construction paper, crayons, workbooks, and coloring books were among the materials mentioned. Blythe Ogilvie, Head of Children's Services, Weber County Library, explained that the RSVP volunteers in her library's grant project identified sources for donations of materials and created workbooks and self-programmed learning packets to help children learn math and reading independently. One librarian interviewed felt that libraries should develop in-house collections of games and toys, while another advocated maintaining a well-stocked paperback collection. Staff at the Brooklyn Public Library hold books at the circulation desk until the following day for children who may not be allowed to check out materials or may not have a library card. This practice encourages children to finish reading a longer book while they are at the library for several consecutive afternoons.

Physical Facility

Concerning the ideal physical facility for unattended children, a separate area of the library was recommended by Levi and Schnick so that children involved in after-school activities would be comfortable and other patrons would not be disturbed. However, Ogilvie felt that the library facility should serve in a coordinating capacity rather than function as the main site for activities for latchkey children.

Policy and Procedures

In regard to latchkey policy and procedures, interviewees emphasized that policy must be clearly defined, that negative policy should be rejected, and that consistency in procedures is a key to success. Ogilvie remarked that librarians should "check their library's mission statement for fundamental guidance when developing policy." For instance, Weber County Library's mission statement specifies that the library will serve, in particular, "segments of the community whose information needs are of greatest concern because the needs of these special groups are not the primary responsibility of other institutions." Specific groups that the library's mission statement lists in this category are preschool children, adults, the handicapped, and minorities. Although latchkey children are not specifically identified as one of these groups, the mission statement does offer guidance. The Weber County Library mission statement implies that latchkey children should be among those deserving special library attention, in that they comprise a particular segment of the population that is not the designated primary responsibility of other community institutions, such as the public schools.

Schnick advised librarians to create a homework council composed of parents, community members, board of education personnel, teachers, representatives from the library board, and high school students. The homework council at the Wallace Branch Library Homework Center functions as a steering committee since it assists the library in planning goals, policy, programs and changes. The council, which meets quarterly, serves as a means for the library to stay in touch with the community. Levi advised librarians to make certain "their legal responsibility is clearly defined in their library policy" and that "legal counsel is obtained" prior to defining policy.

Personnel

Other than urging utilization of volunteers, participants made few recommendations regarding the personnel who serve latchkey children. Several interviewees discussed the background and education of librarians working with children who use the library regularly after school in lieu of child care. Frances Sedney, Coordinator of Children's Services for Harford County Library (Maryland), recommended that "all librarians receive training (workshops, films, lectures) on age-appropriate behaviors and on dealing with children." Ogilvie made a similar recommendation. Crosby advocated that either state library associations or ALA provide a workshop on latchkey children so that librarians from around the nation could share their problems, procedures and successes.

Other Advice: Community Cooperation and a Positive Approach

In the 1988 interviews, participants were asked this question: "In addition to the above, what words of advice would you offer to public libraries having large numbers of children using the library as a substitute for child care?" Advice focused primarily upon the following areas: cooperation between the library and local child care personnel, community support, proactive approaches, and public awareness of the dangers of leaving children unattended. Crosby and Wronka remarked that librarians need to become actively involved with child care personnel by serving on local government or community task forces or coalitions for child care. Barnett suggested that librarians help child care providers by informing them of resources appropriate for these children. Crosby and Schnick stressed obtaining community support and parental backing for library service to latchkey children. The former also advised calling a public meeting to determine how the community could improve the latchkey situation and to ask parents what they would prefer their children do in the after-school hours.

Half of those interviewed stressed the importance of establishing a positive attitude toward latchkey children. Sedney stated that these children should be fully recognized as patrons and have full rights to services because why they are in the library should not be the main concern. Similarly, Levi emphasized that "there should be no double standards and that all children's services should be equally available to all children—attended and nonattended." Crosby advised that children should be treated the same as any other patrons and made to feel welcome by friendly staff. Virginia Walter, Children's Services Coordinator at Los Angeles Public Library, hoped the "category of latchkey children would disappear" and that libraries would adopt a more positive attitude toward latchkey children, rather than single them out and treat them as a stigma.

Sandra Collins, former Children's Services Librarian for Weber County Library, pointed out that, in reality, serving unattended children can be easier than serving children who come to the library accompanied by parents, since in assisting the former there is "no interference in requests for materials/information" or in regard to discipline. Schnick recommended that librarians "take a proactive approach to unattended children by involving the community, obtaining its support prior to problems, and developing a plan, rather than waiting until problems actually occur to take action."

Ogilvie stressed the necessity of publicizing the fact that "it's not okay" to leave children unattended in the library. She related two specific incidents that had occurred in her library because children were being left unsupervised. One involved a stranger who approached an unattended child and the other involved a staff member who tried to correct an unsupervised child. Documenting instances of disruptive behavior, keeping accurate informal records of numbers of children unattended, and obtaining the support of staff, administration and the library board were among Ogilvie's suggestions (Dowd, 1989).

RECOMMENDATIONS OF LIBRARIANS (1990)

In 1990 the author conducted a second survey and other librarians shared their recommendations for library service to latchkey/unattended children in their responses to two open-ended items. (This research is described in Chapter 6.) One question asked librarians for "positive words of advice to a library which has a substantial number of latchkey/unattended children" and the other asked "what, ideally (budget permitting) public libraries should 'do' for this clientele." Responses to both questions were remarkably similar to the advice other librarians had offered two years earlier.

Consider Latchkey Children an Opportunity

The majority of those who offered advice emphasized the importance of viewing latchkey children as an opportunity. Specifically, librarians wrote that the existence of latchkey children gives the library the opportunity to work cooperatively in the community, to turn a captive audience into program potential, and to recruit future library users and book lovers. One librarian remarked: "Be glad they are in the library where they have the opportunity to learn, to stretch their imagination, to come into contact with the positive influence of books." Keeping a positive attitude was seen as essential in working with this service group, along with creativity, flexibility, and a sense of humor. One person advised against creating too many rules but instead emphasizing fun and learning so children will want to spend their time creatively.

Public Relations/Advocacy

After maintaining a positive attitude and considering latchkey children as an opportunity, the librarians' second most important "words of advice," judging from the frequency of their remarks on the questionnaire, pertained to "public relations" or "advocacy." This took the form of cooperation and communication with parents, children, child care providers, schools, legislators, politicians, and the whole community regarding the limits of library service, available library services, and alternatives for these children. Participants advocated that librarians talk with parents, representatives from schools and social agencies serving children, and local governmental officials in order to work out solutions. One respondent remarked: "cooperate your utmost with an extended day care provider." Another stated that it was essential to get involved politically.

Mission, Policies, and Procedures

Additional advice offered by those participating in the survey pertained to the library's mission statement, policies, and procedures. Librarians advocated staff education, especially in regard to laws and policies related to latchkey children, developing policies and procedures, and using the mission statement as a guide to determining the library's appropriate role in serving latchkey children.

Physical Facility

In regard to "space" or the "physical facility," a separate area where children involved in after-school activities would not disturb other patrons was again the main suggestion in addressing the needs of latchkey children. Survey respondents elaborated by stating that there should be areas for: loud, physical exercise; video viewing; listening stations; computer work stations with interactive story programs; quiet supervised study; comfortable lounging; and formal after-school programs. Four persons felt that libraries should designate a separate room for kids, or a reading room for teens equipped with magazines, music, and supervised homework assistance.

Personnel

As in the 1988 interviews, librarians felt that, in regard to personnel matters, utilizing volunteers and educating staff to understand the needs of latchkey children were necessities. However, in 1990 librarians seemed more demanding, recommending additional staff. They specifically recommended that one librarian be solely responsible for after-school programs, that there is one staff member for every tenth person, and that there are enough *paid* staff to work with latchkey children either individually or in groups because one staff member is insufficient to serve the large number of children involved.

Materials

Similarly, librarians in 1988 and in 1990 mentioned, in relation to materials that should be available for latchkey children, arts and crafts supplies for children to use independently, learning games, and a wide selection of books. Personal computers, educational software, and "collection support for latchkey programs housed OUTSIDE the library" were each noted by one respondent.

Programs and Services

Programs and services for latchkey children was the aspect of the latchkey issue receiving the greatest amount of attention from librarians in both 1988 and 1990. In both cases there was agreement on the content of "ideal" library activities for latchkey children. However, more recently librarians described the program and services in greater detail and they recommended a greater variety of activities. The 1990 responses reflected librarians' strong belief that libraries should provide homework assistance or tutoring for latchkey children, as well as after-school clubs, programs, and literature-related craft activities. Again, cooperative programming with other community agencies and serving as advocates for quality child care were highly recommended. One individual stated that librarians should serve on advisory boards, help seek funding, and cooperate with other agencies to offer programs, but let the child care agency take physical care of children. Another wrote that librarians should join with local efforts to provide quality child care and then support those programs. Survey respondents also wanted librarians to offer the following services and programs for latchkey children or for adults who work with them: booktalks, storytelling, puppet shows, a story van for outreach efforts, parenting skills sessions, and training for child care providers in story and book-related activities. Someone remarked however that the "library should not serve as a community recreation center."

Several librarians commented upon the frequency of programs for latchkey children. One stated that two activities should be scheduled each week while two others wanted libraries to schedule a specific program daily (such as "Monday: arts and crafts day; Tuesday: games day; Wednesday: booktalks and book-related video day; Thursday: drama and music day; and Friday: potluck day"). Each of the following were suggested by at least one librarian: programming for latchkey children outside the library; on-site child care; and database lists of agencies/community programs which offer activities for these children.

AUTHOR'S RECOMMENDATIONS (1988)

The following recommendations were developed from the 1988 survey findings to help public libraries clarify their appropriate role in serving latchkey children and facilitate more effective latchkey service:

1. Public library personnel should be better educated regarding appropriate services to latchkey children. Perservice preparation could be included in the content of library courses dealing with children's/youth services or programs, library management, or public libraries. In-service preparation could be offered by an in-house staff development workshop, a program session at the Annual Conference of the American Library Association, or through a correspondence course such as those published in *American Libraries*, which require participants to read certain materials and complete written assignments.

2. Public libraries should develop and publicize specific positively worded written policies and procedures for dealing with latchkey children, whether or not they are currently experiencing this phenomenon.

3. Public libraries should re-evaluate their programs and services for latchkey children, with the goal of providing additional traditional library-related services, including, on a trial basis, information and referral services for latchkey children and their families

through an online computerized community resource database. Nontraditional services, such as security guards or monitors and after-school child care services, should be eliminated.
4. Public libraries should become actively involved in some type of community-sponsored committee/board/task force composed of representatives from neighborhood agencies. The goal of this body should be to explore and provide appropriate services and programs for latchkey children during the after-school hours in order to meet the local area's particular needs.
5. Additional research on the topic of latchkey children in public libraries is warranted, particularly implementation of pilot demonstration projects at various geographic sites of the computerized online information and referral database and of innovative after-school programs. Evaluation should be qualitative, including pretesting and posttesting (Dowd, 1989).

AUTHOR'S RECOMMENDATIONS (1990)

The following recommendations were developed from the 1990 survey findings:

1. Continue to educate librarians about latchkey children. Include current information about these children in library school courses so that graduates will start professional positions with sufficient knowledge. For practitioners, library systems should provide in-service training. Library administrators should encourage librarians to attend sessions about latchkey children at state library association and American Library Association conferences. The profession should also make available descriptions of successful experiences libraries have had in serving latchkey children, so that librarians could gain from reading about what works for others.
2. Encourage librarians to interact with representatives from community agencies regarding latchkey children so that working together with parents, schools, and local agencies, alternatives for children can be developed. Libraries should publicize their services and programs to these community groups. Ideally, librarians could/should represent their agency on a community board/task force/committee regarding latchkey children.

3. Additional research regarding latchkey children in public libraries should be conducted. Interview latchkey children in libraries to learn their perception of the library and their use of it (assuming appropriate permission is obtained). Then undertake a longitudinal study to determine the impact of the library latchkey experience upon children later in life. The major research question might be: How does the library latchkey experience influence childrens' perceptions and use of the public library? Gather data from children participating in formal programs targeting latchkey children which are currently in place in public libraries. Research the preference of latchkey children regarding public library services and programs. The primary goal of the research would be to determine what activities children prefer that public libraries provide for them.
4. Then implement the recommendations obtained from surveying children regarding their preferences for library services and programs at public libraries throughout the country.

REFERENCES

Dowd, F.S. 1989. Serving latchkey children: Recommendations from librarians. *Public Libraries* 28(March/April): 101–06.

Steele, A. Letter to author, 15 February 1990.

Strickland, C. 1988. Young users. *Wilson Library Bulletin* 62(June): 98–99+.

Appendices

Appendix A
1988 Questionnaire

SURVEY OF LATCHKEY/UNATTENDED CHILDREN IN PUBLIC LIBRARIES

PLEASE PROVIDE THE FOLLOWING INFORMATION:

I am responding for one facility (Circle one)   YES   NO

I am responding for a multi-branch system (Circle one)   YES   NO

(If "YES," PLEASE SPECIFY NUMBER OF BRANCHES: ____)

PART I. DESCRIPTION OF THE LIBRARY LATCHKEY/UNATTENDED CHILDREN SITUATION

1. Have you found that latchkey/unattended children are using your library for child care purposes <u>after-school</u> on weekdays? (Circle one)
YES   NO

2. Have you found that latchkey/unattended children are using your library for child care purposes <u>on weekends</u>? (Circle one)   YES   NO

- -
IF YOUR RESPONSES TO BOTH QUESTIONS #1 AND #2 ARE "NO," PLEASE PROCEED DIRECTLY TO PART II.
- -

PLEASE FILL IN THE APPROPRIATE NUMBER OF CHILDREN UNDER EACH AGE LEVEL COLUMN BELOW. PLEASE CONSIDER EACH CATEGORY (e.g., 1 day a week, 2 days a week, etc.) AS EXCLUSIVE AND INDEPENDENT.

Estimate the number of unattended/latchkey children present in your public library during a typical week (excluding summer and holidays) between 3:00 P.M. and 6:00 P.M.

Latchkey/Unattended Children	Under 6 yrs.	7-9 yrs.	10-12 yrs.	Over 12 yrs.
3. one day a week who are	❑	❑	❑	❑
4. two days a week who are	❑	❑	❑	❑
5. three days a week who are	❑	❑	❑	❑
6. four days a week who are	❑	❑	❑	❑
7. five days a week who are	❑	❑	❑	❑

PLEASE CIRCLE THE NUMBER WHICH MOST ACCURATELY DESCRIBES YOUR LIBRARY'S SITUATION

1 = NEVER   2 = SOMETIMES   3 = ALWAYS

Due to unattended/latchkey children at our library, staff have encountered:

8. an opportunity to develop new methods of effectively serving latchkey/unattended children   1 2 3
9. some difficulty in performing regular library services effectively for other patrons   1 2 3
10. uncertainty regarding how to best deal with unattended/latchkey children   1 2 3
11. vandalism/destruction of library property (furniture, walls, shrubbery, etc.)   1 2 3
12. increased overdue and/or lost materials   1 2 3
13. disturbance due to inappropriate behaviors (as running, fighting, moving furniture, throwing paper, etc.)   1 2 3
14. patron complaints concerning unattended/latchkey children   1 2 3

14. patron complaints concerning unattended/latchkey   1 2 3
    children
15. limited or unavailable seating   1 2 3
16. delays or difficulty in closing library when a   1 2 3
    child is left unattended
17. other (PLEASE DESCRIBE): _____

PLEASE CHECK AS MANY AS APPLY

In my opinion, unattended/latchkey children use the public library in lieu of after-school child care because:

18. ❑ their parent(s) cannot afford other day care arrangements
19. ❑ their parent(s) lack information as to other options for care (such as community agency programs, available commercial day care, etc.)
20. ❑ their parent(s) perceive(s) the library as an appropriate facility where children can safely spend a few hours after school
21. ❑ their parent(s) perceive(s) the library as a place where children can learn and extend their education
22. ❑ the public library philosophy toward children has traditionally been that of encouraging children to come to the library
23. ❑ the library is located near school
24. ❑ other (PLEASE DESCRIBE): _____

PLEASE CHECK AS MANY AS APPLY

Factors which aggravate the unattended/latchkey children situation at our library are:

25. ❑ architectural design and layout of the library building
26. ❑ limited number of personnel/staff
27. ❑ limited seating or square footage in the library
28. ❑ other (PLEASE DESCRIBE): _____

29. The main challenge that public libraries have in serving latchkey children is: _____

PART II. LIBRARY POLICY/PROCEDURES CONCERNING UNATTENDED/LATCHKEY CHILDREN

PLEASE CHECK ONE OF THE FOLLOWING

30. Concerning unattended/latchkey children, our library:
    - ❑ has written policy/procedure in effect (IF SO, PLEASE ENCLOSE A COPY WITH YOUR RESPONSE. THANK YOU.)
    - ❑ is in the process of developing written policy/procedures
    - ❑ is considering developing written policy/procedures
    - ❑ has unwritten policy/procedures which are followed
    - ❑ has neither written nor unwritten policy/procedures but needs them
    - ❑ has neither written nor unwritten policy/procedures and does not need them

<u>EVEN IF YOU DO NOT HAVE WRITTEN PROCEDURES</u> for unattended/latchkey children in the library, please describe the procedures which you would follow:

31. if unattended/latchkey children were present at closing time: _____

_____

32. if unattended/latchkey children were being disruptive to other patrons and staff: _____

_____

PLEASE CHECK AS MANY AS APPLY

Written policy/procedures concerning unattended/latchkey children are/would be important because they help to:

33. ❑ standardize procedures for handling unattended children left at closing time
34. ❑ express the library's position on this issue
35. ❑ increase staff confidence
36. ❑ standardize and clarify staff responses
37. ❑ maintain the appropriate and equitable use of the library

38. ❑ express the library's concern for the children's safety and well-being
39. ❑ other (PLEASE DESCRIBE): _____

IF YOU DO NOT HAVE WRITTEN POLICY/PROCEDURES, PLEASE PROCEED DIRECTLY TO PART III.

PLEASE CHECK AS MANY AS APPLY

Our library developed policy/procedures for unattended/latchkey children:
40. ❑ before experiencing a problem
41. ❑ after experiencing a problem
42. ❑ after reviewing policy/procedures of other libraries
43. ❑ after discussing the topic with persons from other community agencies (as police, social services, schools, etc.)
44. ❑ after a library committee/task force met to gather facts or make recommendations
45. ❑ other (PLEASE DESCRIBE): _____

PLEASE CHECK ONE OF THE FOLLOWING

Our library policy/procedures concerning unattended/latchkey children:
46. ❑ have never been used/followed
    ❑ have been used/followed at least once

PLEASE CHECK ONE OF THE FOLLOWING

Our library policy/procedures concerning unattended/latchkey children:
47. ❑ are adequate in meeting our needs
    ❑ are not adequate in meeting our needs (IF SO, PLEASE DESCRIBE):
    _____
    _____
    _____

PLEASE CHECK AS MANY AS APPLY

People are informed of our policy/procedures concerning unattended/latchkey children:

48. ❑ via a sign posted in the library
49. ❑ via word of mouth or talks to schools/community groups/PTA, etc.
50. ❑ via printed material distributed to patrons
51. ❑ other (PLEASE DESCRIBE): _____

PLEASE CHECK AS MANY AS APPLY

Our policy/procedures concerning unattended/latchkey children state that:

52. ❑ children under a specific age (e.g., 6, 7, 8 yrs., or so) should not be left unattended in the library
53. ❑ the library is not responsible for children under a specific age (e.g., 6, 7, 8 yrs., or so) who are left unattended
54. ❑ parents or guardians are responsible for the behavior of their children while in the library

PLEASE CHECK AS MANY AS APPLY

Our policy/procedures concerning unattended/latchkey children specify actions to be taken if the following situations occur:

55. ❑ a child is unattended in the library at closing time
56. ❑ a child is disruptive in the library
57. ❑ a child is identified as a library latchkey child
58. ❑ other (PLEASE DESCRIBE): _____

PART III. LIBRARY PROGRAMS/SERVICES FOR UNATTENDED/LATCHKEY CHILDREN

PLEASE CIRCLE YES OR NO TO INDICATE WHETHER YOUR LIBRARY DOES OR DOES NOT PROVIDE THE SERVICE/PROGRAM AND TO INDICATE WHETHER YOU BELIEVE YOUR LIBRARY SHOULD OR SHOULD NOT PROVIDE THE SERVICE/PROGRAM.

In regard to the following programs or services for unattended/latchkey children, our library:

		PROVIDES		SHOULD PROVIDE	
59.&60.	After-school child care services	Yes	No	Yes	No
61.&62.	Self-help survival skills workshops presented by community agencies on topics as first aid measures, meal preparation, handling emergency situations, etc.	Yes	No	Yes	No
63.&64.	Information and referral services for parents regarding available licensed child care in the area	Yes	No	Yes	No
65.&66.	An on-line computer database community resource file listing activities for latchkey children and their parents	Yes	No	Yes	No
67.&68.	Drop-in activity programs such as arts and crafts projects	Yes	No	Yes	No
69.&70.	Volunteer opportunities for latchkey children, performing library "odd jobs" such as straightening magazines, making name tags for storytimes, shelving books, stamping/labeling, etc.	Yes	No	Yes	No

71.&72. "Warm-line" telephone services by which children can telephone the library, ask about self care survival skills, and receive responses   Yes   No   Yes   No

73.&74. Storyhours, book clubs, films and other traditional library programs specifically to meet the needs or schedule of latchkey children   Yes   No   Yes   No

75.&76. Tutoring sessions conducted by library volunteers who assist latchkey/unattended children with their homework and reading assignments   Yes   No   Yes   No

77.&78. Paired tutoring sessions—an older latchkey child with a younger latchkey child   Yes   No   Yes   No

79.&80. Special programs/services other than those normally provided for non-latchkey children   Yes   No   Yes   No

81.&82. Special security guards or monitors to supervise unattended/ latchkey children in the library   Yes   No   Yes   No

83. An additional program/service which I would recommend public libraries provide for unattended/latchkey children is: _____

_____

_____

84. Some librarians believe that libraries should interact with other community agencies in regard to dealing with latchkey children. Do you feel such interaction is important? (Circle one)   YES   NO
IF "YES," PLEASE DESCRIBE: _____

_____

_____

85. The role of the public library in regard to latchkey/unattended children is: _____

86. Is your library successful in dealing with latchkey/unattended children (Circle one)   YES   NO
    If "YES," please explain what works for you or why, etc.: _____

87. Other general comments concerning latchkey/unattended children:

Thank you for your time and cooperation.

Dr. Frances A. Dowd
School of Library and Information Studies
Texas Woman's University
P.O. Box 22905
Denton, TX 76204
(817) 898-2615

Appendix B
1990 Questionnaire

NATIONAL SURVEY OF LATCHKEY/UNATTENDED CHILDREN IN PUBLIC LIBRARIES

Number of facilities I am responding for: _____

PART I: GENERAL DESCRIPTION AT YOUR LIBRARY

PLEASE SELECT THE RESPONSE FOR EACH ITEM WHICH MOST ACCURATELY DESCRIBES THE SITUATION AT YOUR LIBRARY

1. Latchkey/unattended children are using the library for child care purposes after school or on weekends
   ❏ to a great extent ❏ somewhat ❏ never ❏ don't know
2. The impact of latchkey/unattended children upon the library's personnel and services is:
   ❏ high ❏ marginal ❏ none ❏ don't know
3. In meeting the needs of latchkey/unattended children our library has met with success.
   ❏ strongly agree ❏ agree somewhat ❏ disagree ❏ don't know
4. In comparison with the situation 2 years ago, the number of latchkey/unattended children at the library is:
   ❏ higher ❏ about the same ❏ lower ❏ don't know
5. In comparison with the situation 2 years ago, the level of development of the library's policies and procedures dealing with latchkey/unattended children is:
   ❏ much better ❏ slightly better ❏ same ❏ don't know

IF YOUR RESPONSE TO QUESTION #1 IS "NEVER,"
PLEASE PROCEED DIRECTLY TO PART II.

PLEASE CIRCLE "YES" OR "NO" FOR EACH STATEMENT

Due to latchkey/unattended children at our library, we have experienced:

6. the need to develop new methods of service	Yes	No
7. legal liability	Yes	No
8. medical emergencies/accidents	Yes	No
9. delays in closing due to child left alone	Yes	No
10. increased recruitment of adult volunteers	Yes	No
11. closer interaction/cooperation with schools or representatives from other community agencies	Yes	No
12. a need for increased security measures	Yes	No
13. reallocation of staff to cover after school hours	Yes	No

PART II: PERSONNEL TRAINING AND EXPERIENCE REGARDING LATCHKEY/UNATTENDED CHILDREN

PLEASE CIRCLE "YES" OR "NO" FOR EACH STATEMENT BELOW

I gained an understanding of service to latchkey/unattended children:

14. from library school courses	Yes	No
15. from in-service activities offered at the library system in which I work(ed)	Yes	No
16. at a national or divisional ALA conference	Yes	No
17. at a state library association conference	Yes	No
18. at a local or regional library workshop or conference	Yes	No
19. at an international library conference	Yes	No
20. via reading books or articles in library literature	Yes	No
21. via on the job experience with latchkey children at the library	Yes	No
22. via communication with representatives from community agencies (schools, child care organizations, YWCA, etc.)	Yes	No
23. via reading the ALA Position Paper, "Latchkey Children" in the Public Library, published by ALSC and PLA of ALA	Yes	No

24. via communication (in writing, by telephone, or   Yes   No
    in person) with other librarians to pool ideas
    Other (PLEASE DESCRIBE): _____
    _____

25. The level of my knowledge of library service to latchkey/unattended children is:
    ❑ high ❑ good ❑ satisfactory ❑ inadequate ❑ don't know

26. The MOST VALUABLE METHOD in which I learned about latchkey/unattended children was _____

27. IDEALLY I would like to increase my knowledge/understanding of latchkey/unattended children by doing the following: _____
    _____
    _____

PART III: LIBRARY AND COMMUNITY RESPONSES TO LATCHKEY/UNATTENDED CHILDREN

28. Please describe any successful strategies (in terms of specific services, programs, activities, etc.) which "work" at your library in meeting the needs of latchkey/unattended children or their families:
    _____
    _____

29. Please describe any specific non-library-sponsored activities, services or programs in your community which address the needs of latchkey/unattended children: _____
    _____
    _____

30. Please state the most important positive words of advice you would give to a library which has a substantial number of latchkey/unattended children: _____
    _____
    _____

31. Please describe specifically what, IDEALLY, (BUDGET PERMITTING) public libraries should "do" for latchkey/unattended children:

_____

_____

32. Please describe specifically any cooperative activities with other agencies/institutions in the community which you are involved in on behalf of latchkey/unattended children: _____

_____

_____

FOR EACH TYPE OF PROGRAM OR SERVICE DESCRIBED BELOW, PLEASE CIRCLE "YES" OR "NO" AS TO WHETHER YOUR LIBRARY DOES OR DOES NOT PROVIDE IT TO ADDRESS THE NEEDS OF LATCHKEY/UNATTENDED CHILDREN

33. Self-help survival skills workshops presented by community agencies on first aid, safety, no-cook meals, etc.   Yes   No

34. Information and referral services for parents regarding available licensed child care in the area   Yes   No

35. Database or resource file listing activities for children after school   Yes   No

36. Drop-in activity programs such as arts and crafts projects, films, etc.   Yes   No

37. Volunteer opportunities for children after school at the library   Yes   No

38. "Warm-line" telephone services for children to ask self-care questions   Yes   No

39. Storyhours, clubs or other traditional library programs specifically scheduled at times to meet the needs of latchkey/unattended children   Yes   No

40. Tutoring sessions to assist children with homework or reading assignments   Yes   No

Do you give your permission for the author of this questionnaire to publicize the information you provided by identifying the name of your library system? ❑ yes ❑ no

If "Yes," please sign your name and date below.

Name _____ Date _____

Dr. Frances Dowd
School of Library and Information Studies
Texas Woman's University
P.O. Box 22905
Denton, Texas 76204
(817) 898-2615

THANK YOU FOR YOUR TIME AND COOPERATION!

Appendix C
Annotated Bibliography

This Appendix contains an annotated bibliography of print and nonprint fiction and factual materials for youth about latchkey children.

AUDIOVISUAL MATERIALS

Videos

Alone at Home. 1983. (also in 16mm film). (17 minutes). Alfred Higgins Productions, Inc., 9100 Sunset Blvd., Los Angeles, California 90069, (213) 272-6500.
Told from a child's perspective, this upbeat presentation focuses on types of information needed by older elementary school youth to stay alone while parents work, run an errand, or go out for an evening: coping with fear and boredom, key safety, establishing rules, answering the door and phone, blackouts, first aid, etc. Concludes with a review of main points.

Bright Ideas: Latchkey Kids. n.d. (30 minutes). Myra Lenberg, Cooperative Extension, Skinner Hall, University of Massachusetts, Amherst, Massachusetts 01003, (413) 545-2391.
This television broadcast uses several video inserts to elaborate on points made during the studio discussion. Topics include: benefits and potential problems of self-care, assessing children's readiness for self-care, ways to monitor how well the situation is working, etc. Several children discuss their self-care experiences.

Emergency: Keep Your Cool. 1987. (2nd edition). (14 minutes). Film Fair Communications, Dept L89, 10621 Magnolia Blvd., North Hollywood, California 91601, (818) 985-0244.
Discusses using the telephone to summon help in emergencies.

For Safety's Sake. 1986. (40 minutes). Color. (LCA). Learning Corporation of America, 1350 Avenue of the Americas, New York, New York 10019.
In Part One characters, as Mrs. Friendly and Jack and Jill, demonstrate accident prevention and emergency preparedness in regard to strangers, fires, etc. Part Two contains information on kitchen safety and preparing meals. Noteworthy for its

inclusion of first aid, and the suggestion that children enroll in a Red Cross course and obtain CPR experience. Stars Gary Coleman.

Home Alone: A Kid's Guide to Playing It Safe When You're on Your Own. 1987. (30 minutes). Color. Hi-Tops Video, 2730 Wilshire Blvd., 5th floor, Los Angeles, California 90403.

Involves Malcolm-Jamal Warner and his friends in staged but realistic situations designed to model basic skills in answering the phone and door, avoiding an emergency, and making constructive use of time. Unique in that it shows the incorrect way of handling the situation, then demonstrates the correct way, reviews the points made, and finally asks viewers what they would do.

Home Alone: You're in Charge. 1986. (also in 16mm film). (19 minutes). Color. Barn Productions, P.O. Box 5667, Pasadena, California 91107.

Animated friends, such as talking telephone and sink, teach Tracy, a latchkey child, how to handle a variety of situations she encounters.

Latchkey Kids: Give'em a Break. n.d. (9 minutes). Community Service for Children, 431 East Locust Street, Bethlehem, Pennsylvania 18018, (215) 691-1819.

Lara Jill Miller of NBC's "Give Me a Break" describes guidelines school-age child care programs should follow to meet the developmental needs of children ages 5 to 13. She also suggests activities with parent involvement.

Latchkey Series: Four Part Video. 1985. San Antonio Cares Resource Center, 1411 North Main, San Antonio, Texas 78212, (512) 271-3902.

1. *Playing by the Book.* (8 minutes).
   Covers home safety, coping with emergencies and "house rules."

2. *Who Makes the Rules?* (7 minutes).
   Explores feelings of students about staying home alone or caring for siblings and suggests ways to cope with family conflicts.

3. *Help Is Just a Phone Call Away.* (9 minutes).
   Encourages students to differentiate between emergency and non-emergency situations. Emphasizes staying calm and knowing how to use the telephone for help.

4. *When You're the Boss.* (8 minutes).
   Explores some problems in caring for younger children and suggests ways to make the experience safer and more enjoyable.

Nutrition on the Run. 1988. (48 minutes). Sunburst Communications, Room Q 7575, 39 Washington Avenue, Pleasantville, New York 10570.

Especially helpful for home-alone kids who prepare their own snacks. Encourages teens to question the nutritional quality of the foods they eat and buy.

Take Charge! 1988. (20 minutes). Color. Community Service. Attention Connie Wingfield, Baltimore Gas and Electric Company, P.O. Box 1475, Baltimore, Maryland 21203, (301) 234-6313.

As viewers follow two latchkey narrators—a black girl and white boy—around Baltimore, situations, (such as lights going out and losing the housekey) are presented in a "What would you do?" question and answer format. Then the video depicts how to best handle each episode. A special feature is the inclusion of telephone numbers of services available in the Baltimore area which provide options to self-care.

16mm Films

Better Safe Than Sorry. 1987. (17 minutes). Film Fair Communications, Dept. L89, 10621 Magnolia Blvd., North Hollywood, California 91601, (818) 985-0244.
Dramatized vignettes of potentially dangerous circumstances, such as encountering a stranger at the door, are followed by common-sense rules for personal safety to match age levels.

In Charge at Home. 1986. (also available in video; in Spanish; and in captioned version). (21 minutes). Color. Film Fair Communications, Dept. L89, 10621 Magnolia Blvd., North Hollywood, California 91601, (818) 985-0244.
Creates positive feelings for viewers by depicting how four multi-ethnic latchkey children, representing a variety of family lifestyles, deal with realistic problems and develop responsibility when they are home alone. Vignettes include handling the key; having a contact person rather than a parent; emergency first aid; chores; homework; answering the telephone and door; fixing snacks; coping with fire, plumbing, and electrical emergencies; and use of leisure time.

Kids After School. n.d. (30 minutes). Volusia County Extension Home Economists, University of Florida, 3100 East State Road 44, DeLand, Florida 32724, (904) 736-0624.
Six lessons demonstrate self-care skills for third graders, including washing dishes, making beds, clothing repair, safe practices, nutritious snacks, and using the microwave.

Lord of the Locks. 1985. (also available on videotape). (30 minutes). Produced by Kansas Committee for the Prevention of Child Abuse. Distributed by KCPCA, 112 West 6th Street, #305, Topeka, Kansas 66603, (913) 354-7738.
Highlights the seriousness of self-care and the need for responsible actions, both by parent and child, via two magical characters, Lord of the Locks and his friend, Ariel. The humorous storyline illustrates possible dangers and responses.

Mickey's Safety Club: What to Do at Home. 1989. 16mm film. Coronet/MTI Film and Video, 108 Wilmot Road, Deerfield, Illinois 60015-5196.
Humorously illustrates how young latchkey children can be safe at home.

Taking Responsibility: On Your Own at Home. 1986. (also in video). (12 minutes). Color. Coronet Film and Video. Dept. L 89, 108 Wilmot Road, Deerfield, Illinois 60015, (312) 940-1260.
In an animated fairy tale setting a princess in her castle copes with dragons at the door, scullery fires, and other dangers, using the same problem-solving skills adults use when home alone.

What Ever Happened to Childhood? n.d. (45 minutes). Churchill Films, 662 North Robertson Blvd., Los Angeles, California 90060.
Portrays the rush children are in to grow up, as well as home-alone children and their problems. Interviews older home-alone kids responsible for younger siblings while parents work.

Filmstrips

Home Alone: Prepared for Today. 1986. (3 filmstrips with 3 cassettes, each 10 minutes). Boy Scouts of America, Audiovisual Service, 1325 Walnut Hill Lane, P.O. Box 152079, Irving, Texas 75015-2079.
(Includes *Home Alone, Fix a Meal and Care for Younger Children,* and *Home Safety and Know Your Neighborhood.*) All deal with being alone at home until parents arrive from work. In *Home Alone* a girl discusses entering her home alone, chores, and phone rules. *Home Safety* deals with fixing your own snack and leaving the house. *Fix a Meal* shows how an older child entertains and feeds a younger sibling.

Latchkey Series. 1985. (4 filmstrips with 4 cassettes, each 10–13 minutes). Color. Marshfilm.
In this series child narrators explain and demonstrate the problems, concerns, and feelings of children in self-care.

BOOKS FOR CHILDREN

Fiction Titles

Bunting, Eve. *Is Anybody There?* 1988. Lippincott. Grades 4–6.
Although Michael, a 13-year-old latchkey youth, is independent, just before Christmas he has the creepy sensation someone is watching him. A high interest/low reading level novel.

Carris, Joan. *When the Boys Ran the House.* 1982. Lippincott. Grades 3–4.
When their father is out of town and their mother becomes ill, four brothers manage the household by themselves.

Clark, Margaret Goff. *The Latchkey Mystery.* 1985. Dodd. Grades 3–4.
Minda and her friends begin a neighborhood watch when a series of robberies frighten everyone in their suburban Florida community.

Cleary, Beverly. *Ramona Forever.* 1984. Morrow. Grades 2–4.
Ramona, now in third grade, convinces her parents that she and her sister Beezus no longer need a sitter after school, and the two work together—sometimes smoothly, sometimes not—at getting along on their own.

Clifton, Lucille. *My Brother Fine with Me.* 1975. Holt, Rinehart, and Winston. Grades K–2.

In the summer, Johnette, an 8-year-old black girl, watches her 5-year-old brother, Baggy, while both their parents work, in this story about sibling rivalry and dependence.

Delton, Judy. *Angel in Charge.* 1988. Houghton Mifflin. Grades 3–5.

Ten-year-old Angel learns to care for herself and her 4-year-old brother, Rags, when their inept and accident-prone babysitter is hospitalized and their mother is in Canada.

Gerson, Corine. *How I Put My Mother Through College.* 1981. Atheneum. Grades 3–5.

After their newly divorced mother decides to go to college, Jessica and her brother Ben take on the management of their household.

Haas, Dorothy. *Tink in a Tangle.* 1984. Albert Whitman. Grades 3–4.

Tink's attempt to run a beauty shop, (as her single-parent mother does), provides the background for just one of the humorous incidents she gets into in this story about a girl forced to entertain herself while her mother works.

Hamilton, Virginia. *Sweet Whispers, Brother Rush.* 1982. Philomel/Putnam. Grades 6–9.

Through the ghost of her dead uncle, Tree works out the frustration she feels about her mother's long absences and having to care for her retarded brother. A good example of complete responsibility for a sibling and the problems it may cause.

Kibbe, Pat. *My Mother, The Mayor, Maybe.* 1981. Knopf. Grades 3–5.

When Dorothy Pinkerton agrees to run for mayor of Cranberry Falls, her children, especially 10-year-old B.J., do all they can to help her win.

Knox-Wagner, Elaine. *An Apartment's No Place for a Kid.* Albert Whitman. 1985. Grades 2–3.

When her divorced mother gets a job transfer, Kelley must adjust to being a latchkey child in an apartment in the city.

Koningsburg, E.L. *Up from Jericho Tel.* 1986. Atheneum. Grades 4–6.

Jeanmarie Troxell and Malcolm Soo are both bossy latchkey children who want to be famous. Tallulah, the aged actress they meet, tells them what it takes to make a star and sends them among a group of colorful street performers to search for a missing necklace.

Love, Sandra. *But What About Me?* 1976. Harcourt, Brace Jovanovitch. Grades 3–7.

Lucy, upset when her mother returns to work, falls into a series of misadventures that get her into trouble, including a fire accidentally started in a closet.

Moore, Emily. *Just My Luck.* 1983. Dutton. Grades 3–5.

Ten-year-old Olivia, whose mother and father both work and whose best friend moved away, meets a funny-looking boy who joins in her obsessive quest for a dog.

Schnick, Eleanor. *Home Alone.* 1980. Dial. Grades 1–3.

In this beginning reader, Andy gradually learns to deal with his loneliness and fears in the time between the end of school and his mother's return from work. He does exactly as he is instructed—locking up behind himself, calling his mom, and performing the duties described in the note she left.

Shreve, Susan. *How I Saved the World on Purpose.* 1985. Holt, Rinehart, and Winston. Grades 2–4.

Altruistic 9-year-old Miranda, the protagonist, has two older brothers to care for her when her mother decides to go back to work, making her a latchkey child. (Her father is a lawyer.) After meeting a young boy, Joey, who stays home alone, she starts a club for latchkey children, and with her father's help arranges publicity and rents space for a program.

Stanek, Muriel. *All Alone After School.* 1984. Albert Whitman. Grades 1–3.

When his mother goes to work but can't afford a babysitter, Josh shows resourcefulness and independence and slowly develops confidence about being on his own after school in an empty apartment. His mother prepares him to stay alone—instructing him about safety, dialing 911 in an emergency, etc. He goes directly home after school, unlocks the door, locks it again, calls his mother to tell her he's home, does his homework, sets the table, and plays with games.

Terris, Susan. *The Latchkey Kids.* 1986. Farrar, Straus and Grioux. Grades 4–6.

Due to their father's depression and their mother's new full-time job, Callie and her younger brother, Rex, become latchkey children and have a difficult time adjusting.

Nonfiction Titles

Chaback, Elaine. *Official Kids Survival Kit: How to Do Things on Your Own.* 1981. Little, Brown. Grades 3–7.

A handbook of practical advice on accidents and emergencies that happen everyday when children are home alone, and how they can be handled.

Hautzig, Esther. *Life with Working Parents.* 1976. Macmillian. Grades 4–7.

Reassuringly presents sensible directions about work priorities, safety measures, homework suggestions, use of household appliances, meal preparations, pet care, money, babysitting siblings, and things to do for fun. Includes recipes and craft instructions.

Kyte, Kathy. *In Charge: A Complete Handbook for Kids with Working Parents.* 1983. Knopf. Grades 6–9.

Chapters deal with coping with stress, caring for clothes, cleaning, cooking, coping with fire and plumbing emergencies, and organizing the latchkey experience.

Leiner, Katherine. *Both My Parents Work.* 1986. Watts. Grades 1–6.

Narrators between the ages of 5 and 14 describe their lives as children of working parents.

Monroe, Judy. *Latchkey Children.* (The Facts About Series). Crestwood House. 1989. Grades 3–5.

Discusses various aspects of the lives of latchkey children, such as why they must come home to an empty house, how they interact with brothers and sisters, how they can use the telephone to find help in emergency situations, and how they spend their time.

Swan, Helen. *Alone After School*. 1985. Prentice-Hall. Grades 4–10.
Comprehensive source dealing with parental guilt, emotional health, physical safety, first aid, cooking, and siblings.

Appendix D
Latchkey Organizations and Agencies

AgeLink Connection, Center for Improving Mountain Living, Western Carolina University, Cullowhee, North Carolina 28723, (704) 227-7492.
Connects in various ways older adult caregivers with children needing after-school care: in homes, by telephone, and through after-school activities.

American Association of University Women, State College Branch, P.O. Box 735, State College, Pennsylvania 16801, (913) 677-5555.
Sponsors PhoneFriend, an after-school telephone help line for children at home without adult supervision.

American Child Care Foundation, Inc., Roberta L. Newman, President, 7927 Jones Branch Drive, Suite 600 South, McLean, Virginia 22102, (703) 758-3583.
A nonprofit organization dedicated to promoting the development of a broad range of quality child care services.

American Home Economics Association (AHEA), 1555 King Street, Alexandria, Virginia, 22314. (800) 252-SAFE.
Together with the Whirlpool Foundation, sponsors Project Home Safe, a national education and advocacy program on behalf of latchkey children and their families.

American Library Association (ALA), 50 East Huron Street, Chicago, Illinois 60611, 1-800-545-2433.
Publishes the "position paper" *"Latchkey Children" in the Public Library.*

Boy Scouts of America, National Office, 1325 Walnut Hill Lane, P.O. Box 152079, Irving, Texas 75015-2079, (214) 580-2000.
Offers "Prepared for Today," a self-help survival skills booklet (available in several languages including Hmong, Cambodian, Vietnamese and Laotian) designed to help 6- to 12-year-olds cope with being at home alone, and which covers safety rules, emergencies, meals, and problem solving.

Camp Fire Boys and Girls, 4601 Madison Avenue, Kansas City, Missouri 64112, (816) 756-1950.
Offers "I Can Do It," a self-reliance program for latchkey children in second through fourth grades, through local Camp Fire Councils.

Center for Advanced Study in Education (CASE), The City University of New York (CUNY) Graduate Center, 33 West 42nd Street, New York, New York 10036, (212) 719-9066.

Sponsors the Early Adolescent Helper Program. Also has available 2 videotapes, "Helping Hands" and "Youth Meets Experience," brochures, and guides which explain the program. One guide is called "Latchkey Helpers: A Guide for Program Leaders."

Center for Early Adolescence, University of North Carolina at Chapel Hill, Suite 211, Carr Mill Mall, Carrboro, North Carolina 27510, (919) 966-1148.

As part of the Department of Maternal and Child Health at the University of North Carolina at Chapel Hill, the Center disseminates information, such as resource lists and bibliographies, that deal with school-age and early adolescent children.

Family Day Care Check-In Project, Fairfax County Office for Children, 10396 Democracy Lane, Fairfax, Virginia 22030, (703) 218-3800.

Provides a comprehensive package of materials for agencies and organizations interested in adapting the Family Day Care Check-In Project in their communities.

Girl Scouts of the United States of America, 830 Third Avenue, New York, New York 10022, (212) 940-7500.

Offers "Safe and Sound at Home Alone," an activity booklet for children 6–12 who spend a period of time at home alone or with younger siblings. The booklet covers home safety, first aid, decision making, health foods, and games.

Houston Independent School District, 3830 Richmond Avenue, Houston, Texas 77027.

The Lighted Schoolhouse is offered at Gregory-Lincoln School, (713) 521-0935. Sharon Burney is the coordinator.

Houston United Way Neighborhood Centers, Inc., 3410 Fannin Street, Houston, Texas 77004. (713) 236-8377.

Sponsors Chatters (Children Home Alone Telephone Reassurance Service), a warm line children can call.

Independence, Missouri School District, 1231 Windsor Street, Independence, Missouri 64055, (816) 833-3433.

Dr. Robert Henley, Superintendent of Schools, offers the School of the 21st Century, a concept developed by Dr. Edward Zigler.

Kansas Child Abuse Prevention Council, 715 West 10th Street, Topeka, Kansas 66612. (913) 354-7738.

Offers "I'm in Charge," a family-based self-care education course for upper elementary school students and their parents.

Lone Star Council of Camp Fire, 4209 McKinney Avenue, Suite 100, Dallas, Texas 75205, (214) 521-CAMP.

Sponsors KIDTALK, a telephone reassurance line for latchkey youth.

Metropolitian Cooperative Library System, 2235 North Lake Avenue, Suite 106, Altadena, California 91001, (818) 798-1146. ATTN: Gini Bennetsen.

Offers a National Clearinghouse on Library Latchkey Children. Representative samples of policies and procedures from cities throughout the country regarding latchkey children in public libraries are available.

Murfreesboro City School System, 400 North Maple Street, P.O. Box 279, Murfreesboro, Tennessee 37133-0279, (615) 893-2313.

Has available a videotape entitled, "Success Is Spelled E.S.P.," which describes their before and after school program which involves Middle Tennessee State University students in tutoring latchkey youth.

National Association of Elementary School Principals, 1615 Duke Street, Alexandria, Virginia 22314-3483, (703) 684-3345.

In 1988 almost 1,200 principals of grades K–8 who were members of this international professional education association completed the survey regarding the need for "before- and after-school child care" included in the NAESP publication, *The Communicator*. (Highlights are presented in Chapter 3 of this book).

National PTA, 700 North Rush Street, Chicago, Illinois 60611, (312) 787-0799.

Professional organization for parents, teachers, and others concerned with bridging the gap between home and school for the welfare of youth.

North Carolina State University, Agricultural Extension Service, P.O. Box 7605, Ricks Hall Annex, Raleigh, North Carolina, 27695-7605, (919) 737-2770.

Designed the following educational materials: *Self-Care Skills for School Kids*, a guide to help parents assess their child's readiness for self-care; *When I'm in Charge*, a 4-H parent-child home project guide that uses puzzles, stories, and games to convey self-care concepts and skills; and *4-H Cares*, a guide to expanding 4-H Club work to school-age child care settings, such as extended school programs, family day care and community agency programs.

School-Age Child Care Project, Center for Research on Women, Wellesley College, 828 Washington Street, Wellesley, Massachusetts 02181, (617) 431-1453.

This national information and technical assistance resource center, which started in 1979, is committed to promoting the development of programs and services for children between the ages of 5 and 12, before and after school.

Sugar Mill Elementary School, 1101 Charles Street, Port Orange, Florida 32119, (914) 756-0491.

Implemented an extended day Theatre Arts Program as part of a demonstration drug and alcohol abuse grant activity for high risk youth.

United States National Commission on Libraries and Information Services, 1111 18th Street, N.W., Suite 310, Washington, D.C. 20036, (202) 254-3100. Dr. Peter Young, Executive Director

Works with ACTION regarding Intergenerational Library Assistance Project RSVP grants which address unattended children in public libraries.

Uptown Center Hull House, 4520 North Beacon, Chicago, Illinois 60640, (312) 561-3500.

Operates "Grandma, Please," a telephone reassurance line staffed by senior volunteers.

YMCA of Hamilton/Burlington, 500 Drury Lane, Burlington, Ontario, Canada L7R 2X2, (416) 632-5000.

Offers an after-school program called C.A.R.E. (Children's Afterschool Recreational Enrichment) geared to 10 to 12 year olds and their parents.

Appendix E
Names, Addresses, and Telephone Numbers of Public Libraries in Case Studies

Atlanta-Fulton Public Library
One Margaret Mitchell Square, N.W.
Atlanta, Georgia 30303-1089
(404) 730-1700

Baltimore County Public Library
320 York Road
Towson, Maryland 21204-5179
(301) 887-6100

Charles County Public Library
Charles and Garrett Streets
P.O. Box 490
La Platta, Maryland 20646
(301) 934-9001

Cleveland Heights-University Heights Public Library
2345 Lee Road
Cleveland Heights, Ohio 44118-3993
(216) 932-3600

Cleveland Public Library
325 Superior Avenue
Cleveland, Ohio 44114-1271
(216) 623-2800

County of Los Angeles Public Library
7400 East Imperial Highway
P.O. Box 7011
Downey, California 90241-7011
(213) 940-8462

Crawford Public Library
Second Street
Crawford, Nebraska 69339
(308) 665-1780

Dekalb County Public Library
1300 Commerce Drive
5th Floor
Decatur, Georgia 30030
(404) 371-3045

Durham County Library
Stanford L. Warren Branch
1201 Fayetteville Street
Durham, North Carolina 27707
(919) 560-0270

Fort Erie Public Library
136 Gilmore Road
Fort Erie, Ontario, Canada L2A 2M1
(416) 871-2546

Free Library of Philadelphia
Logan Square
Philadelphia, Pennsylvania 19103-1157
(215) 686-5322

Geauga County Public Library
Geauga West Library
13455 Chillicothe Road
Chesterland, Ohio 44026
(216) 729-4250

Greenville County Library
300 College Street
Greenville, South Carolina 29601
(803) 242-5000

Havre-Hill County Library
402 Third Street
Havre, Montana 59501
(406) 265-2123

Huntsville-Madison County Public Library
915 Monroe
P.O. Box 443
Huntsville, Alabama 35804-0443
(205) 532-5940

Long Beach Public Library and Information Center
101 Pacific Avenue
Long Beach, California 90802
(213) 437-2949

Los Angeles Public Library
630 West Fifth Street
Los Angeles, California 90071-2097
(213) 612-3200

Montclair Free Public Library
50 South Fullerton Avenue
Montclair, New Jersey 07042
(201) 744-0500

Muskegon County Library
Norton Shores Branch
705 Seminole
Muskegon, Michigan 49441-4797
(616) 780-2322

Omaha Public Library
Charles E. Washington Branch
29th and Ames Avenue
Omaha, Nebraska 68111
(402) 444-4849

Prince George's County Memorial Library
Hillcrest Heights Branch Library
2398 Iverson Street
Temple Hills, Maryland 20748
(301) 630-4900

Rolling Meadows Library
3110 Martin Lane
Rolling Meadows, Illinois 60008-2698
(708) 259-6050

Sacramento Public Library
Martin Luther King Regional Library
7340 24th Street Bypass
Sacramento, California 95822
(916) 421-3151

St. Joseph County Public Library
122 West Wayne Street
South Bend, Indiana 46601
(219) 282-4646

Salt Lake County Library
South Jordan Library
10300 Beckstead Lane
South Jordan, Utah 84065-8801
(801) 943-4636

San Marino Public Library
1890 Huntington Drive
San Marino, California 91108
(818) 282-8484

Santa Clara County Free Library
1095 North Seventh Street

San Jose, California 95112-4434
(408) 293-2326

Seattle Public Library
1000 Fourth Avenue
Seattle, Washington 98104
(206) 386-4100

Volusia County Public Library
City Island
Daytona Beach, Florida 32014-4484
(904) 252-8374

Washington, D.C. Public Library
901 G Street, N.W.
Washington, D.C. 20001
(202) 727-1101

Weber County Library
2464 Jefferson Avenue
Ogden, Utah 84401-1248
(801) 627-6913

Index

Compiled by Estella Bradley

A+ after-school program in Hawaii, 35
Accidents among latchkey children, 16
Act for Better Child Care Services, 8
ACTION, 105, 106, 107
Adventure Addison, 47–48
Advertising directed toward latchkey children, 18
After-school child care programs
  examples of, 33–41
  NAESP survey on, 32–33
  sponsors of, 32
  types of, 31
Age-segregated housing, 8
AgeLink, 41
Agencies involved with latchkey children, list of, 198–200
Agencies providing school-age child care, 31
Ages of latchkey children, 4, 6–7
Aizawa, Herman, 35
Alcohol abuse, educating youth about dangers of, 38
Alcohol use by latchkey children, 15
Alternative terms for latchkey children, 4
American Association of School Administrators, 4
American Child Care Foundation, Inc., 63
American Home Economics Association (AHEA), 55, 105, 108

American Library Association (ALA), 77, 105, 111
American Red Cross course on Basic First Aid Training, 47
Annotated bibliography for youth about latchkey children
  books for children, 194–97
  films, 193–94
  filmstrips, 194
  videos, 191–93
Apartment sites, child care programs at, 40
Army posts, provision of school-age child care, 31
Atlanta-Fulton Public Library (Georgia), 127
Austin, Texas, EARTHNAUTS program, 35–36

Baltimore County Public Library (Maryland), 132–33
Barnett, Sally, 116, 166
Beams, Lynda, 15
"Being In Charge" self-care training course, 44
Beneficial impact of the latchkey experience, 18–19
Bibliography for youth about latchkey children
  books for children, 194–97
  films, 193–94

bibliography for youth about latchkey children *(continued)*
    filmstrips, 194
    videos, 191–93
Block parents, 54
Bookmobile service for latchkey children, 124
Books for youth about latchkey children, annotated list of, 194–97
Boston, availability and cost of care for school-age children, 8
Boy's Clubs of America, school-age child care provided by, 32
Boys and Girls Clubs C.A.R.E. programs in Ontario, 37
Buddy system for latchkey children, 43
Burney, Harry, III, 38

Cactus Club of Osborn School District in Phoenix, Arizona, 34
California Media and Library Educator's Association (CMLEA) Reading Interest Survey, 121
Camp Fire, Inc.
    school-age child care provided by, 32
    survival skills program developed by, 46
C.A.R.E. (Creative Afterschool Recreation and Enrichment) project, 37, 158–59
Case studies of library programs for latchkey children
    addresses and telephone numbers of libraries studied, 201–03
    Atlanta-Fulton Public Library (Georgia), 127
    Baltimore County Public Library (Maryland), 132–33
    Charles County Public Library (Maryland), 133–34
    Cleveland Heights-University Heights Public Library (Ohio), 141–42
    Cleveland Public Library (Ohio), 142
    County of Los Angeles Public Library (California), 116–17
    Crawford Public Library (Nebraska), 137
    DeKalb County Public Library (Georgia), 127–28
    Durham County Library (North Carolina), 140–41
    Fort Erie Public Library (Ontario, Canada), 158–59
    Free Library of Philadelphia (Pennsylvania), 145–49
    Geauga County Public Library System (Ohio), 142–45
    Greenville County Library (South Carolina), 149–50
    Harve-Hill County Library (Montana), 136–37
    Huntsville-Madison County Public Library (Alabama), 115–16
    Long Beach Public Library and Information Center (California), 117–18
    Los Angeles Public Library (California), 118–20
    Martin Luther King Regional Library (California), 120–23
    Missouri libraries, 134–36
    Montclair Free Public Library (New Jersey), 139–40
    Muskegon County Library (Michigan), 134
    Omaha Public Library (Nebraska), 138–39
    Rolling Meadows Library (Illinois), 128–30
    Sacramento Public Library (California), 120–23
    St. Joseph County Public Library (Indiana), 130–32
    Salt Lake County Library (Utah), 150–51
    San Marino Public Library (California), 123–24
    Santa Clara County Free Library (California), 124
    Seattle Public Library (Washington), 153–57
    Volusia County Public Library (Florida), 125–27
    Washington, D.C. Public Library, 124–25
    Weber County Library (Utah), 151–53
Census Bureau estimates of numbers of latchkey children, 6

Center for Improving Mountain Living (CIML) AgeLink program, 41
Charles County Public Library (Maryland), 133–34
Charlotte, North Carolina, number of latchkey children, 7
Child care, availability of, 8
Child care programs
  at apartment sites, 40
  employer-sponsored, 39–40
  examples of, 33–41
  at housing projects, 40
  intergenerational programs, 40–41
  NAESP survey on, 32–33
  self-care supportive programs. *See* Self-care supportive programs
  sponsors of, 32
  types of, 31
Child molestation risk to latchkey children, 17
Children Home Alone Telephone Reassurance Service (CHATTERS), 52
Children in self-care. *See* Latchkey children
Cigarette smoking by latchkey children, 15
Cleveland Heights-University Heights Public Library (Ohio), 141–42
Cleveland Public Library (Ohio), 142
Cody-Fuller, Carolyn, 150
Collins, Sandra, 168
Color Me Safe, 55
Combination adult care and self-care programs, 51–54
Communities, recommended strategies for, 63
Community characteristics, effect on adjustment of latchkey children, 20
Consequences of leaving children in self-care
  deleterious versus beneficial effects, 12
  difficulties in school, 17–18
  drug and alcohol use, 15
  effects on libraries, 22
  effects on parents and their work, 22
  emotional effects, 13–14
  health effects, 19
  safety risks, 16–17
  sexual activity, 15–16
  susceptibility to advertising, 18
  television viewing of inappropriate programs, 15
Corporation for Public Broadcasting booklet for latchkey children, 55
County of Los Angeles Public Library (California), 116–17
Cranston, Senator Alan, 117
Crawford Public Library (Nebraska), 137
Creative After School Recreation and Enrichment Pilot Projects, 37, 158–59
Crosby, Kathy, 164, 167, 168

Dallas, Texas
  number of latchkey children, 6–7
  YMCA school-age child care programs in, 36
Day care, availability of, 8
Definitions
  children in self-care, 3–4
  latchkey children, 3, 5
  library latchkey child, 77
DeKalb County Public Library (Georgia), 127–28
Department of Labor report on children in self-care, 6
Developmental readiness of children for self-care, 42
Developmentally Appropriate Practice in School-Age Child Care Programs, 57
Dodd, Senator, 8
Doorkey children, 4
"Dorks," 4
Drop-in programs, 134–36
Drug abuse, educating youth about dangers of, 38
Drug use by latchkey children, 15
Duckett, Gay Nell, 149
Durham County Library (North Carolina), 140–41

Early Adolescent Helper Program, 52–54
EARTHNAUTS after-school care, 35–36

Educational progress, effect of self-care on, 17–18
Elementary school principals, views on before- and after-school care, 32–33
Elementary schools, private, extended day care programs of, 32–33
Emergencies, ability of latchkey children to deal with, 17
Emotional effects of self-care on children, 13–14
Employees, effects of having latchkey children on, 22
Employer-sponsored child care, 39–40
Employers, recommended strategies for, 69–70
Extended School Program (ESP) in Murfreesboro, Tennessee, 33–34

Family Day Care Check-in Project in Fairfax, Virginia, 51
Fears experienced by children in self-care, 13–14
Federal government, recommended strategies for, 70–71
Fiction, Kart's evaluative criteria for, 114–15
Films for youth about latchkey children, annotated list of, 193–94
Filmstrips for youth about latchkey children, annotated list of, 194
Firearms, prevalence in homes of latchkey children, 16
Fires, risk among latchkey children, 16
First aid training for latchkey children, 47
Food companies, expenditure on advertising directed toward children, 18
Fort Erie Public Library (Ontario, Canada), 158–59
4-H Club, 138
Frazier, Louise, 109, 110
Free Library of Philadelphia (Pennsylvania), 145–49

GAB (Grandparents and Books), 118
G.A.S.P. (Great After School Program), 128–30
Geauga County Public Library System (Ohio), 142–45
Geographic mobility, 8
Girl's Clubs of America, extended day services of, 32
Government, recommended strategies for, 70–71
"Grandma, Please," 51
Grandparents and Books (GAB), 118
Greenville County Library (South Carolina), 149–50

Harve-Hill County Library (Montana), 136–37
Hawaii's A+ after-school program, 35
Health of latchkey children, 19
H.E.L.P. (Homework Enrichment Library Project), 156–57
Helpers Promoting Reading, 53
Hillcrest Heights Branch Library Home Safe program, 109–11
Historical background of the phenomenon of latchkey children, 4
Historical view of public library service to children, 80–82
Home economists, recommended strategies for, 68
Homelessness, 8
Homework Enrichment Library Project (H.E.L.P.), 156–57
Homework Help Centers, 127
Homework Help program, 151–53
Homework Helper Program, 139
Homework Hotline or Walk-In, 140–41
Homework libraries, 127–28
Housing projects, child care programs at, 40
Houston, number of latchkey children, 7
Houston Independent School District Lighted School House, 39
Huntsville-Madison County Public Library (Alabama), 115–16

I Can Do It program, 46
"I'm In Charge" self-care training course, 44
Illinois Department of Children and Family Services, 8

Institutions of higher education,
  recommended strategies for, 71
Intergenerational programs
  AgeLink, 41
  "Grandma, Please," 51
  RSVP Intergenerational Library
    Assistance Project, 106–08,
    136, 137, 138, 141
  Shared Heritage Intergenerational
    Child Care Program, 41
  types of, 40–41
Intramural program for latchkey
  children, 65–66

Jackson, Tennessee, parks and
  recreation program, 35

Kansas Committee for Prevention of
  Child Abuse, 44
Kart's evaluative criteria for fiction,
  114–15
Kart's evaluative criteria for nonfiction,
  115
KEY/H.E.L.P. Project, 156–57
Keys for Kids curriculum kit, 45
KIDLINE, 50
Kids-on-Kampus centers, 34–35
K.I.D.S. program, 46
Kids Smarts for Working Parents, 54–55
"Kids with Keys," 123
"Kids with Keys...Parents with
  Jobs...Who's in Charge?", 69
KIDTALK, 50
Kildee, Senator, 8

Latchkey children
  ages of, 4, 6–7
  alternative terms for, 4
  annotated bibliography for youth
    about, 191–97
  definition of, 3, 5
  effect of being. *See* Consequences of
    leaving children in self-care
  effects on parents and their work, 22
  factors contributing to prevalence of,
    7–8
  historical background of the
    phenomenon of, 4
  numbers of, 4–7
  organizations and agencies involved
    with, 198–200
  in public libraries. *See* Public
    libraries
  research on. *See* Research on
    latchkey children
  socioeconomic status of, 3
  strategies for dealing with. *See*
    Recommended strategies for
    dealing with latchkey children
*"Latchkey Children" in the Public
  Library,* 77, 78, 111–13
Latchkey intramural program, 65–66
Latchkey Kids Program, 149–50
Legislation
  Act for Better Child Care Services, 8
  recommendations for, 70–71
  Texas Senate Bill 914 on out-of-
    school care, 33
Levi, Selma, 165, 166, 167, 168
Levine, Michael, 43
Lewis, Ida, 110
Libraries. *See* Public libraries
Library latchkey child
  definition of, 77
  problems posed by. *See* Public
    libraries
Lighted School House program, 39
Literacy Volunteers of America, 139–40
LOCATE: Child Care Referral Service,
  132–33
Long Beach Public Library and
  Information Center (California),
  117–18
Long, Thomas, 6
Los Angeles Public Library (California),
  118–20
Loughran, Ellen, 165

Marketing directed toward latchkey
  children, 18
Markey, Penny, 116, 117
Martin Luther King Regional Library
  (California), 120–23
Metropolitan Cooperative Library
  System, 108
Metropolitan Life Study of American
  teachers, 6
Midwest study of adjustment of
  latchkey children, 20–21
Minneapolis area, number of latchkey
  children, 6

Missouri libraries, 134–36
Montclair Free Public Library (New Jersey), 139–40
Moore, Anne Carroll, 81
"Movies and More," 125
Murfreesboro's Extended School Program, 33–34
Muskegon County Library (Michigan), 134

National Association of Elementary School Principals (NAESP) survey on school-age child care, 32–33
National Association of Indepen-dent Schools, 32
National Clearinghouse on Library Latchkey Children, 105, 108
National Commission on Libraries and Information Science (NCLIS), 105, 106
National Committee for the Prevention of Child Abuse, 44
National Institute of Latchkey Children and Youth, 6
National Institute on Drug Abuse, 15
National Parent Teachers' Association (PTA)
   estimate of children in self-care, 6
   recommended strategies for local organizations, 63
   recommendations for parents of latchkey children, 69
National survey of latchkey children in public libraries
   findings of
      1988 survey, 86–93
      1990 survey, 97–102
   follow-up interviews with selected librarians
      1988 survey, 94–95
      1990 survey, 100
   methodology of
      1988 survey, 85
      1990 survey, 96
   questionnaire used
      1988 survey, 177–85
      1990 survey, 186–90
   reasons for conducting
      1988 survey, 84–85
      1990 survey, 95–96
   summary of
      1988 survey, 93–94
      1990 survey, 102–08
New York City, number of latchkey children, 7
Nonfiction, Kart's evaluative criteria for, 115
North Carolina study of school adjustment of latchkey children, 19, 20, 21
Numbers of latchkey children
   estimates of, 6–7
   problems in determining, 4–5

Ogilvie, Blythe, 166, 167, 169
O'Hagan, Deidre, 139
Omaha Public Library (Nebraska), 138–39
On Your Own training program for latchkey children, 45
Organizations, recommended strategies for, 62–63
Organizations assisting librarians in serving latchkey children
   ACTION, 105, 106–08
   American Home Economics Association (AHEA), 105, 108
   American Library Association, 105, 111–13
   National Clearinghouse on Library Latchkey Children, 105, 108
   National Commission on Libraries and Information Science (NCLIS), 105, 106–08
   Whirlpool Foundation, 105, 108
Organizations involved with latchkey children, list of, 198–200
Orr, Cynthia, 143
Osborn's Cactus Club, 34

Palmer School of Library and Information Science, 113
Parent Teachers' Association (PTA)
   estimate of children in self-care, 6
   recommendations for parents of latchkey children, 69
   recommended strategies for, 63
Parents
   effect of latchkey children on work performance, 22
   recommended strategies for, 69

Peer pressure
  susceptibility of latchkey children to, 21
  to try drugs and alcohol, 38
Pets as companions for latchkey children, 42–43
PhoneFriend, 14, 49
Physical education teachers, recommended strategies for, 65–66
Plummer, Mary Wright, 81
Police Partners survival training program for latchkey children, 46
Policies of libraries for dealing with latchkey children
  findings of survey of librarians, 88–89
  recommendations from survey of librarians, 166–67
  recommendations of the American Library Association, 112–13
  survey questions on, 180–82
Predictors of adjustment of latchkey children, 20
Prepared for Today program, 45
President's Citation for a Private Sector Initiative, 49
Preteen Project, 142
Prince George's County Memorial Library (Maryland), 108
Principals, views on before- and after-school care, 32
Private elementary schools, extended day care programs of, 32
Procedures concerning latchkey children
  findings of survey of librarians, 88–89
  recommendations from survey of librarians, 166–67
  survey questions on, 180–82
Programs for latchkey children
  case studies. *See* Case studies of library programs for latchkey children
  findings of survey of librarians, 89–90, 99–100
  recommendations from librarians participating in the 1988 survey, 164–66
  recommendations from librarians participating in the 1990 survey, 171–72
  survey questions on, 183–85
Programs for school-age child care
  examples of, 33–41
  NAESP survey on, 32–33
  sponsors of, 32
  types of, 31
Project Home Safe, 19, 55–57, 63, 105, 108–11
Project LEAP: Learn, Enjoy, and Play at the Library, 145–49
PTA Communicator, 15
PTAs. *See* Parent Teachers' Association (PTA)
Public libraries
  categories of use by unattended children, 77
  challenge posed by latchkey children, 87–88
  effects of latchkey children on, 22–23
  estimates of latchkey children in, 86
  factors aggravating the latchkey situation, 87
  history of philosophy of service to children, 80–82
  impact of latchkey children in, 86, 97–98
  interactions with community agencies, 90–91, 101–02
  national survey of latchkey children in. *See* National survey of latchkey children in public libraries
  personnel training and experience regarding latchkey children, 98–99
  policies and procedures for latchkey children, 88–89
  problems posed by latchkey children, 78–79
  programs and services for latchkey children, 89–90, 99–100
  reasons for use by latchkey children, 86–87
  recommendations of librarians for community programs and services for latchkey children, 71–72

Public libraries *(continued)*
  response to latchkey children. *See* Case studies of library programs for latchkey children
  role in regard to latchkey children, 91
  success in serving latchkey children, 91–92, 100–01
Publications for latchkey children and their working parents, 54–55

Quality Criteria for School-Age Child Care Programs, 57
Questionnaires used in survey of latchkey children in public libraries
  copies of, 178–90
  preparation of, 85

Raymond, Joan, 39
"The Reading Connection," 121–23
Recommendations for future library service to latchkey children
  from librarians participating in the 1988 survey, 164–69
  from librarians participating in the 1990 survey, 169–72
  from the author, 172–74
  general guidelines, 163
Recommendations from public librarians for services for latchkey children, 71–72
Recommended strategies for dealing with latchkey children
  for communities, 63
  for employers, 69–70
  for home economists, 68
  for institutions of higher education, 71
  for organizations, 62–63
  for parents, 69
  for researchers, 62
  for school administrators, 64–65
  for school counselors, 67–68
  for school librarians, 67
  for school physical education teachers and recreation leaders, 65–66
  for state and federal government, 70–71
  for teachers, 66–67

Recreation leaders, recommended strategies for, 65–66
Research on latchkey children
  based on surveys of librarians. *See* National survey of latchkey children in public libraries
  content analysis of materials directed toward the latchkey child, 113–15
  limitations of existing studies, 12–13
  recommendations for future studies, 23–24
  recommended strategies for, 62
  studies indicating a beneficial impact of the latchkey experience, 18–19
  studies indicating a detrimental effect of the latchkey experience, 13–18
  studies indicating no impact of the latchkey experience, 19
Reston Children's Center Family Satellite Program, 51
Retired Senior Volunteer Program (RSVP). *See* RSVP
Rodman, Hyman, 57
Rolling Meadows Library (Illinois), 128–30
Rossnagel, Elizabeth, 158
RSVP (Retired Senior Volunteer Program)
  Intergenerational Library Assistance Project, 106–08
  participation in after-school program, 137
Rural New York State, study of latchkey children in, 20
Ruskind, Mary, 139

Sacramento County Kids-on-Kampus centers, 34–35
Sacramento Public Library (California), 120–23
Safe at Home program, 45
Safety risks of latchkey children, 16–17
St. Joseph County Public Library (Indiana), 130–32
Salt Lake County Library (Utah), 150–51
Salvadore, Maria, 125

San Marino Public Library (California), 123–24
Santa Clara County Free Library (California), 124
Sava, Samuel, 33
Schnick, Christine, 165, 166, 167, 168
School
 adjustment of latchkey children to, 19, 20
 effect of self-care on children's success in, 17–18
School administrators, recommended strategies for, 64–65
School-age child care programs
 examples of, 33–41
 NAESP survey on, 32–33
 sponsors of, 32
 types of, 31
School counselors, recommended strategies for, 67–68
School librarians, recommended strategies for, 67
School of the 21st Century, 38
Seattle Public Library (Washington), 153–57
Sedney, Frances, 167, 168
Self-care supportive programs
 buddy system, 43
 determining developmental readiness for self-care, 42
 survival skills training, 43–47
 telephone hotlines, 48–51
 use of pets as companions, 42–43
Senior volunteers. *See* Intergenerational programs
Services for latchkey children
 case studies. *See* Case studies of library programs for latchkey children
 findings of survey of librarians, 89–90, 99–100
 recommendations from librarians participating in the 1988 survey, 164–66
 recommendations from librarians participating in the 1990 survey, 171–72
 survey questions on, 183–185
Sexual activity of latchkey children, 15–16

Shared Heritage Intergenerational Child Care Program in Iowa, 41
Single-parent families, 7–8
Smoking by latchkey children, 15
Socioeconomic status of latchkey children, 3
S.P.L.A.S.H. (Seattle Public Library's After School Happenings), 153–56
Sprint, 14
State and federal government, recommended strategies for, 70–71
Stefansson, Jody, 123
Sugar Mill's Theatre Arts Program for children at risk, 37
Survey of latchkey children in public libraries. *See* National survey of latchkey children in public libraries
Survival skills training for latchkey children, 43–47

Teachers, recommended strategies for, 66–67
Teen Scene Club, 133
Telephone hotlines and warmlines
 description of, 48–49
 examples of, 49–51
 recommendation for a national children's hotline center, 71
Telephone plus counselor programs, 52
Television
 advertising directed toward latchkey children, 18
 viewing of inappropriate programs by latchkey children, 15
Texas Association for School-Age Care (TASAC), 63
Texas Senate Bill 914 on out-of-school care, 33
"Three O'Clock Club," 125–26
T.I.M.E. (Teen Issues Made Easy), 141
Tobie Grant Homework Library, 128
Training for providers of school-age child care, recommendation for, 71
Training of librarians to deal with latchkey children, findings of survey of librarians, 98–99

Training programs for latchkey children, 43–47
Tucson Association for Child Care (TACC), 50

U.S. Army policy on school-age child care, 31
U.S. Department of Health and Human Services Office of Substance Abuse and Prevention, 38
University of Arizona study of medical risk to latchkey children, 19
University of Chicago study of day care, 8
University students, participation in after-school programs, 34

Videos for youth about latchkey children, annotated list of, 191–93
Volusia County Public Library (Florida), 125–27

Washington, D.C. Public Library, 124–25
Weaver, Rocky, 165
Weber County Library (Utah), 151–53

Wellesley College center for Research on Women, 71
What If I'm Home Alone?, 55
Whirlpool Corporation latchkey-oriented educational guides, 55
Whirlpool Foundation, 56, 105, 108
Wisconsin study of susceptibility of latchkey children to peer pressure, 21
Women in the workforce, 7, 8
Working mothers, number of, 7, 8
Wronka, Gretchen, 164, 168

YMCA, school-age child care programs offered by, 32, 36, 37
Yolo County Kids-on-Kampus centers, 34–35
Youth Homework Tutoring Center, 126–27
YWCA, school-age child care programs offered by, 32

Zigler, Edward, 38
Zucker, H., 64

FRANCES SMARDO DOWD

Frances Dowd is an associate professor in the School of Library and Information Studies at Texas Woman's University. She has taught courses in children's and young adult literature and programs, library management, public libraries, and literacy programs. Prior to teaching at the academic level, she was a professional children's librarian, early childhood specialist, and assistant manager in Dallas public libraries, as well as a second grade teacher in Baltimore. In 1982, under the name Frances Smardo, she coauthored the monograph, *What Research Tells Us About Storyhours and Receptive Language*. In 1991 she was included in *Who's Who in the South and Southwest*. She received a Master of Arts in Library Science from the University of Denver and a Ph.D. from the University of North Texas, with a major in early childhood education.

www.ingramcontent.com/pod-product-compliance
Lightning Source LLC
Chambersburg PA
CBHW050138240426
43673CB00043B/1715